Shirley & MARTY

AN UNLIKELY LOVE STORY

Shirley & MARTY

AN UNLIKELY LOVE STORY

Shirley Jones & Marty Ingels

with Mickey Herskowitz

S.P.I. BOOKS

A division of Shapolsky Publishers, Inc.

Shirley Jones & Marty Ingels

S.P.I. BOOKS
A division of Shapolsky Publishers, Inc.

Previously published in hardcover by William Morrow and Company, Inc. in 1990

ISBN 1-56171-236-1

For any additional information, contact:

S.P.I. BOOKS/Shapolsky Publishers, Inc.
136 West 22nd Street
New York, NY 10011
212/633-2022 / FAX 212/633-2123

Printed in Canada

10 9 8 7 6 5 4 3 2 1

SHIRLEY:

To all my children:
Shaun, Patrick, Ryan, David, and Marty

MARTY:

To both my mothers

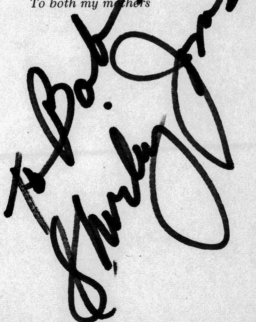

Acknowledgments

A BOOK IS A COLLABORATION in the truest sense, and not simply the product of one, two, or three brains and souls. Dozens of friends, old and new, and family members contributed their time and memories and support. They are too many to single out by name, but they know who they are and what they gave and, we hope, how much their efforts were appreciated.

Our special thanks must go to Ron Kenner, who served as our ears in the very beginning, recording so many interviews and transcripts that they literally filled a trunk.

Fifi Oscard, a sweet friend and agent for thirty-three years, not only encouraged this book but made it happen, along with some of the meaningful events described in it.

Lisa Drew was a sympathetic editor and a decisive boss, the latter when it really counted. Her assistant, Bob Shuman, helped keep open the lines of communication. Ellenor Whitty reorganized a trunkload of material. And Michelle Lichlyter spent hours under the gun, running the final drafts of the manuscript through a computer.

Contents

The Telephone Call

THIS IS A FAITHFUL TRANSCRIPT of a conversation that actually took place between Marty Ingels, in Los Angeles, and his mother, Minnie Ingerman, in New York. It offers, in less than two minutes, what Marty feels is a microcosm of his life.

MINNIE: Hello, is that you?
MARTY: It's me.
MINNIE: Good. How are you?
MARTY: Well, I'm . . .
MINNIE: Is Shirley there?
MARTY: She's in Florida.
MINNIE: What's in Florida?
MARTY: Shirley.
MINNIE: Oh. Listen, they have a show here. It's called *Jeopardy!*
MARTY: I know it.
MINNIE: You know it?
MARTY: It's here, too.
MINNIE: So you know?
MARTY: Know what?
MINNIE: About the question.
MARTY: What question?
MINNIE: I got a humdred calls. Everybody—the neighbors—Evelyn called.

MARTY: Who's Evelyn?
MINNIE: You don't know her.
MARTY: So what?
MINNIE: The whole world called me.
MARTY: I give up. Tell me.
MINNIE: The other day—yesterday. They asked a question. First they pick a category, then they ask a question.
MARTY: Yeah, so?
MINNIE: The question was: "Who is Shirley Jones married to?"
MARTY: So?
MINNIE: I'm so proud of you, darling. You're so famous. Everybody knows you. I can't walk on the streets. The whole world.
MARTY: Did they get the answer?
MINNIE: Who?
MARTY: The people, the contestants. Did they answer the question?
MINNIE: No. One even said the wrong name.
MARTY: Wonderful.

February 1990

Shirley & MARTY

AN UNLIKELY LOVE STORY

1

A Fire in the Night

THE PHONE RANG in the dark, sprawling, two-story home in Beverly Hills around four in the morning of December 12, 1976. The least appropriate person to take the call, Marty Ingels, answered the phone.

Ingels had been romancing Shirley Jones, mother of three of the Cassidy brothers, for not quite a year. Shaun, Patrick, and Ryan were in their rooms, asleep. Shirley was in the master bed beside Marty, untroubled, stirring, not quite awake.

Ingels was trying to shake the label of a rejected, out-of-work comic, and his presence at that time, in that house, was a source of mystery and discomfort to Shirley's friends and advisers. The call was from Bernie Gross, a theatrical manager who qualified on both levels. He was sorry to call at such an indecent hour, sorry to disturb them, but there had been a fire in his neighborhood . . . the fire trucks were parked in front of Jack Cassidy's building. Probably means nothing, and I'm sure everything is okay, said Bernie, but I thought, in case you hadn't heard . . .

Marty said, yeah, yeah, thanks, rolled over, and went back to sleep. On information so thin and vague, he did not even bother to wake Shirley.

That Ingels was at ease making this decision tells us a great deal about the nature of what had become a most unorthodox love triangle. Shirley Jones was, and is, one of America's sweethearts: an angel-faced, overnight star in the movie version of *Oklahoma!* and, in her more mature years, mother of the Partridge family on television. She had, at twenty, married Jack Cassidy, who would squander his great talents on booze and transient women, and throw away his life with a flair the Irish seem to carry off better than anyone.

Beautiful, talented, and sensible in most other matters, Shirley picked two men in her life whose emotional swings went off the chart.

Marty Ingels was funny and caring and bursting with a need to be accepted. He had co-starred with John Astin in a television sitcom called *I'm Dickens, He's Fenster.* The show was canceled, and his career had gone down the plumbing after he suffered a nervous breakdown, showing the first signs of it in public on the Johnny Carson Show. He left the set in a panic; nearly everyone thought it was an act—not especially funny, but no worse than some of the comics who try to impress Johnny.

Jack Cassidy was born to be a matinee idol; he played John Barrymore on the screen—and off the screen, he played him better than Barrymore had. Jack came from a modest, angry Irish-Catholic background. He reinvented himself. His goal was to overcome and obliterate those roots by becoming the ultimate debonair swinger. He wore thousand-dollar suits when you could buy a Volkswagen for not much more. At his peak, his limo bills ran three thousand dollars a week.

With his wavy blond hair, blue eyes, and gleaming teeth, he looked like an eight-by-ten glossy. Those who knew them both insisted that Jack was a more naturally gifted actor, and singer, than Shirley. But he became more self-destructive as the years passed without a major triumph, and as the shadow of Shirley Jones lengthened. He was a favorite on Broadway in such plays as *Wish You Were Here.* He won an Emmy for his role in *The Andersonville Trials* on television, and briefly he co-starred with Paula Prentiss in a series, *He & She.* But the big success that would have validated his work, and his life, escaped him.

Within the trade, and in that odd contract that artists enter into with their audiences, Cassidy was not especially well liked. He possessed the Burt Reynolds sense of humor long before Burt happened along; the "Aren't-I-Beautiful" shtick. It was easy to believe that Cassidy meant it.

He was, parenthetically, the ideal husband for Shirley Jones in her twenties. He was her mentor, wonderful on the social circuit, popping the champagne cork and charming friends and guests with the aplomb of a David Niven. What Cassidy was unable to handle was life at the nine-to-five gut level. He talked often about his fear of aging. Of course, he joked to his friends, he would never live to worry about it.

The drinking and the chasing grew more frenetic. If ever a woman had gone through life wearing blinders about a man, it was Shirley Jones. When he did not come home for days or nights at a time, she didn't challenge him. He said he was working. In Hollywood, actors sometimes do. She never tried to analyze what went wrong with the marriage. In fact, very little had, until she began to develop her own point of view and her spotlight outgrew his. It was a sad and glaring weakness of Jack Cassidy that he could hardly abide success in those closest to him.

Cassidy walked out on Shirley after seventeen years, during which she had ignored the humiliations he sometimes seemed to create for the sport of them. In the six months after their divorce was final, Jack begged to come back . . . even as Marty Ingels, the zany intruder her friends disliked, love-bombed her with marriage proposals. And there the relationships hovered and tangled, up to the night the phone didn't stop ringing.

The second call came in twenty minutes later. Bernie Gross had more news: The fire *was* in the building where Jack leased a penthouse apartment. A body had been discovered. Ah, but Jack's car, his Mercedes convertible, a classic car, was missing from the garage. A neighbor recalled he had made a date to drive to Palm Springs with friends. No, it was unlikely that the charred corpse the paramedics had brought down the service elevator was Jack Cassidy. The inspectors were already trying to determine how the fire had started. For now, they knew only that the flames had gutted the apartment, and the intense heat had melted the victim's gold chain and watch and burned away his face. Dental records would be needed to identify the body.

But thought you would want to hear the latest. . . .

Earlier that evening, Marty and Shirley had gone out to dinner, stopped by a party, strolled along the streets of Beverly Hills, admired the Christmas decorations in the shop windows, and soaked up the tenderness of the night. At two o'clock, they ducked into a pancake house to put off going home. It was no more than two blocks from Jack's building. A little later, they heard the sirens of fire engines, felt the adrenaline rush that sound nearly always arouses, and then forgot it.

As the morning light turned the sky to shades of gray, no one slept in the home that Jack Cassidy had picked out and Shirley's money had purchased. Accounts of the fire had been reported on radio and the day's first telecasts, and spread by word of mouth. The calls were coming in every few minutes; Bernie Gross from the scene, various friends as the news reached them.

Now they knew the body had been removed from Jack's apartment; the fire had started there. Still no identification had been made, no conclusions drawn. It was not unknown for Cassidy to hear a hard-luck story in a bar and, overcome with emotion and a fifth of scotch, invite a stranger to spend the night as his guest.

Shirley tried to put out of her mind the idea that the dead man was her ex-husband. It could not be Jack. There was the evidence of his missing car, his Mercedes convertible. He had to be away. But someone was dead, and her grief, although detached, was no less real. She could imagine the screams, the specter of a death we all fear, to be burned alive.

Shaun, seventeen, Patrick, fourteen, and Ryan, the youngest at nine, had joined Marty and Shirley downstairs in the living room. They sat with backs as straight as a nine-iron. There is no way to hold a light, relaxed vigil, and no one doubted what kind of vigil they had begun.

David Cassidy waited at his own home for the call he hoped would confirm that his father had turned up safe and unaware. In some ways, their relationship had been the most complicated of all. David was seven when Jack divorced his mother, a dancer named Evelyn Ward, after falling in love with a teenaged Shirley Jones.

In a roomful of family, Marty continued to take the calls. It had to be awkward for him, but if the others felt anything, it was relief, not resentment. That was Marty. A dinner check, a telephone, he had a long reach.

The police and fire inspectors were checking out the car. Of course, it was possible Jack had loaned the car to someone. A houseboy ran errands for him. While the car remained missing, there was hope.

In the morning, they began combing the dental records. There was no point in anyone trying to identify the body. Still no final word. Everyone clung to the car as the key . . . as their best hope. In the living room, the five of them sat and waited, the silence as heavy as smoke.

One tries to imagine what thoughts invade a woman's mind, wondering if the man she loved, who taught her to love, who in the end hurt and disappointed her, was alive or dead. Shirley remembered their one futile attempt at a reconciliation. Twice since then they had dated, met for dinner to see what was there for either of them. Marty had agreed, had nervously urged her to test herself. When Jack asked her out a third time, Marty drew the line. If she didn't know by now, she never would, he argued. And she knew. She had seen Jack deteriorate, his behavior grow more erratic, with episodes of running naked into the night. She feared that in one of his drunken tantrums he might injure the children.

Shirley said no. That call, that plea, had come on the afternoon of the night of the fire. It was the last time they would ever talk:

^^^^

I loved Jack, but I was no longer *in* love with him. Nor did I feel I could live with him again. As long as he was unstable, mentally, I would have worried that his drinking, his carelessness, might endanger the children. It had been his decision to leave the first time, and mine to get the divorce. He was going through a period of saying, "Let me come back. I need you, and I want to come back." I told him he knew how I felt. You don't stop loving someone after seventeen years, but we had been through all this.

And at the end of the conversation, Jack was very specific: "This is the last time I'm going to ask you. You belong with me, Mouse. And you know this is the last time . . . I'm not going to ask you again." He wasn't talking just about dinner, of course. He was talking about our lives.

vvvv

Marty had pursued Shirley, had in fact launched a relentless campaign to win her affection, after a chance encounter the week she made up her mind to file for divorce. Little by little, he worked his way into her embrace, and finally into her home. "I knew I wanted to live with her," he said, "but I also knew it was too early to ask. So I did it a shirt at a time. I'd carry shoes under my jacket one trip, socks and sweaters another, cuff links and stuff in my pockets. This went on for a year. By the time I actually asked her, I had moved everything but my piano. She had no idea how it got there."

Shirley remembers it this way: "I never knew what to expect with Marty. From the moment he appeared, he just never went away." With a giggle, she added, "I had no choice, you see. No choice at all."

Now he sat with Shirley and three of her sons through hours of communal fear. Ingels knew his disadvantages. He had not yet won over the boys, certainly not to the point where they would expose their emotions in front of him. Compared to the handsome, dashing, almost regal father they had known, the Cassidy brothers regarded Marty, in his words, as "an odd Jewish uncle you hide in the attic."

The brothers sat on one couch, Marty on another, holding Shirley, her cheek pressed against his chest. Marty recalled the night he worried himself nearly sick that she would go back to Jack.

~~~~

We sat in that very room, and Shirley began by saying, "We're not married, you understand," and I understood it very well. She was leading up to telling me that Jack had
~~~~

called and asked her to have dinner with him. She said, "I have to do it, this once. How do you feel about it?"

Now that was a very hard moment for me. I didn't want her going out with Jack. I didn't want to lose her. At the same time, I didn't want to live under that shadow, knowing she might love somebody else. With great difficulty, I said, "Shirley, not only do I say you can go, you have to go. Having you is of no value unless you feel free of Jack. You have to decide if you still love the man, if you have to be with him." The words sounded noble, but my heart was sinking.

It was not an easy night. I had plans for all kinds of things to do and, of course, did nothing. I just walked back and forth, waiting for her to come home. My thoughts bounced from strength to desperation and a dozen scenarios of what might be happening out there. She had made no real commitment to me. It was eleven o'clock, twelve, one. Finally, she walked through the door, crying. I ran to her, and we hugged. She kept crying and I was holding her, and stroking her, and in my brain I'm asking, What kind of crying is this? I mean, who was it for, Jack or me? Was I in or was I out? It was terrible.

Finally, she sat down. In a funny way, the tears were good. If she had walked in and said everything was fine and gone upstairs to bed, it would have bothered me more. It turned out she was crying because Jack had deteriorated so. He was in bad shape, frantic, not coherent. She said, "It hurts because I feel so much for him, and he's in such pain, so lost, and he needs someone." There was no soap opera here. She felt for him as a human being. And at that point, she said, "I agonized all night. But I know now that I will never live with Jack again. I love him and I cry for his pain, but I am no longer in love *with* him. He will never come back to this house."

~~~~

It was midday when Marty took a call from the coroner's office. They had examined a signet ring, overlooked at first on a blackened hand curled into a claw. The only piece of jewelry to survive the fire, it bore the crest of the Cassidy clan. He had given a shield to each of his sons.
~~~~

Marty hung up the phone and looked from face to face. No one needed to hear his next words—"They've identified the body. It's Jack." They knew from his own expression. And he stood there, not knowing what to do or say or how to help.

~~~~

Everyone shrieked. It was like one shrill voice. Then, interestingly, each of them got up and went to a different room to cry, privately, on their own. Shirley went to her room, Patrick went to another. Ryan went upstairs. Shaun went into the kitchen and closed the door and bawled. It just came blasting out through each door, from all those different rooms. And I was alone, and torn, not certain what my role was; how to comfort these grieving boys who might not even want me around. Later, I drove to the burned-out apartment. Ryan, the youngest, came along, with the understanding he would stay in the car.

I got off at the penthouse. The door was open. The place was a black simmering cave, reeking, with smoldering ashes everywhere. The firemen were still investigating, poking around in the ruins. There was nowhere to walk without something crumbling around you. It was gruesome. Where the couch had been, only the springs were left. That was where Jack had been when the fire started. The firemen said, without a doubt the blaze had been caused by a cigarette that fell under a cushion. It had been there even before he went out for the evening. Years earlier, a psychic had actually predicted the way Jack would die—from a fire started by a lighted cigarette.

He had fallen asleep, but it was clear he did wake up and started crawling toward the balcony, instead of the door. We don't know if he was confused and turned in the wrong direction, or if he was just trying to get to the air. That's where they found him, on the floor facing the balcony.

~~~~

Meanwhile, Cassidy's secretary had dropped by the building, spotted Ryan waiting in Marty's car, and invited him to go upstairs with her. When they walked in, Ingels was furious, but the damage was done. Ryan saw it all through nine-year-old eyes, the charred walls, the wire springs that had once been a couch, a roomful of ashes. Marty hurried him out of there, but the boy would revisit that scene in his nightmares.

The investigators had begun to trace Jack's movements. He had been scheduled to drive that day to Palm Springs with friends. They never located him. He went out on the town, tried to get a party going, stopped in several bars, left one with two men nobody knew and who were never seen again. The Mercedes turned up in the garage later in the day.

His last stop had been to an Italian restaurant that had been a favorite of his and Shirley's, Dominick's, directly across the street from Cedars-Sinai Hospital. The owner was a wonderful Italian character who would close the restaurant and take off for six months to go fishing. When he returned and opened the door, everyone knew he was back. One of those places with six tables and no sign outside. If you didn't know it was there, you couldn't find it. Months later, the owner called Shirley and told her he thought he might have been the last person to see Jack alive. He said Jack had been acting crazy.

~~~~

There were rumors that the fire had been deliberate. The police were interested in Jack's remark to Shirley that this would be the "last time" he asked to come back. But I don't think people usually commit suicide by setting themselves on fire. True, he dreaded growing older. I found that sad. His career was starting to move again. He would have been a hot actor as an older man. Absolutely, he would have been Rod Steiger with looks. But he had a compulsion to overcome a poor childhood, and be elegant, know all the good wines and all the beautiful ladies. That was his mask, and it separated him from reality. There was no day-to-day living with Jack. Shirley lived with a wonderfully exciting man who loved parties, who bought drinks on the house, and wore a silk bathrobe to bring in the paper from his doorway.
~~~~

But in life there are times when you have to be good at calling the plumber, and nailing the fence, and taking the kid's knee to the right doctor. And there was no Jack there.

~~~~

In the few days leading up to Jack Cassidy's funeral, Shirley's friends, her business manager, her agent, all were dropping hints that it would be best if her companion did not attend. Three times she raised the question, and asked what he thought. Of course, the politic thing would have been to stay away. A funeral was not Marty's idea of a good time. He also had his own demons to deal with, his own phobias, although he had managed through a pure act of will to so far conceal the depth of them from Shirley. Still, he somehow instinctively knew that there was something terribly wrong about not being with the woman he loved on that sad day.

The medical term for one of his problems was *agoraphobia*—a fear of leaving a familiar setting. Going out, anywhere, was often harrowing for Marty. This time he was adamant that he would go. The fears, for once, dissolved. The more outside pressure he felt, the stronger his determination to be there, alongside Shirley.

~~~~

Several of Jack's friends called and told me directly not to go. Some of the calls were anonymous. Some I thought were threatening. That was when I told Shirley they would have to call the SWAT team to keep me away. I loved her. I had to be there. If people were going to look at me funny, so be it. I knew it would take a certain kind of strength to show up and face his friends when a lot of them perceived me as Jack's rival, as having taken her away from him, neither of which was true.

The assumption was that we had hated each other. Not on my part. Jack, who referred to me as "the boy," clearly felt some contempt for the man he saw as a raspy-voiced, funny-faced slapstick Brooklyn comic. And yet the wife he left, and now wanted back, seemed to be in love with me. It had to be embarrassing to him.

It does not take long for news, good, bad, or sexy, to get around Hollywood. Jack had thrown a few zingers at me, and he had to endure a few of his own—from more or less neutral sources. At a roast one night for Burt Reynolds, Jack tossed off a line at the expense of the honoree. And Reynolds retorted, "And while you're up here, Marty Ingels is walking around in your bathrobe and slippers." The whole town seemed to know about it the next morning.

Another time the word got back to me that Cassidy, drinking one night with friends, let some of his pain surface. "Yeah," he told them, "she's living with that Jew comic." That one got me. It was time to deal with it, and I called him on the phone. Right off, he seemed bewildered. But I plunged right in. I said, "Jack, look, I'm living in your house, with your ex-wife and your children, but I am not your enemy. I didn't take any of these people away from you. I met them after all that. And if I should get lucky enough to become Shirley's husband and the stepfather of your kids, who I think are terrific, I'll do my best to take good care of them. And I still won't be your enemy. I know more about the painful position you're in than Shirley. I was right there myself, maybe worse, not two years ago. So, please Jack, don't fall into that traditional trap of squaring off with me because I'm the new kid on the block.

"That would be a mistake. And don't get me wrong, Jack. I heard all about the 'Jew' talk at the party. I'm more than prepared to meet you on any battlefield you choose. Tonight. Right now. You pick the alley. But the truth? I can think of a lot better ways to solve a problem than breaking bones. I have always admired you—actually been in awe of your talent. And I don't see why any of that should change now. You want to talk to Shirley? You want to see your kids? You want to find out what's going on here? Call me. Here's my phone number. All things considered, Jack, it's better to have a friend on the inside. If you want one, you got it."

I think it was the first time Jack Cassidy was rendered virtually speechless. What he mustered was a thank you; he said he appreciated a call he thought had to be difficult to make. (How right he was.) Finally, he said he might take me up on my offer. Of course, he never did. Perhaps pride, and certainly time, kept him from it.

With those mixed feelings, I went to the funeral of Jack Cassidy. The crowd was large. To my own astonishment, I had to choke back tears. (How would I explain *that* to anyone?) Really, I had a hard time dealing with my own feelings about Jack. You fall into these natural outside roles. My role was, I got the girl, I won. But, in fact, I would listen in the evening to some of their records, and I melted hearing them sing together. Their voices were magical together.

At the funeral, they played all his favorite music, and friends told loving stories. And there I was, sitting with his radiant wife and four beautiful boys. All the work was done, and there I was with the gifts. I was sad and humbled and proud and scared and shaky, all at the same time. All of it while keeping my face a mask for the cold mob around me and the constant photo flashes. I would have traded anything for a few old friends.

~~~~

As they left the cemetery, some of Jack's closest friends edged over to Ingels and told him, in effect, this was not a day in the park, and we respect you for standing up and doing what you did.

If little in Cassidy's last years had been simple or tranquil, his death would not change the pattern. First, there was the matter of his will. Shirley was struck from it, not to her surprise, and Shaun's name was deleted from Jack's insurance policies. The month Jack had executed a new will, he and Shaun happened to be quarreling. The other sons received payments of fifty thousand dollars each. Everything else went to Jack's friends and his secretary.

It was a sad and curious irony that on the day of his death, Jack was not on speaking terms with two of his sons, David also having disappointed him in some way. In the weeks after their father's funeral, the boys each carried away a distinct and separate impression. Ryan, the baby, nurtured a fantasy about the perfect father. Patrick, the most emotional,
~~~~

seemed to be hit the hardest. Shaun had to fight off his anger; as the eldest living at home, he had seen the whims and mischief and occasional madness.

Then there was David. To nearly everyone's consternation, Jack was intimidated by the success of David Cassidy as a teen idol. Unable to enjoy it, to take pride in it, to love David even for his inherited talent, Jack withdrew from him. To the extent that each of the Cassidy boys lacked a compatible, ongoing relationship with his father, each suffered in his own way.

Jack Cassidy had died two weeks before Christmas in 1976. Not many years later, before Father's Day, Ingels found an old photograph in an album of Jack Cassidy as a very young man, so handsome it almost hurt to look at him. He had four copies framed and gave one to each of Jack's sons. "I really wasn't trying to win points," he said. "It was far beyond all that. I was in many ways obsessed with the responsibility of keeping their father bright and alive for them. If nothing else, it was an easy way for me to puncture the myth—those involuntary roles, again—that I was intimidated by, and at odds with, the memory of Jack Cassidy."

What you had here was a gorgeous blond shiksa, a Jewish comic consumed with her and looking for another line of work, and, mind it or not, a ghost. To his credit, Marty didn't mind. He would marry her, the perfect mother of television's Partridge family, and he knew he would catch hell for it. "With a person as wholesome as Shirley," he analyzed his position, "there is a strong sense of possessiveness on the part of the public."

The year of the fire there were lives to be led, to restart, to rearrange. At the center was a love story with a twist. Marty Ingels had met and fallen wildly in love with Shirley Jones. Actually, what he did was fall wildly in love, first, and then arrange to meet her. From then on, and forever, he knew he would be in some kind of competition with Jack Cassidy.

2

To Paris with Love

AN ASSISTANT IN HER AGENT'S office, Selma Linch, spoke the single most dangerous sentence one can say to a restless, curious, blossoming young woman of nineteen:

"Don't fall in love with him, Shirley. Every girl who meets him does." As an afterthought, Selma added, "And he's married."

The warning was related to the actor who would be her leading man in the touring version of *Oklahoma!*, Jack Cassidy. Shirley was recast in the role of Laurey, the part that had made her an instant star in the motion picture, opposite Gordon MacRae.

She had eagerly accepted a two-for-one offer: to tour Europe in the Rodgers and Hammerstein musical classic, and at the same time promote the motion picture. Now she was in New York, in the winter of 1954, to begin rehearsals for the road company; it was the most exciting time of her life. Up to then, however, it was a life that had not strayed far from Smithton, Pennsylvania. Smithton was a town so small you could start a crime wave by stealing a chicken.

She had been the school beauty and an honors student, and had gone on to win the Miss Pittsburgh Pageant. Now she was the "Cinderella" Girl who in her first audition captured the part of Laurey in *Oklahoma!* She was not, as the press reported and many believed, too good to be true. Rather, she was just good enough to be true.

She returned to Selma's remark, prepared to be skeptical. "What is so marvelous about this Jack Cassidy? What makes him so special?"

Selma said, "He's very handsome, and he's extremely talented. But forget that. Just remember the part about his being married." And Shirley Jones, the innocent from the outback of Pennsylvania, tried to remember. . . .

^^^^

We were to rehearse in New York for six weeks before the play opened in Paris. I walked into the theater with a friend for the very first reading, and it began to sink in that I would be working with all these *stage* people. Rod Steiger was playing the role of Jud, the part he had done in the movie, and he was the only person there I knew. I could feel a lot of eyes on me. I was this fairy-tale princess Hollywood had discovered. It's funny. Most actors on Broadway are in awe of people who have starred in movies. And in Hollywood, as soon as someone is successful, he or she talks about going back to Broadway, where the real acting is.

The routine was for each member of the cast to be introduced onstage, and make a brief speech on your character and how you might play it. My friend Sari Price, who was in the chorus, asked if I had seen my leading man. I said, "Yes, when we came in, I saw him talking on the phone." I meant it in a sarcastic way, as if to note that he wasn't being very professional. She said, "Oh, God, Shirley, he's gorgeous." I said, "I don't think he's so much. Everyone keeps telling me how marvelous-looking he is. If you want to know the truth, he's really too pretty." I really was not attracted to that type of man . . . or, at least, I didn't think I was.

Just then he got up and walked all the way across the stage, smiled, and said, "Hi, I'm Jack Cassidy." And I replied, "I know who you are." By that time, I had talked myself into being half-mad at him. So there were some chemical forces at work already. Everything about him, his presence, his looks, the way he talked, gave off this cloud of sophistication. Then he sang . . . and in spite of myself, I all but fell out of my chair. It was so schoolgirlish. It was like the

"Trolley Song" had gone off in my head. It was knight-in-shining-armor time, the way I suddenly saw him.

The nicest part was that he didn't come on strong. He didn't pounce. He was, absolutely, the perfect gentleman. He was married, but it seemed to be common knowledge that he wasn't living with his wife. I would turn twenty on the tour, and he was twenty-eight. And I thought of him as an older man. I asked him his age, and he laughed. He told me I was still a child, but he said it kindly, not in a patronizing way. Obviously, the attraction was there.

Our director then was Rouben Mamoulian, who had directed the original Broadway version of *Oklahoma!* He had been a favorite of Garbo, Dietrich, Hedy Lamarr, Gene Tierney, Bette Davis. He was out of the old Viennese school of the boots and pith helmet and a whip he could crack for effect. After we did our first love scene, Mamoulian chided us in his thick accent: "Now, now, dollinks, ve only fall in luff in the play. It is only on the stage that ve do this. Do not take this vit you outside." We all laughed.

No one could say I hadn't been warned. Wise girl that I thought I was, I avoided Jack. He lived in New Jersey, and I had my apartment in the city, and we went our separate ways after rehearsal. Three days before the cast and crew were to fly to Paris, there was a party on an excursion ship that sailed along the Hudson River. It was to be Rodgers and Hammerstein night, and everyone was invited. I decided not to go with a date. I knew Jack would probably be there, and if I had a date, I wouldn't be able to dance with him. Of course, I was right. We both came alone, and we danced, and that night was the first time I had been physically close to him.

When I went home that night and started packing for the trip, my friend said, "You know, you better be careful. You're really going to get in hot water." I said, "I'm okay. I'm not involved." She wouldn't drop it: "He's a married man, Shirley. He's a lot older and has been around." I told her not to worry. I wasn't being defiant. I just was not receiving.

We flew to Paris on a military air transport, the most uncomfortable form of flight ever designed. We ate box lunches, lots of them, because the flight lasted over twenty hours. In Paris, we stayed in a quaint hotel on the Left Bank with one tiny lift and rooms too small for those who shared them. Jack was gallant. He talked his roommate into offering Sari and me their room, which had a larger closet and more walking-around space. He insisted we trade, noting that we had more clothes and more things to spread around. Fifteen years later, he would never have made such a gesture, because he had more clothes than anyone.

His kindness created an opening, and he suggested that the four of us go out to dinner to celebrate our first night in Paris. His roommate, a popular actor named Will Kuluva, went off with Sari, promising to catch up with us later. Jack made reservations for the two of us at the restaurant atop the Eiffel Tower.

Of course, the rest was right out of *Modern Romance.* I was in heaven. He introduced me to his world. I had my first order of escargots, my first martini, my first champagne. We literally talked the night away. Jack was predictably the most articulate, the best-read, the most romantic man I had ever met. (No great distinction at that point in my untraveled life, but still I was impressed.) He quoted at length from Thoreau. He had no interest in politics or religion or economics, but he could argue about them endlessly.

He had been in show business since he was fourteen. He had married at twenty-one, had a child, a baby, David. I knew the story—perhaps not all, but as much as Jack wanted me to know. I accepted it.

Evelyn Ward was a dancer, dark-haired, exotic-looking, much favored by photographers who described her as a cross between Linda Darnell and Hedy Lamarr. She once replaced Gwen Verdon in a show called *New Girl in Town,* but my guess is—and I know David believes it—that she gave up her career to raise her child.

As Jack represented it, they were chorus kids in a show that was on the road for twenty weeks. When the run ended, they decided to get married. It was as if they had said, Well, the show has closed, what else have we got to do? Nothing is ever quite so clear as when we attempt to justify ourselves. No doubt Jack skipped rather lightly over the feelings that may have been there once. But whether they were in love or just lonely, they were both young and sweetly irresponsible. They really didn't know each other.

That night in Paris was not a night for questions. We finished dinner, danced, then met Will and Sari at a cabaret where we danced and drank and talked some more. The club was called Charlie's, but Charlie, the owner, wasn't a man. She was a lesbian well known in Paris's arty circles. I was getting a lot of education in one night.

About five in the morning, the sun started to come up, and Will hailed a taxi to take us back to the hotel. Jack asked me if I would mind walking, and I said I'd love to, and we let them go. We walked from the Right Bank, across the Seine, a long, slow, incredible, wordless walk. It was a wonderful, once-in-a-lifetime feeling. The milkmen were just getting up, and the young people on their bicycles, some with loaves of bread under their arm, were pedaling to school or to jobs. I was seeing all the things you hear about Paris: people putting the flowers out, sweeping the sidewalks, unshuttering their shops; artists setting up their easels to catch the early light.

I felt overwhelmed. There had been crushes and boyfriends, but nothing that felt as this did. I didn't know whether it was Jack, or being in Paris, or being so far from home and singing in a hit musical, or all of these. We just walked hand in hand, saying nothing, until we reached the hotel, and went up together in the tiny lift. At the door, I fumbled for my room key, and he gave me a light, feathery kiss. Then he said, "I'm going to marry you."

And I said, "You're already married."

"I know," he said, and he walked back to the lift.

Sari had been waiting in the room nearly an hour, after her cab ride. She was breathless to hear what had happened. I told her Jack said he was going to marry me. I don't think I believed him, and I might have been amused, except for the way he said it. Sari cringed. "Oh, Shirley," she said, "I'm so worried about you. He's going to break your heart. You're going to be in for a terrible time. Please, please, don't fall in love with him." She meant well. They all did. It was already too late.

vvvv

Twenty years would pass before her friend's prediction would come true. As bad as the bad times would get, for all the pain she and Jack would share, none of it would outweigh the happy times or make Shirley wish she could erase the past.

The show moved on to Rome. There were morning swims and picnics on the beach and performances on the stage that seemed to improve as their love affair picked up speed. It was so obvious what was happening that the rest of the crew worried about the consequences, if the two of them had a fight.

Romance between co-stars is supposed to be a theatrical cliché, or myth, or both; the leading man and his leading lady usually wind up loathing each other. But it happens. Bette Davis married Gary Merrill, her co-star in *All About Eve*. Sophia Loren and Cary Grant fell in love. And heaven knows Liz Taylor and Richard Burton could not get enough of each other.

A fear of being hurt was not enough to keep Shirley from accepting the risk. Jack kept telling her he intended to get a divorce when they returned to the States. News of the romance had crossed the Atlantic, upsetting her parents, her friends, her agents. Everyone made virtually the same argument: He's charming, he's married, it was Paris in the spring, you can't possibly believe that old line about getting a divorce, can you?

^^^^

I told myself, If that's how it turns out, I will have no regrets. I had a marvelous romance, and I learned from it. When the tour ended and the cast returned to New York, everything was on hold. We would be separated for the next three months. I continued on to California to begin rehearsals for my next picture, *Carousel*. Jack went into a play called *Witness for the Prosecution* at the Bucks County Playhouse.

Meanwhile, Evelyn had moved out of the house in West Orange, New Jersey, taking the baby and moving in with her parents. I see no purpose in rationalizing all these years later what took place. I knew how it looked to Evelyn, that I had broken up her marriage, stolen her husband. How she must have hated me for it. Deep down, I think she understood that Jack did not want to continue the marriage, and wanted to end it years earlier. He had carried on a number of affairs, and I imagine Evelyn knew about every one of them. To her, at first, I was just another of his casual ladies. Time and the scoreboard were on her side. He always came back . . . until now. This time he said he wanted a divorce. He wanted to marry someone else.

For three months, Jack and I wrote long, mushy letters and spent a fortune on the telephone, and then one day he knocked on my door and announced; "I'm divorced. We went to Mexico and got a Mexican divorce."

vvvv

They didn't rush into marriage. Shirley Jones didn't rush into anything. Her career was booming, and instinctively she felt an obligation not to embarrass Evelyn Ward. A year and a half after his divorce, Jack Cassidy and Shirley were co-starring in a musical called *The Beggar's Opera* in Cambridge, Massachusetts, in the theater on the Harvard campus. Their characters were married onstage every night in the play. And there, in August of 1956, in that oh-so-traditional New England setting, they agreed to wait no longer.

On short notice, Shirley had a wedding dress made, flew her family and best friend to Cambridge, and planned a formal church wedding. They were married at two o'clock, did an early show at six, and then enjoyed a reception at the town's Old World hotel, the Ritz. Her agent, Gus Shirmer, arranged for the champagne and a catered supper.

For their wedding night, Jack had reserved a bridal suite, with a grand piano in the living room. Under the heading of "It Seemed Like a Good Idea at the Time," Shirley suggested that they invite Gus, who was staying in the hotel, to join them for a champagne nightcap. For her trousseau, Shirley had packed a pair of see-through black lace baby-doll pajamas, with matching black high heels. Jack saw them laid out on the bed and slipped into them, put on a shower cap, and opened the door to Gus Shirmer, who seemed to take the outlandish getup in stride. He knew actors.

Gus had a glass of champagne. And another. He showed

no interest at all in leaving. Cassidy kept saying, "Listen, don't you think it's time to give us a little privacy now?" "That was how we spent most of my wedding night," Shirley recalls, "drinking champagne with my agent."

Her storybook romance would have a nice, new beginning, with one exception. . . .

^^^^

The night before the wedding, Evelyn called and said that David was hysterical over the news, and how could he do this to him? Jack would have to come to New York and explain to his son what it all meant. He was shaken by the call. Who could be indifferent to the torment of a seven-year-old? I heard him say, in measured words, "Evelyn, I will not, I cannot, leave now. You are going to have to handle this. You have to prepare the boy for the fact that I am marrying someone else."

She was furious, unsparing in blaming Jack for whatever had gone wrong: He was a bad father, a bad husband, and a worthless person. That night was the beginning of a long vendetta between them, a vicious turn they had taken, with David always the pawn. Evelyn felt betrayed, and she was embittered. Perhaps she had reason to be. I didn't know, still don't, what the past had been for them. I knew they had separated twice and gotten back together. After the divorce, she went back to work, and in those formative years David was partly raised by his grandparents, who were lovely people.

Jack paid alimony and child support until Evelyn remarried, and then the alimony was waived. Later, she took us to court twice to raise her child support. I was successful then, at the height of my movie career, and although Jack was not working consistently, I'm sure she felt we both owed her.

The scene in court was brutal. Jack had to take the stand and testify, in effect, that I was keeping him. I had to confirm that he had not earned more than a certain modest amount of money since our marriage. All of which was true, but to be in the witness box and say it, confront it, was a hard moment for both of us to choke down.

Evelyn claimed his earnings had been understated. The records were introduced into evidence and supported our sworn testimony. She lost the suit, but it was no victory for us. I felt guilty over her need to seek additional child support. I loved David and wanted to help care for him, but by then Jack was so vindictive toward his ex-wife, he would not give an inch.

vvvv

A second Cassidy family would soon appear: Shaun in 1958, Patrick in 1962, and Ryan in 1966. A pattern also emerged, of feast and famine. Each pregnancy would deprive Shirley of nearly a year of work, and their savings would shrink to perilous lows. These were years when Jack continued to struggle to find his niche, to get his career untracked.

His frustrations mounted, and slowly the marriage changed. Shirley did not see the changes coming, nor did she judge their meaning. It had all been idyllic at the outset, when Jack could play her Pygmalion. . . .

^^^^

His dream for me was to reshape me, remold me. He constantly encouraged me to read more, to learn to paint, attend the theater, play the charming Perle Mesta hostess and entertain his friends. He wanted a sophisticated woman of the world, a courtesan. He admired that kind of woman, but he didn't marry one. He married a little girl from Smithton with big eyes, and he drove her off in his car, not a carriage.

The irony was that the moment I took one step forward, moved one iota from that sheltered small-town ingenue, he rebelled. From the moment I had something to say, had my own feelings to express, Jack felt threatened.

As his career stalled, Jack was angry and frustrated, and between us small problems escalated into large ones. I didn't look at them as problems at the time. I only knew that Jack wasn't doing the work he wanted to do, a mystery to both of us. Our earnings fluctuated wildly; still, Jack had little respect for money, and we spent it as though oil had been discovered in our backyard.

We always had spacious backyards, three large homes in the span of a few years. We never lived more above our means than when we purchased a mansion on two acres from Merle Oberon, on Copa de Oro, in the hills of Bel Air. At the time I was pregnant with Patrick, with no prospect of any immediate work. We had not yet sold our former home on Miraga Drive, and soon after we moved in, Jack left for New York and a good but low-paying part in a play called *She Loves Me.*

I was alone in this mansion with servants' quarters and no servants, with formal gardens to maintain, much more house than I could live in, much less keep up, about to have a baby, when the great fire of 1962 swept Bel Air. The flames leaped across the hills, destroying every home on Bel Agio Road, and raging through Copa de Oro, miraculously stopping at the edge of our property. All the landscaping, including the poolside area, was gone.

I was evacuated from the house, taking with me my four-year-old son, my schnauzer, my bird, my address book, and the Oscar I won for *Elmer Gantry.* We moved in with friends and listened to the reports on radio of the fight to contain the fire. It went on for days, an inferno, frightening and awesome. I called Jack in New York and told him we had to sell the mansion. He wanted to know why we didn't just sell the other one.

I said, "Because it burned halfway to the ground." There was little left on Miraga Drive except a scorched shell and a few charred timbers and a small mountain of ashes.

As one might expect, after the fire there was no stampede among buyers eager to move into the neighborhood. It would not occur to me until many years later that of all nature's forces, fire would be a devastating symbol in our lives.

We lived in the mansion for not quite two years. That was a strange, seesaw period. We were in the center of Hollywood's strongest concentration of glamour, and yet well removed from it. We knew that Jerry Lewis lived on St. Cloud, down the street, and the Robert Stacks lived in the next block. But we had no real contact with them. It was not the kind of neighborhood where you made friends, where someone knocked on your door to borrow a cup of sugar.

We did make the party rounds on occasion. Jack loved to go out, and we were on most of the lists, a fringe benefit of my having co-starred in two recent box-office hits, *Music Man* and *Elmer Gantry*.

We were invited to a party one night at the home of Ross Hunter, a producer and director of great range, who had made, among many films, *Lost Horizon*, and the Doris Day–Rock Hudson comedies. He was Lana Turner's mentor, admired by actresses of a certain age for his flair with lighting and wardrobe, his ability to make the ladies look beautiful.

The party was after the premiere of a movie starring Susan Hayward, I think, and the guests were seated around a long banquet table. I had just been nominated for an Oscar in *Gantry*, and was receiving more than my share of the attention. Jack at that point felt very neglected. Everyone was talking movies, about this star and that, and the other guests had more or less dismissed him. He felt very much the out-of-work actor, and the more he drank, the deeper he sank. Someone said to me, in an offhand way, "Tell us how it feels to be nominated for an Oscar."

It was a question that required no answer; many in the room knew how it felt. But Jack rose unsteadily to his feet and shouted, "*I'll tell you about it!*" He was in the kind of drunken mood where anything you say sounds brilliant in your own ear. He went on and on, repeating himself: "Yeah, I'll tell you about it. I think you're a phony, Ross Hunter. A big goddam silver-plated phony. I think this business, this whole stinking business, is run by phonies . . . phony, fake, synthetic Hollywood." He went on and on, unable to make his point, obviously way off base. Finally, Ross Hunter stood and silenced him with one withering remark: "Thank you, Mr. Norman Maine."

I suppose most of us do that, but more so in Hollywood, the references to movie scenes and characters. Of course, the line referred to the husband in *A Star Is Born*, a drunken has-been who, having wasted his own career, devotes himself to making a star of his wife. That was not our scenario, but others could read into it what they wished.

Jack's unhappiness was no longer possible to ignore. He had built a workshop behind the house, and passed his time designing or refinishing furniture. To my dismay, he began to talk about remodeling the house, and each day new pieces of machinery would arrive for his workshop.

"How are we going to remodel this place," I asked, "when we don't have enough money to pay our bills?"

If money was the topic, Jack simply tuned you out. He didn't want to hear about it. He was a charmer, a man of fantasies. He dreamed about having a farm in Vermont. Twice a year he would bring it up: All he needed was one good part in a film, one big payday, and we'd be packing off to Vermont.

When he wasn't pining for his dream of the hour, his decisions were usually based on logic. If I tried to change him, it was in that direction. I wanted a real husband, a real father. He accused me of trying to stifle his ego. The day I asked him about paying our bills, he said in a voice that was aching, "You want me to be Robert Young in *Father Knows Best*. I'm never going to be that, Shirley. You may be able to take everything else from me, but you're never going to take my dreams away."

We did not jabber endlessly about self-esteem in those days, but one needn't know much psychology to recognize the damage done to a proud man whose wife was, for a time, the breadwinner.

vvvv

The critics had been generous about his role in *She Loves Me*, and he won a Tony Award, a nice boost for his ego. Yet his success there didn't travel to Hollywood, which never really found a way to use him. He was a difficult man, but the problem was technical. He had become a fine actor, but he didn't fit any category. Unfortunately, he happened along at a time when the day of the matinee idol was nearing an end. The Barrymores, the Errol Flynns, the Tyrone Powers, were finished. Jack was classically handsome, and more so in his later years, in an era when Walter Matthau led Hollywood's trend to a different look.

So Jack was cast in the roles of the pretty-boy villain, the homicidal maniac, or the homosexual in episodic television shows. Of all the ironies, he was just beginning to get decent movie offers when he died.

^^^^

He had hit bottom at about the same time I was reaching a peak, gaining a new national audience with *The Partridge Family* in the early 1970s. Not only was it a hit, but there was the pure fun of working with my stepson, David. It didn't occur to me then how rough our successes might be for Jack. That may sound insensitive, but I thought there were compensations, namely, my need for him. I would have given up everything immediately if there was a chance of that solving Jack's problems. I understood that this business was up one day and down the next, and I really believed his turn would come. Thinking that, I may have missed how wounded he really was. At home, Daddy was not in a very good humor, and I constantly had to make excuses for him. He had a lot of bitterness in him. He was very fastidious, and wanted everything in its place. When you have little boys, that isn't always an attainable goal. If one of them left a toy out, he went into a tirade. It had nothing to do with the toy, everything to do with the fact that he wasn't working, he was home all day, every day.

Whatever problems Jack had, I didn't think I was one of them. There were so many warning signals around I don't know how I missed them, but I did. Even when the strange behavior started, I was slow to feel alarm. In Hollywood, you do not overreact because someone seems strange.

I know now that he suffered a great amount of guilt, and not only in his relations with his sons and me. He had never made peace with his family. He did not attend the funerals of either his mother or his father. He had little contact with his brothers, one of whom was an alcoholic who used to show up drunk at the stage door and embarrass him.

He was agnostic, but spent an excessive amount of time searching for something to replace religion in his life. He had been born into a devoutly Catholic home, and on her deathbed his mother begged him to come back to the church. He was so opposed to it, perhaps to any organized faith, that his feelings bordered on hatred. I never knew the source of those feelings. The subject would make him irrational.

In time, he developed an interest in psychic phenomena. He was fascinated by the spirit world, mystics, the writings of Edgar Cayce. He read everything Cayce wrote, and toward the end of his life carried one of Cayce's books around with him wherever he went.

His lack of a religious base, his inability to reconcile with his family, his fear of growing old, all combined to leave a great emptiness inside him. And in the stereotype of the man nearing fifty, he kept shopping around for something, or someone, to fill the void.

vvvv

Shirley gave Jack a generous amount of what lovers in the next decade would refer to as "space," perhaps too much. She understood, or thought she did, his prowling, his endless searching for answers that were just out of reach. She was not aware that one of Jack's searches had succeeded.

He was keeping a mistress.

The other woman was much on his mind when he suggested, on what seemed a moment of impulse, that he take Shirley out for pizza. If he had offered her a diamond, Shirley could not have reacted with more enthusiasm. In fact, she had been worrying. Jack seemed cold and withdrawn in that summer of 1971, and she could not account for it. After weeks of being virtually ignored, she craved his attentions. This would be a treat.

He was smitten by a young actress then featured in a network adventure series, and paid the rent on a plush apartment where they conducted their romantic interludes. They were well matched. She offered the promise of youthful passion, and he the reality of an unemployed actor's most negotiable asset, lots of free time. He intended to disclose none of this to Shirley, however. He had covered his tracks at the expense of an ever-guiltier conscience, and this was why he needed a rare night out with his wife. He wanted something from her. He wanted more of that space.

^^^^

I don't think Jack ever meant to get a divorce. He had so much guilt, he in no way could carry on a big affair and still be with me. I'm not talking about one-night stands.

Not that I was unwarned. My friend Betty kept saying, "Shirley, you're making a mistake. He's too sure of you. You're not playing the game well enough. You need to give him a taste of his own medicine. All he knows is that you're here, you're happy and contented."

I laughed and said, "Well, I am, most of the time."

That was before the night I caught him with a pretty girl in a Mexican restaurant, the Cafe Escobar, in Beverly Hills. Jack was in an acting class and starting to write a play, and it wasn't unusual for him to say, "I'll be home about eleven. I'm going to stop at So-and-so's office to dictate a few lines of dialogue."

It was on one of those nights that friends called and asked me to meet them for dinner. Then we stopped off at the Cafe Escobar for drinks. We were sitting there when suddenly in strolls this brunette with my husband. I watch them slide into one side of a booth, never so much as glancing around.

My friends had seen them, and there was no point in trying to conceal my shock. The café had a piano and a three- or four-piece mariachi band, and my companions were waiting to see how I would react. I didn't know. How does anyone handle such a situation? All I knew for sure was that he was sitting in a café with a woman, and she wasn't me.

But my friends were, I suspect, itching for a scene. They said, "Why don't you get up and sing with the band?"

Ah, that should be interesting, I thought, because our table was behind his, and he hadn't yet seen me. So I got up and very casually walked up to the band, introduced myself, and started to sing. I sang two songs, and the first was, "It

Had to Be You," and from the opening notes I saw him freeze. But he was cool, and he slowly turned around just to be sure who it was, and he saw it was me. Then he turned right around and continued his conversation with the girl. I am certain they were not talking nearly as fast as his mind was moving.

I had downed a few drinks and was clearly upset. I didn't quite finish the second song, "Blue Moon." I stormed off the stage and walked over to the booth and said, "Well, fancy meeting you here. Just one of those things, is it?"

Again, calmly, Jack said, "Shirley, this is So-and-so."

I said, "I don't care who she is," and after a few more biting words I ran out of the restaurant. He came after me, and we stood there on the sidewalk, and it was the first time in our marriage I ever really let him have it. I was screaming in the street, "You son of a bitch, how could you?"

"Let me explain."

"There is no explanation."

"She's So-and-so's secretary."

"Bullshit."

So it was that kind of scene. It was one of the few times I fought with him. I turned and left him standing there, and he took the girl home. Later, he gave me a very breezy story—she had been taking dictation for him, it was past quitting time, they went out for a cup of coffee. I didn't believe him, but from then on I never asked Jack questions.

That and much more was in the background when we dressed to go out. It seems silly now, my sitting there, happy as a lark, just enjoying his company like two kids on a pizza date. For weeks, we had communicated so little, now I was eager to catch up. And when he finally spoke he said:

"Mouse, you know I have to leave you."

I thought he meant he was going back on the road, or back to New York. I asked him what he meant.

He said, "I mean, I really have to leave. We have to separate."

I couldn't believe it. It was as if we had suddenly developed a language barrier. All I could think to ask was "Why?"

He said, "It's not you. There isn't anybody else, but I have to be . . . I just have to be myself. I just gotta do it, and I got to do it now."

I felt as though I had been gored in the stomach by a bull, a reaction I was determined to conceal. I didn't ask him not to go. I wouldn't plead with him. Actually, I couldn't speak. I was devastated. I just sat there, hearing him say the most words he had said to me in a month: "We'll tell the kids together. I'll get an apartment or a small house somewhere. It will take me a couple of weeks to get myself together and find a place, and I'll try not to upset anything. I'll try to stay out of your way until then."

Several times I asked if there was another woman. Each time he said no, there wasn't. "I don't want a divorce. It's not that, either," he said. "I just need to be by myself."

The next two weeks were tense and nearly intolerable. One of my friends called him on the phone one day and said, "Jack, why are you doing this?" He said, "I don't know," and started to cry, on the phone. "I don't know why I'm doing this."

Later, he told someone else, "If she had just once said please, don't go, I don't think I would have." But I didn't. As much as I was absolutely dying inside, I couldn't bear to have him stay when I believed that he didn't want me.

When he left, he rented a house way out in Hidden Hills, in the valley. There was no understanding, no promises, no expressions of wishes well meant. He was out of my life for most of 1972, and I went through all the cycles. Anger and hurt. He's really an idiot. He's a son of a bitch. What the hell made him leave? I had been true and honest, a marvelous wife, a wonderful mother. I had supported him in every way for seventeen years. Then you stop and think, It takes two people, and if he needs someone else, maybe I'm doing something wrong.

It was not long before I learned there was another woman, after all. He had always been honest with me about his flirtations. So there was a momentary shock, but no big one. The instinct I acted on was to see a psychiatrist for the first time to find out who I am.

It helped. In my first interview, I told the doctor my story and ended it by saying, "I just don't understand." And he smiled and said, "What you mean is, what's a nice girl like you doing in a place like this?" We both laughed.

There are no lightning bolts of wisdom at the end of therapy. Wisdom isn't what you need. Reassurances are. It was basically his decision. I was still a good person. I hadn't failed.

And better yet, I thought, My God, this man had everything. He had me, three beautiful sons, a marvelous home in Beverly Hills. We worked well together. How could he give up so much?

Within the year, he wanted to come back. He was more attentive now than he was the last year he lived with me. He would come to see the kids and call, and gradually the tension eased off. Slowly, I started to date. A doctor, a tennis pro, a few here and there. I began to enjoy that part of it. Suddenly, it was nice to be told how attractive I was.

Finally, Jack called one day and said, "We have to talk." I met him for lunch, maybe dinner, and he said, "I want to come back. I still love you. I never stopped loving you. I had to get away, but it's all over. I'm a better person now. I can be a better husband to you, a better father to the kids."

Of course, that was what I had been waiting to hear, because I never stopped loving him. I even understood his secret girlie. She was a brunette with blue eyes, in some ways childlike. She told him how she always fell asleep in front of the Christmas tree because she never wanted to go to bed on Christmas Eve. He liked that in her and, of course, she was probably in awe of him, as I had been. I guess I didn't give him those things anymore, and that was what he missed, and needed. The moment I started to grow up, he couldn't handle it.

In a way, through his description, I saw myself as I used to be. I had been the other woman once, in someone else's view, not mine. So I understood. What Jack had to understand was that there had been changes in my life, and I liked them. I learned how to live pretty much on my own. I had opinions, and I tapped into a strength I didn't know I had. I liked having more control. And if Jack wanted to come back, it would be on my terms. We were not going back to the relationship we had.

I told him the children and I couldn't walk on eggs around him anymore. He had to be a husband and a father. No more tennis games and nights out with the boys where the children and wife were excluded. He agreed, and it was done.

I told the doctor I was taking him back, and although you ordinarily have to put a gun to their heads to get an opinion, he did not hide his distress. "You are not going to change that man," he said. "Don't go back into this marriage thinking you can."

Jack came home, and he immediately began to work on writing and producing an act the two of us would take on tour. It was to be our show, and we called it *The Marriage Band.* We were excited, starting over, working together the way we had when Shaun was just a baby.

We played Las Vegas, the Cocoanut Grove, theaters in the round, hotels, all kinds of rooms, finally ending the tour after three months at the MGM Grand in Vegas. But the excitement, the fun, was short-term. For the first time, I started to see a personality change in Jack. The act had gone well, I thought, even though Jack had strained his vocal chords, the result of a three-or-four-pack-a-day cigarette habit. Nat (King) Cole had recently died of throat cancer, and the doctors had warned Jack that he had to stop smoking. His chords already had what they described as a white film on them.

We were playing the McKinley Theater in Warren, Ohio, when I really began to observe a person I didn't know. We had just checked into the hotel and put up our bags when Jack left the room and went for a walk. After about an hour, he burst into the room, and his eyes were strange, glassy, almost transparent. I asked him if anything was the matter. "Mouse," he said excitedly, calling me by my nickname, "you won't believe it. There is a large oak tree down the street, at the square, and on my walk I stopped and stood there, and my mother spoke to me. She spoke to me."

He had this faraway look in his eyes, and I asked, "Jack, what are you saying?"

He said, "You have to believe me. I heard her voice." He took a pack of cigarettes out of his pocket and crushed it in his hand. "She said these are going to kill me." And he tossed the crumpled pack into the wastebasket.

I said, "Um, honey, I, I, uh—that's remarkable." I didn't know what to say. His face had changed. I had never seen that look in his eyes. But I thought, Well, if it got him to quit smoking, some good would come out of it. And then the mood was gone—his eyes cleared, and it was as if he had just emerged from a trance. We had about an hour to get ready for the show, and we went on without any hitches.

From that point, he would go in and out of these spells. I cannot say with any certainty that drugs were not involved. I never saw him take anything other than medication for his throat, or an occasional upper, Dexedrine or Dexamil, to help keep him up (the kind of pill college kids were taking when they needed to stay up to cram for an exam).

I never knew him to smoke marijuana or take cocaine. He drank heavily, and either he knew not to mix stimulants or he didn't need anything else.

He was preoccupied now with his mother talking to him from the grave, and her warning that cigarettes would lead to his death. He was in contact with her on a frequent basis, or so he indicated. Whatever was taking place in Jack's mind, he was more at peace than he had been in years. He was convinced he had communicated with the spirit world.

One day he brought me a small metal paperweight with a sculpted spider on top. "This is for you, Mouse," he said. "This is a symbol."

I said, gently, "What kind of symbol, Jack?"

"*Charlotte's Web,*" he said. "Don't you remember the children's story, about the spider?"

I had no idea where this was going. Then I asked if he was thinking about a cartoon. He nodded at the spider: "Well, that's Charlotte."

I said, "It is?"

Then it dawned on me. His mother's name was Charlotte. He saw his mother reincarnated as a spider. Whatever delusions he had, she was in them. It probably would have been much easier on Jack if he had just gone to the funeral.

By the time we made our second appearance in Las Vegas, Jack had signed to do a movie with Clint Eastwood called *The Eiger Sanction.* He commuted every day from Las Vegas to the film's location in Death Valley. He had to be up at five in the morning to catch a helicopter, then back in the evening for our show. That schedule went on for weeks, and Jack was exhausted to the point of danger. We had rented a house near the hotel, and I went up to the bedroom when it was time to dress for that night's show. He was sitting in a corner, totally naked, reading a book.

I said, "We have to go and do the show, Jack."

He looked up at me and said, calmly, "I know now that I'm Christ."

I do not mean this disrespectfully, but I doubted that Christ did supper clubs. I tried not to panic. I had a desperate need to get help for Jack and, in a corner of my mind, I wondered what to do about the act. I said, "Jack, honey, I've got to go and get a doctor. I'll be right back."

There was no point in trying to trick him, I thought. One never knew with Jack. He might say yes, he would like to have a doctor see him, or he might laugh it off. I went into another bedroom to call, and Jack, who had taken the key from my purse, locked the door from the outside. So there I was, stuck in the bedroom, with no way out. I was having an anxiety attack of my own. I didn't know what he would do. I just knew that he was in the middle of a full-blown breakdown.

Quickly, I dialed my business manager, Howard Borris, in Los Angeles, and described what had happened. I said, "He needs to be hospitalized, and I don't want him put away here in Las Vegas. He needs to be taken home."

Howard did not waste words. "I'll be there in an hour," he said. "I'm leaving for the airport now." Then I called home and talked with Shaun, who was then sixteen, to explain what was happening. He offered to fly out, but I said, "Honey, it's okay. Howard's coming. We just need somebody to take Daddy home."

By that time I was a wreck, shaking, crying, unable to convince Jack to open the door. I kept repeating myself, "Please, let me out," but there was no response at all. Within an hour, Howard arrived on a private jet. Now Jack was locked in his room, and Howard talked to him through the door: "Jack, get your clothes, you and I need to go home. Shirley can do the show tonight, and we only have a couple days left."

The show featured a dozen dancers and singers, six men and six women. It was a musical narrative that took a couple from their first meeting through their marriage and first child. The music and the costumes were lovely.

I went out on the stage that night and announced that Mr. Cassidy was ill and unable to perform. If the audience would bear with me, I would *try* to give them a complete show. I said, "It's about love and marriage, and it was written for two people. So if it strikes you as funny in the wrong place, you'll know that I'm trying to sing both parts."

And I did, by myself. They loved it. By making that short speech, I had let the audience know I was trying something that was nearly impossible, and they were with me the entire time.

We canceled the remainder of the contract, but I needed another day to settle our business, pack up our belongings, and move out of the rented house in Las Vegas. When I returned home, I learned that Jack had refused to see a doctor, or a psychiatrist. He sat around in a bathrobe with nothing on underneath, and when people came to the door, he would just drop his robe and walk past them into the street. Whoever was available would bring him back.

He agreed to see a doctor, an analyst, and I sedated myself with the hope that this would soon pass. It did not. One night, in late 1973, I walked into the house after a concert, and he had fires blazing in every fireplace. I mean roaring fires. Two downstairs and one in the master bedroom. Fires everywhere, dancing higher and higher, while Jack kept throwing in more paper and more wood.

And again he was running around without his clothes. It was around two in the morning, and the children were asleep. Each time that I thought he could not frighten me any worse, we seemed to break the record. I was sure he would burn the house down. He was totally out of it, mesmerized by the fire:

"Isn't it beautiful?" he said. "This is the way we all should be. Look how peaceful the flames are."

My mind could no longer make the jumps necessary to keep up with Jack. It turned out that he was expressing his anger, at me—for sending him home and canceling the remaining shows in Las Vegas. He was very coldly berating me: He had lost face and would never work again, and it was my doing.

At that hour, after two, I called my psychiatrist, Dr. Rosengarten—for me, not for Jack. I was beside myself. I told him exactly what had happened, and what was said, and concluded, "I don't know what to do." He said, "Just stay there. I'll be right over, and I'm bringing an ambulance."

vvvv

When Shirley went back downstairs, she managed to stop him just as Jack was trying to set fire to the coffee table. She knew she could no longer protect him, or even put his welfare ahead of her own. His mind was slipping away into some dark corner she had no way of entering. It didn't matter what caused his condition, too much booze or too little sleep or an industry that refused to acclaim him.

What mattered were the three sons who were asleep in their beds. She now had to choose between salvaging something with Jack and the security of her children.

^^^^

I was scared, petrified. I honestly didn't know what he was capable of doing at that point. I knew he had a gun. I wasn't sure where he had put it. If he was angry enough with me, would he use it? I didn't know, but I was convinced that if I failed to act now, some harm would eventually come to the boys.

The doctor arrived and the attendants in their white coats, and they put him into a straitjacket. As they did, the haze seemed to lift, he grew calm, and with pleading eyes he asked, "Mouse, are you really going to let them do this? Are you going to let them take me away?"

I turned away and covered my face, the tears soaking my hand. It was dawn now, and I will never forget that morning as long as I breathe. As they led him to the ambulance, he was furious, glaring at me. "I'll never forgive you for this," he swore.

I wanted him to be admitted to Westside Hospital, a private psychiatric facility, and I started to climb in the ambulance with him. He would have no part of it. He said, "I don't ever want to see you again. Get out of my life."

I rode in the car with the doctor and followed the ambulance to the hospital. I had to sign the commitment papers. His words rang in my ears: "Are you really going to let them do this to me?" I got through it the only way I could, by thinking of the kids and their safety. I signed my name and waited for the doctors to finish their consultation.

Jack's own psychiatrist arrived and said that he would prescribe Lithium for him. He had diagnosed him as manic-depressive and thought the drug would help control his mood swings. He had been going through a major nervous disorder, reasonably normal for months, then suddenly—swoosh—another person would be there.

He had the right to check himself out of the hospital after seventy-two hours, and he did. I went to visit him each of the three days he was there, knowing he would not speak to me, that we would just sit and stare at each other for twenty minutes to an hour.

I would not wish that experience on any woman, seeing the man you've loved and lived with most of your life, the father of your children, with raw hatred in his eyes. He blamed me so, for taking away his pride. I asked God if I had done the right thing. Did I really have any choice?

Jack refused to take the Lithium; he didn't want to be on any drugs. But he did agree to check himself into Cedars-Sinai Hospital, voluntarily, for treatment. He had a therapist working with him, and we talked every day, and slowly the ice melted. He joked about his progress; they had been making leather novelties, and he was good at it. He was always adept with his hands. He wanted to see the boys, even though he knew he would be embarrassed being visited as a mental patient. I told them, in the gentlest way I could, that their father had suffered a nervous collapse, brought on by exhaustion and overwork, and he would be well soon.

Of course, Shaun, as the oldest, knew how far from the truth my explanation was, but he spared his brothers.

Jack stayed at Cedars-Sinai two weeks, checked himself out, and flew to New York. He registered in an expensive midtown hotel and began spending money as though they might stop printing it at any second. I received the bills.

At some point, he called me and said, "Please, Mouse,

get a divorce. You have to get a divorce for your sake." I knew by now we had played out the string, and to prolong matters would merely inflict more pain. I said, "Yes, I really do." Suddenly, I could see us losing the house, and our children could end up with nothing. I hired a lawyer and started divorce proceedings.

Two months later, after I had filed for the divorce, Jack flew back to California. He had rallied, had made a personal comeback, and all things considered looked well. He asked me to have dinner with him "to talk"—old times not forgotten.

He took me to a little restaurant on King's Road, and after we got past the polite chitchat, he said, "I really mucked things up. I really mucked it up, didn't I?

He wanted to know if we should make one more try to get back together. I said, "Frankly, Jack, I'm not sure that you would accept or even like the woman that I am now. I'm not sure that I'm the person you were in love with."

He said, "I know what you mean."

It was a strange moment. For someone who had been such a forceful and manipulative presence in my life, he was now so passive, so oddly agreeable, going along with whatever I said.

"I could never go back to the way it was, Jack."

He said, "I couldn't either, Shirley," and I knew it was the last time we would have that discussion.

vvvv

Shirley had in fact struck up a recent relationship with the man who would become her next major project, Marty Ingels. Few women ever had gone to such extremes. "All Jack wanted to do," she said, laughing, "was live life to the hilt. And Marty wanted to be Kafka's cockroach."

3

Is There Sex After Marriage?

IN ALL OF HIS YEARS as a humorist, a stand-up comic, and a bedside philosopher, Marty Ingels has concluded that sex is not the answer. But it does raise some interesting questions while you are waiting for whatever the answer turns out to be.

After a terrific start, sex virtually disappeared from his first marriage, along with his first wife, the former Jean Brett. They stuck it out for nine-and-a-half years, and today Marty still has an enduring respect for Jean as a sharp, talented lady and a patient, nurturing person.

When they met, in the late 1950s, Ingels was one of the hottest comedy prospects around. But not surprisingly, then and later, he spent a disproportionate amount of his time literally picking himself off the floor. After two decades of therapy and endless hours of soul searching, he still hasn't a clue as to what made him the way he is—riddled with complexes and insecurity.

This is an excerpt from one of his sessions with his analyst:

Marty: "If you say Jean was really my mother, and Shirley was my mother, why wasn't my mother ever my mother?"

Doctor: "Schmuck, you don't want a seventy-year-old mother, you want a thirty-year-old mother."

Much about Marty Ingels is admirable, some of it lovable. He is brutally self-honest, creative, persistent, street-smart, almost never aware of what time it is. He is also a world-class worrier, a hustler filled with so much raw energy he comes at you like a ball of rolling knives.

How he met and wooed his first wife tells you two things about him: his resourcefulness and his occasional disregard of the rules. He met her in one of the traditional ways. She was dating his best friend.

Certain women were always attracted to Ingels, sensing how vulnerable he was. He was born with a sweet Cabbage Patch Kid face. You look at that face, and you know instantly that when he was a boy, Marty's aunts and uncles were always pinching his cheeks.

He had a miserable childhood, always feeling ignored or overshadowed by a model older brother, Arthur. Out of that experience came his comedy, which led him to Hollywood, where he found Jean Brett. Of course, he didn't have to look far. She had been dating his roommate, a lanky New Yorker named Lloyd Rubin, who worked as an accountant for one of the movie studios.

~~~~

Lloyd was very strange with women. He would meet them in singles bars in out-of-the-way places like Alhambra. He'd go to these small towns because Hollywood made him nervous. He thought everyone he met in Hollywood was a movie star.

So he kept talking about this girl, Jean. It was all I heard . . . Jean, Jean, Jean. She was married once, now she's not. She's terrific. He kept telling me so much about her that I became fascinated, and I sneaked her telephone number from his book one night, and at two o'clock in the morning I called and talked to her. Well, we had a long discussion about Lloyd, how crazy he was, and she got a kick out of that. I laughed. She laughed. We got along great.

I said I would call her the next night, and I did, and every single night after that for weeks. And always late at night. I'd wait until Lloyd left, and after she came in from her dates. We got to be really close, just on the telephone, sharing the trivia that happened to us that day. We established something that would end up being the prevailing
~~~~

theme of our marriage, which I guess was unhealthy, in many ways. We were both scared to death of the arena out there—the jungle. And rather than brave it alone, we chose to hang on to each other.

This went on for months. We had never met, but I couldn't wait to run home and call her every night. It was crazy—but it was great, indirect and easy. I didn't have to *be* anything. I just went with my voice and my brain, and my natural nutsy impulses, and she loved it.

I really never felt I could cut it in person. That's why I developed so many indirect ways of communicating with the world. Telephone calls were great. Letters were great.

As a kid, I went to all the meat-market dances, and that was agony for me. The rules were to stand there and parade your stuff, when maybe you thought your stuff sucked. And I did. I always thought I was ugly as sin, and really I wasn't. I mean, I look at the pictures now and see that I was a cute kid. But I felt ugly. So I met girls at the library, in the subway stations, in the back of the supermarkets, places where I could catch them off guard.

So one day, four o'clock in the morning, Jean and I were talking fervently. And just out of the blue, connected to nothing, I said, By the way, where the hell do you live? She blurted out the address, the location, the directions, and we both knew without saying a word that I would be there momentarily. At four-thirty in the morning. I got in my car and pointed myself to who-knows-where, to meet who-knew-what, and what-the-hell-for? Now that's a lonely guy.

~~~~

Only a powerful urge could have motivated Marty. Driving around in the dark was very low on his list of fun things to do. Shortly after he moved to California, he got lost one bleak and rainy night trying to find his way home. He pulled into a gas station to fill his tank, and ask for directions to the San Bernardino Freeway. It was late, he was nearly out of gas, and the fear of being abandoned alone and far from home—which was so ingrained in him—had left him tongue-tied.
~~~~

When the attendant walked up to his window, Marty asked, "Do you know where . . . ?" And he couldn't get the words out. He couldn't say "San Bernardino." He did fine with the "San" part, but no matter how many times he started over, he couldn't say the rest. Finally, the attendant asked him to move his car away from the pumps so he could serve the people who had pulled in behind him.

"In the trip from your brain to your mouth," he says, "the brain is the editor, the mouth is just the actor." One of them wasn't working. Marty moved his car, parked, leaned his head against the wheel, and cried. "It was terrible," he remembers. "Just terrible."

~~~~

Somehow I found my way to the address Jean gave me. She lived in a small guest room in the back of a little yellow house. I made my way slowly along the narrow side path. It was pitch-black, but for the glaring white bulb over a screen door. I tapped on it. Almost instantly, it opened, and there in a half-blurry shadow she stood. Neither of us said anything. We just stood there. Then I pushed the door open and just grabbed her. We kissed again and again, there in the dark by that half-open screen door, and never stopped. We made love right there. It was spectacular.

That was probably the last time we made love, mad, spontaneous love. The sexual thing with Jean and me ended right away because we became buddies. I don't know why it was so great that first time, but it never was again. She wanted it. I wanted it. But the heat was gone. I had sexual desires all over the place, and she did, too, but we didn't have it together.

If I had known that would be the case, what happened would still have happened. I went back to my apartment that day and picked a fight with Lloyd. He moved out. Then I called Jean and said, "Hey, guess who needs a roommate?" She said, "How about me?" And she moved in. Not long after that, I landed my television series with John Astin, and there we were—little Jean Brett from Alhambra and her movie-star roommate.
~~~~

Jean was Italian, bright, articulate, with a tremendous figure, beautiful hair, great eyes and mouth, and the best sense of humor ever. But she didn't like her nose. She kept a list of all the things she wanted to change in her life, and first on the list was her nose. She was a changer. To a fault. Anything and everything she saw as wrong went on her change list. Amazingly, she actually went down that list and tackled them one by one. Second on the list was her relationship with her mother. Her father had abandoned all of them when she was fairly young, and she found herself stronger than a very erratic mother who attempted suicide several times. She intended to fix all that. Jean's agenda was a big one.

Her face. Her family. Her career. I told her flatly she was not to have her nose fixed. I had seen too many of those operations bungled. I said, "You don't need it. You're beautiful the way you are." Then one day she came home with bandages all over her face. She had done it. And it worked. She was gorgeous, with a Marlo Thomas or Audrey Hepburn look, dark eyes, dark hair, elegant.

She quickly became a top photographer's model in California and then New York. We were married for nine years, and it was wonderful in many ways. She provided a home wherever I went, city to city, job to job. Always in the audience for the television shows I did, she made me feel secure. It had the look of a perfect marriage—funny guy, beautiful girl—and we were on everybody's party list. Except for the sexual part, which never improved, we *were* a perfect marriage. We loved to be together. We laughed, had a good time . . . and gave each other the protective armor we needed to brave the Hollywood jungle.

All through the 1960s, Ingels was on the verge of breaking through as a major comedy talent; the next Jerry Lewis, many said. Another Red Skelton. (His face, in those days, was a dead ringer for Red's.) Lewis took credit for discovering Marty, and put him in two of his movies.

But Marty's impulsive and often self-destructive ways were

a source of endless frustration for his agent, an especially nice man named Lenny Kaplan. Marty once showed up two hours late for a meeting with a CBS executive who planned to offer him a deal. "If he really wanted me," Marty told the dejected Kaplan, "he would have waited."

They never heard from the man again. "Marty really didn't want to go to that meeting," said Kaplan. "He was afraid to go. He could have conquered the world. But somehow . . . deep down, it wasn't really what he wanted. The natural stuff that he used to come up with was hilarious. Just sitting there talking to him, you could pee in your pants.

"He could have been one of the biggest comics, I think, in the world, if he had worked at it. That drive to succeed, he never put into his talent. He put it into all the outside factors, like his stationery and sending out gifts and writing letters. That's what he did with his time. He never worked on developing the talent part."

Lenny also represented Jean Ingels, during and after the marriage. "Commercials, a little acting, mostly modeling jobs," he says. "A very pretty girl. I knew for a long time Marty was sleeping on the couch or on the floor. I didn't exactly get what was going on with them."

Most of the time, Marty didn't know either, but he went with the flow, and it was good.

~~~~

I made a movie in Europe called *If It's Tuesday, This Must Be Belgium*, as close to a hit as anything I ever did. It developed a kind of cult following. The producers threw Jean in with a small part, and it gave us a sweet opportunity to work together and see the world at the same time.

The female lead was Suzanne Pleshette, a really terrific lady, but she was not happy about Jean being too close to the camera. In truth, they looked too much alike. So they debeautified Jean. She had to wear her hair pulled back and no makeup and a frocky dress, and ended up sitting in the back of the bus. But at night when we would go out with the cast, she became her natural knockout self, and I can remember everyone being repeatedly dazzled by that transformation.
~~~~

I was very proud of Jean. Of course, most of my friends tried to make a move there. They were all over her. Then we'd leave a party or a dinner and go home and have our giggles. And drift off to a sexless sleep. I know. It was nuts, but for us it seemed to work.

As I said, Jean was hungry to improve herself. She dove headfirst into everything—psychiatry, meditation, *est*, primal scream. Then she painted for a while, feverishly. And the fix-up list continued. Music, school, tennis, house. And I guess I should have looked at the list a little more carefully, because next to number nine it read, "Husband."

And while I never really wanted to think about it, that one was inevitable. Change husband.

Then things began to deteriorate. As is nearly always the case when there are frustrations between two people, we started to fight. About little things, about nothing. One of us always wanted to go when the other wanted to stay, those kinds of quarrels. Of course, we didn't have that one sure makeup place other marriages had, the bedroom. So even our good times would end in a scrap. One of them was about her career. I wouldn't admit it then—maybe I didn't see it—but I know now that her prospects were intimidating to me. Her jobs took her away from me, and I needed her, perhaps too much.

One morning she was looking through her photo portfolio, into which all models put their whole goddam life. Years of collecting one-of-a-kind color blowups that gradually make up a collage of priceless audition samples, taken from every angle and in every outfit at every location imaginable. Her three-ringed bible.

We were fighting about something, I forget what. And my eyes suddenly focused on the book. I felt an unreasoning anger rising in me. "It's that book," I said. "Your life is that fucking book." I ripped it out of her hands, raced to open the front door, and flung the book end-over-end into the air. I truly didn't think about the swimming pool. And that's where it landed. Right in the pool. All those precious pictures. In a flash, we both raced to the edge to scoop it up and start peeling the sheets off one another. We saved most of them. But a big part of us ended that day.

For that and countless other reasons, it was time for Jean

to leave. One day she showed up during my appointment with the therapist and virtually wept for "permission" to leave. I had hoped the doctor would take my side and say, "No, hold on, you have a good relationship here." Instead, I was crushed to hear him say, "What makes you think you have to ask permission to leave someplace? If you feel it isn't right for you, leave. You must leave. You don't need my permission, or even your husband's."

She reacted as if a great weight had been lifted from her shoulders. I had never seen her so free. In the car driving home, she just stared out the window and kept repeating, "Of course, of course. Why didn't I see it before?"

She began preparing to leave. My first clue came from the newspapers spread over the kitchen table, with the apartment ads circled. I started getting sick . . . headaches, chest pains, nausea, dizziness, and worse. Terrifying panic seizures. Doctors call it "separation anxiety," fear of being abandoned.

All very psychological, but the symptoms are no less real to the person who has them. If one has led a relatively normal, healthy life, it may be impossible to imagine a panic so acute one can't carry on the simplest chores.

If my helplessness was supposed to stop her, it didn't. The marriage was closing out. For nine-and-a-half years, we had clung to each other like two shipwrecked souls. The marriage lasted as long as we both needed it, and Jean stopped needing first. It was that simple. Just being Marty Ingels's wife, sitting there in Merv Griffin's audience, wasn't enough anymore. She was ready for her turn. She knew it, and gradually I did, too.

I envied her in many ways. Words could change her. Jean would read a book, *How to Win Friends and Influence People*, or *I'm OK—You're OK*, and suddenly everything around her would be better.

I could read six hundred books and still be unable to cut back on Twinkies. I still can't change any of my habits, and I've had most of them since I was a child.

It may sound cruel to suggest that she had to step over me to walk out of the apartment, but that's what happened. By the time she left, I was floor-bound, curled up in an old blanket like a homeless pup. I had virtually blocked the door with my body. Yet she had to leave for her own survival. She stopped in the doorway for one, lingering moment, while her taxi waited. There was a lot of her that still loved a lot of me, but in my heart I really didn't want to drag her down.

She looked at me and said, "I'd like to take Gypsy with me."

I said, "No, the dog stays here."

There was no argument. "Okay," she said. "I'll need about eight weeks to get adjusted, and then you can bring the dog over to see me." That was vintage Jean.

She did it just like that. After eight weeks, she called, as she said she would, and I stopped by. When she opened her door, she reached out and said, "Hello, Gypsy. Hello, sweetheart."

~~~~

Marty Ingels tells weird and hysterical stories, and sometimes they have the added advantage of being true. He may be the only person alive who blames Albert Schweitzer for the breakup of his marriage, and even in this claim there is at least a shred of truth. . . .

~~~~

I was to speak at a very elaborate, black-tie dinner at the New York Hilton, honoring a philanthropist named Simon Musselman. Jean and I were seated at the upper tier of a raised dais, in full view of about fourteen hundred black-tied New York luminaries. As was our custom, we whispered witty remarks to each other while awaiting my turn at the mike.

At one point, one of the speakers compared the honored guest to his friend "the immortal Albert Schweitzer."

Out of that innocent if flowery comment came a scene that would drive the final nails in our marital tomb. Jean started it by whispering out the side of her mouth, "Albert Schweitzer? That's some stretch from Simon Musselman."

I whispered back, "Albert Schweitzer? So who the hell was Albert Schweitzer, really?' "

Jean: "What do you mean, 'Who the hell was Albert Schweitzer?' "

Ingels: "Exactly what I said. Who the hell was Albert Schweitzer, and what did he ever do besides play the organ and hang out with the lepers?"

Jean: "Oh, wonderful. What did Albert Schweitzer do? Oh, nothing. Just probably the greatest missionary of the twentieth century."

Ingels: "So what the hell is a great missionary? Just a priest with a press agent."

Jean: "Are you crazy? Did you ever hear of the Nobel Peace Prize?"

By now our voices were rising, and the speaker, a few feet away, was shooting nervous looks in our direction. In the front tables of the audience, heads turned and people were craning their necks.

Ingels: "You call me crazy? You worship some whacko jungle shut-in because your mother told you to and—"

Jean: "At least, my mother reads."

Ingels: "Yeah, maybe the racing form."

Jean: "Why, you miserable son of a bitch . . ."

With that, Jean jumped to her feet, grabbed her purse, knocked over my water glass, pushed her chair aside, and left the dais. With every eye in the room on her and the speaker standing there, flustered, she marched up the aisle and out the ballroom. There was nothing I could do, as she walked through the dumbstruck crowd. I was the next to speak, which I did with aplomb, all things considered.

Jean didn't make scenes for effect. By the time I raced home to our rented apartment on Central Park South, the closets were open and Jean was gone.

Three days passed without a word. I was frantic. A friend of mine was a cop, and we checked out all the major hotels, even the hospitals. Nothing. Finally, on the fourth day the phone rang. It was her. "I'm at a hotel on Fifty-seventh Street. Will you come get me?" It was a rickety old place used mostly for show-biz rehearsals. When I walked into her tiny room, she was in bed in the dark, but there was a spotlight placed curiously on the floor near the door, its beam reaching my stomach. I asked what that was all about, and she said she was afraid one of the short Puerto Ricans who lived in the hotel might try to break into her room. She figured the light in his face might surprise and discourage him. That was also vintage Jean. She was back, but I knew she wouldn't stay long.

~~~~

During roughly the same period that Shirley Jones and Jack Cassidy were struggling, unsuccessfully, to ride out their troubles. Marty's career had hit a wall. His TV series had been long since canceled, a lot of his calls were not being returned. He was about to crash.

The Ingels divorce was uncontested. It had been a marriage without a legacy, without children, no permanent victories, just two decent people who held on as long as they could.

Jean wanted no settlement, and Marty had none to give. But he was yet to let go, calling when he could, visiting when he could, driving by when he could just to look at her windows and steal another memory of the warmth and home and security he felt with her. He brought gifts, and left notes. Anything to manipulate her feelings. But Jean wasn't buying.

Not in the worst months after she left, or later, would he ever have any negative feelings about Jean. In 1980, after he had been happily married three years to Shirley and reestablished himself as a business-celebrity matchmaker, he heard one more time from Jean:

~~~~

I had always felt that the way Jean and I parted left something unfinished. She wouldn't take any of my money, little as there was. She left feeling guilty and asking for nothing. She said, "I'll leave the same way I came." But I felt deeply about the selfless nine-and-a-half years she had given me. I knew someday I would find the natural opportunity to make that up to her.

Perhaps this was it. She called, and we agreed to have lunch. It was nice. No awkwardness. She looked sensational, as always, and she still talked a mile a minute. Then she mentioned college.

"College?"

"Yes, night school. I've decided I want to be a psychologist."

A little bulb lit up in my head. I thought that was a gritty thing to do. "Yeah? You're actually going to college. About how much will that whole thing cost?"

She said six thousand dollars, and the light got stronger. It just popped out: "Listen, what if I made that a gift to you? Just paid for your college courses."

Jean was never a taker. Nor had she attracted many givers. She was never the type who would be taken care of by a man, with one guy sending her rings and another paying her rent and a third giving her furs. So this was not a comfortable spot for her. Her eyes grew wide. "You want to give me six thousand dollars, now? You would do that for me?"

I nodded my head. And so it was done.

The next day, I had my bookkeeper draw up a check for six thousand dollars and had it messengered to Jean's little house in the Valley. (Buying that house was probably the wisest move she ever made. She bought it shortly after she left me, with a down payment of four thousand dollars. The house is probably worth $400,000 today.)

In a small but satisfying way, I had settled some unfinished business. Now I had a different kind of problem. Should I tell Shirley? How could I not tell her? I even called long-distance to seek an opinion from my mother, Rego Park's one-woman crisis clinic. She gasped that familiar Jewish gasp and predicted that Shirley would divorce me when she found out.

I wasn't sure of anything, but I knew I had to tell her. It was a quiet Sunday night. I asked her to sit down. And I laid the whole thing out for her.

She sort of blinked, startled. She knew how I felt about my ex-wife, that I respected her, and there was nothing else involved.

"What was it for?" she asked.

"She's gone back to college to get a degree. I felt I owed her something. I mean, the girl gave me nine years of her life, and she got nothing out of it. Nothing. She supported me emotionally for so many years, and spent her own money on so many things. I was a bad deal for her."

Shirley smiled. "She saw you coming," she said, in a teasing, not unkind way.

"What do you mean?"

"Don't you think that may have been what she had in mind when she called?"

I said, "No, I really don't. Shirley, she didn't ask for anything. I was the one who brought it up."

"Maybe she knows what a soft touch you are."

I felt a little defensive, so I said, "Shirley, look, you have absolutely no obligation in the world to be a part of this six thousand. It's my ex-wife. I have some money in New York that's not community property that my uncle invested for me. I'll get it from there."

She thought about it for a few seconds, and then said, with no hesitation, "No, a little part of me is glad that you're the kind of guy who would do that."

No more was said. It felt good to be able to offer someone a gift that she needed, with no strings attached. And in a way, it finally closed that chapter in my life.

~~~~
~~~~

4

When Marty Met Shirley

IT WOULD BE HARD to imagine anything good coming out of what had been, up to then, the worst week of Marty Ingels's life—which says a great deal right there.

His wife of nine years had walked out. The bank had foreclosed on his home, and he had moved into a cheap apartment in a nondescript building. His new Cadillac had been repossessed one night while he slept. And he knew he could no longer live off his exposure from having starred in a television series. It was Marty's theory that for a year after your show had been canceled, you were still a celebrity. He called it "coasting." That week his year was up.

Out of all that misery, with more to come, something good happened. Shirley Jones happened. But that is getting ahead of the story. The low point came that same week, when Ingels suffered a nervous breakdown on the Johnny Carson Show. It was a comic's nightmare, a page out of *Pagliacci:*

~~~~

I felt as if everything I had was gone. Yet I don't recall being despondent. Comedy is the best distance keeper, and I was good at repressing my feelings. It was not a good time, but I kept thinking I was doing okay.

I should have paid more attention to my "little anxieties," which were taking more and more forms. Stomach pains,
~~~~

skin rashes, heart palpitations and, always before a performance, short dizzy spells. As a result, show business was just no fun anymore. Gradually, it had become a sheer agony, and I never stopped long enough to deal with it. There were suddenly no want-to's in my life, only have-to's, places I had to be, people I had to please, goals I had to reach. Without fully realizing it, I was in a state of major panic from morning to night.

On top of all that, the business itself was frustrating and fragile. The opportunities were there and gone in a minute, and every year there was a new crop of younger and brighter comics breathing down your neck and ready to take over.

If that wasn't actually the way it was, this was the way I saw and felt it. The absence of control over your own destiny grinds you down. Working, not working. If you are a comic, your guts and your rent are always on the line. Finally, I had to take a Valium to go anywhere, and I'm not a pill person. It was getting more excruciating every day.

Now *The Tonight Show* called. That was every comic's "big" shot. I had been on a few times before, usually when one of their regulars had to cancel out. But it never really happened there for me.

For all that the country loved him, Carson struck me as tied up and nervous inside, as I was. I was moving like mad with the other talk shows—Merv Griffin, Dick Cavett, Les Crane, Virginia Graham, all pussycat people who dug my humor and whose shows, of course, would all hit the network skids. So I never felt really comfortable with Carson.

I know he felt that way with me. I didn't do his kind of comedy, and he seemed offended by my insecurity. The word was he thought I "spilled my guts too much." He actually ended up putting me on the show's "don't book" list, which was funny in a way, because this night I was going to blow myself out of the water forever, all by myself.

I went on and did my routine. My timing was a little off, but it wasn't bad. The applause was pleasant, I went to the couch, and the next guest came out. I think it was Buddy Rich, the drummer. I was just sitting there, listening, when it started. From the fingertips of my right hand to my right shoulder, a kind of muscle reflex, a "tingling." I'd had it before, but this one wouldn't stop.

I had experienced the whole range of anxiety things. I was driving once and the entire street seemed to turn sideways and I felt as if I was driving on a wall. Basically, your mind is saying, "You're a nobody, you can't cut it."

At first I thought, well, maybe the audience wouldn't notice, but I was quivering. I couldn't sit still, and so I sat on my hand. Instead of regaining control of myself, the shaking began spreading to the rest of me—up my left leg to my left shoulder, and now across my chest and up my neck. By now, the entire right side of my body was trembling uncontrollably, and the audience was starting to whisper and giggle. They thought I was doing a shtick. Carson wasn't happy. He gave me a look that said, "Oh, Ingels is really hitting bottom, reaching for a cheap laugh. . . ."

I was terrified. I thought I was having a stroke. My vision started to blur, and I began to feel myself passing out. I knew I had to get out of there. If I was going to die, I didn't want it to happen on network TV. So I stood up—ever a comic—and made a joke about always wanting to use Johnny's private john. I literally left them laughing. I staggered to the curtain, held on just long enough to kind of spin around—the audience thought it was my finale—and fall to the floor backstage. A couple of the stagehands helped me to my car. I was conscious, but that's all. A couple of them drove me home, carried me up the stairs (I wouldn't take the elevator) and into my apartment. They gently laid me down in front of the television set, turned it on, covered me with a blanket, and left, glad to get the hell out of there. I can't blame them.

I tried to sleep, hoping that whatever this new siege was, it would be gone by morning. It wasn't. Nor the next. And more or less crawling to the bathroom and the kitchen, I stayed on the floor in that blanket in front of that blaring TV for what seemed to be an eternity.

~~~~

For the next nine months, Marty Ingels dropped out of sight. He doesn't recall leaving his apartment for anything, except to sneak downstairs for the mail, praying no one would see him. He went weeks without shaving or bathing, with-
~~~~

out answering the phone. He spent most of his days and nights hugging his floor. He ate mostly candy and Saltines, except when a neighbor, a young girl named Myra, dropped by to bring him soup or an occasional hot meal. She lived in the building and was herself an invalid, suffering from kidney disease, dependent on a home dialysis machine. She gave him nourishment, no lectures or questions. He promised himself that if he recovered and was financially able, he would return the gift and help support her for the rest of her life. And so he has.

While Marty was crawling around on his carpet and working up the will to call his psychiatrist, Shirley Jones was coping with her career and life as a single parent. There was no reason for their paths to cross. But they did.

~~~~

It isn't cancer and I didn't think about death. But anxiety is an awful disease because you have no idea why you are so fearful. It just takes you apart piece by piece and renders you totally unable to deal with simple things. I felt physically unable to stand. Not knowing what caused me to be on the floor, I didn't know how I was going to get up.

Down there on the floor, life became a series of sunsets and sunrises. I slept little, if at all, waking up at all hours, anxious every day to see the first television news at four-thirty, which told me another business day was over. No more dragons available until tomorrow.

I kept the phone on the floor next to me, but I dreaded the rings. They meant it was someone out there wanting me for something I could no longer do. The calls from agents dropped off gradually, as did the rest of them. My father was gone. My mother called occasionally, aware that "something was wrong." Years later, my brother, a New York dentist, told me that he was secretly in touch with my psychiatrist during that period, and at one point the doctor said, "We'll know in a month or two, one way or another."

My brother said, "Know what?"

"Whether or not Marty tries to take his own life."

To this day, that call astonishes me, that any of them were
~~~~

thinking in such terms. In spite of whatever I was going through all that time on the floor, I never thought of suicide. To the contrary, I was trying desperately to hold on to the little life I felt left. I managed to persuade a doctor friend to visit my apartment once. He did whatever cursory examination he could and assured me I had nothing terminal.

But my emotional paralysis continued. There was one sweet and isolated attempt by a fellow comic, a friend of mine named Sandy Baron, to pull me out of the pits. Sandy, who had a history of his own with agoraphobia, showed up one night banging at my door. When I opened it, he said he was stranded downstairs without his car and he had to get to Robertson and Wilshire streets in ten minutes. I thought he was crazy. I explained my condition, but he paid it no mind and pressed his predicament until I put on my robe and hobbled with him down to my garage. I hadn't even seen my car in weeks. I was hoping it wouldn't start, but it did, and in a few minutes we were at Robertson and Wilshire.

"Okay, you're here," I said.

"Okay," he said, "take me back."

"Take you back? What are you talking about?"

"Well," he said, smiling, "I just wanted to prove to you that you *could* get up if you really wanted."

It was sheer genius what he tried, and better than all the doctors I had consulted because he had shown real caring—rare for this town, certainly rare for me. He was right, but it didn't work. I wasn't ready to abandon my Linus blanket. (This isn't a psychiatric term. I picked it up from the comic strip *Peanuts*. But the principle is the same.)

I don't think I saw Sandy again after that, and I never really thanked him for what he did. Sandy, wherever you are, thanks.

At one point, some months later, I put a call through to my doctor and cried, "I don't know what to do. I'm afraid to go anywhere, but I can't stay here the rest of my life. I gotta do something."

"Start with one little step," he said. "Shave, for instance. Get to the bathroom and shave. It'll be a beginning." I decided to try it. I actually crawled to the bathroom and shimmied up the sink to the mirror. I hadn't seen myself in months. And I suppose when you are sick mentally, you are sick all over. It was startling. My eyes were bloodshot, my skin was yellow, clumps of hair had fallen out. I was all bent over like a hunchback. I had a full beard. It was like looking at your reflection and seeing Howard Hughes.

The next day, I called my doctor and shouted, triumphantly, "I shaved. I shaved. Now what do I do?"

He said, "Go somewhere. Anywhere. Just get in your car and go."

That was when I started looking through my mail. And one morning it just appeared, an invitation to an art exhibit to be held on Michael Landon's front lawn. The idea appealed to me because the gathering would be outside, near to the curb and my car, where I could make a quick run for it if I panicked. I decided right there, this was the one. The moment when I would reach out to the real world again.

I had about a week before the event, and I actually spent it rehearsing for my reentry. The first day I spent going back and forth to the elevator, and then down to the lobby. That was a big step for me. (Around the world three times, and now I was cheering myself for taking an elevator four floors to the ground. Great.) Then from the lobby to the garage . . . and to my car, again and again, until Sunday came and I was ready.

The things I remember doing then seem even weirder to me now, but I'd be lying if I left them out. Such as, putting my clothes on *over* my pajamas, so I could feel secure and still connected to my warm floor. I climbed in my car, drove around the block, pointed it toward the freeway, and started to shake. I turned back toward the apartment building, and the shaking stopped.

I circled the block again, and again, knowing I had only two options: my room or that party. Finally, I knew I had to go on or continue to be a prisoner in my room. In a cold sweat, I drove to Michael Landon's house.

There was the usual line of cars and attendants at the front gate. I had a five-dollar bill in my pocket. When the attendant opened my door, I slipped him the five and said, "Do me a favor. Keep my car right here in front. I want to pick up a quick painting and split."

I wasn't sure I could make it down the graded grass walkway to where the crowd was milling around. I leaned up against the car first, waiting to give myself a push, a little momentum. That's when Jim Garner walked past, and Pat Boone, and Betty White. There were a couple of cute cracks about me lounging peacefully on the hood of my car. Funny, the way things look, and the way they really are.

A minute later, I had my thrust, and I was tripping down the path winding to the party. And I guess the next forty seconds were about to change the whole course of my life. As I rounded the bend, there was Shirley Jones coming from the other side. And I rolled into her like a wrecking ball knocking down a building. She fell back onto a chaise longue and, before I could say or do anything, there was a crowd of princely types lifting her up and brushing her off. It was then that I got a chance to look into her eyes.

At the risk of sounding like a Hallmark card, there was something in her eyes that spoke to me. Later, she would tell me that week had been a particularly awful one for her. She had filed for divorce, and accepted the fact that her marriage to Jack Cassidy was over. She had come to this party for much the same reason I did.

It was a terrible time for her, and two or three friends hovered around her protectively. She was having what I call a "Gentile" nervous breakdown. That's where you get a sharp headache on the right side for about forty minutes. You take two Bufferin and you're fine by dinnertime. The Hebrew kind has you waking up in a Beirut motel, with lobotomy scars and the deep conviction that you are Woodrow Wilson.

I'm not a devotee of holistic medicine, nor am I psychic, nor do I transmit messages for the God people. At that moment, I wasn't even sure I could stand without losing my balance, but I was sure that I was seeing something in the eyes of Shirley Jones that said, "*I need you.*"

What I said was, "I'm sorry, hello. My name is Marty Ingels." She smiled that radiant smile. "Yes, I know," she said. All at once, I had the collected works of several dead poets I wanted to quote, but before I could get another word out, her palace guard had gathered her up and ushered her out to the car. I did yell some stuff after her, and I could hear her yelling back, "Later, Marty, later." Later, indeed.

Then and there, I was convinced that the first giant stride in my recovery would be to find that lady again. I knew full well if I suggested such a thing to anyone, they would have said I was out of my mind.

And, of course, I was.

~~~~

Shirley's account of that meeting differs only slightly: "I saw him trip getting out of his car. I knew who he was. I had seen him on Dickens and Fenster. He looked at me, with those giant brown eyes, and it was like a cartoon, where the light bulb goes *ping*! It made me giggle. I could hardly keep from staring, it was that overt.

"After the crash, he introduced himself and said something, and I tried to answer, but people kept getting between us."

His reaction was absurd in the context of his own problems. "I really felt she needed me and that I could help her." He spent the next six weeks trying to contact her. He went to libraries to read whatever they had on Shirley in their magazine files. He carefully tore out the photographs of her for a collage he was creating, sitting alone at night, thinking of all the things he would say to her if he could. With all other avenues closed, he slipped twenty dollars to a secretary at the William Morris Agency to sneak into the private files and get her home phone number for him. He started calling, leaving messages with her maid.

~~~~

I knew I would be talking to her one day, and I started making elaborate notes of exactly what I wanted to say. Meanwhile, the picture collage was getting bigger and bigger—and really lovely. I was still mostly on the floor, but now I had something I really wanted to do. And it was literally getting me on my feet.

The day she finally returned my call, my notes were gigantic and wonderful, but I was in the bathtub, three rooms away from my desk. I said, "Shirley, this may sound funny, but would you mind if I put you on hold? I've got some notes on this, and they're in the other room." I knew she thought I must have just flown in from Pluto, but I ran to the other room, dripping wet, naked, and nearly as innocent as a newborn babe, retrieved the notes, and started reading.

I had all these things I wanted to say, what I saw in her eyes. I really wanted to start all over and bring her one of those purple corsages and take her to the prom and a hay-ride and all that. All of it was in my speech, which I had been rehearsing now for six weeks. I was doing great. I knew she would listen. She might send an ambulance to take me away, but I knew she wouldn't hang up. I'm three quarters of the way into it, zeroing in on why the two of us deserved a shot, when she cut right in. "Wait a minute," she said. "If all this is to ask me to dinner or something, that's fine, I accept."

As fine as that sounded, it wasn't exactly as I had planned. "Uh, Shirley," I said. "I just have one paragraph to go. Would you mind if I finished it?"

~~~~

So began one of the least likely romances ever recorded in the motherland of romantic fantasy. On their first dinner date, Marty remembers taking Shirley on a scenic drive through the Hollywood hills. She remembers looking for a restaurant, not finding one, and not getting to eat. He remembers driving back to the street and sitting there, talking, savoring the fact that Shirley made no move to get out of the car. . . .

~~~~

When I was a kid growing up in Brooklyn, the measure of how well you did on a first date was how fast the girl leaped to the handle of the car door when you took her home. In my history, most of them used to leap out before the car had fully stopped.

But here, the lady wasn't making a move. I was doing great. I started opening up, telling some old stories. Now we have been sitting there for over half an hour. She still hasn't moved toward the door. Boy, this was my night. She was hanging on every word. I'm not George Hamilton. I'm not prepared for success. I thought to myself, My God, we're going to have children right here in the car.

I'm a guy who, all of his life, had to fight for every inch. Now I have America's sweetheart in the car and it is two o'clock in the morning and she can't get enough of me. I'm running out of jokes. Finally, she turns and says, "Listen, it's getting late. Maybe you'd better take me home."

"Home? What do you mean?" I said. "Isn't *this* your home?"

"Oh, no," she said. "I live two blocks down that way and one to the right."

~~~~

Whatever the world record is for Most Hilarious Second Date, Ingels had to be a contender. He was convinced that this would be his big romantic home run. And he had a plan. He made a dinner reservation at a restaurant atop one of Hollywood's swank hotels. At the same time, he reserved a posh suite in the same hotel, overlooking the city's vista. He spent the day setting it up: dinner table for two on the balcony, chilled wine, and instructions to have the steaks in the warmer precisely at nine. In the bedroom, he had a stereo with all of Shirley's favorite songs and, on the wall, a giant blowup poster of the two of them together (which Marty had pieced together from separate photos.) The plan was to take Shirley first to the restaurant, which he counted on to be crowded and noisy, and then, after agreeing that the place was unsuitable, he would just whip the key to this magic lair, not two floors away, out of his sleeve.

Marty takes it from there. . . .

~~~~

In the restaurant, I pressed my first-plan button: "Gee, this place is awfully stuffy," I said, looking around me. "No, it isn't," she said. "It's kind of nice."

"You don't understand," I said. "It's too crowded in here, too hard to talk. I know a much nicer place." (Suddenly, I had this awful picture of those wines turning tepid and my steaks shriveling to a cinder.)

"Well," she said, humoring me, "maybe so. Where are we going?"

We were on schedule again. "You'll see," I said. I led her to the elevator, waved my fingers in a circle in front of the panel of floor buttons, and said, "How about fourteen?" (Our suite number was 1408.) She followed me down the long corridor, finally to the heavy double doors marked "1408." I made another magic wave with my hand, produced a metal key from the air, and put it in the lock. The key wouldn't turn. I tried again, but no go. The door was double-bolted. Good grief. What happened?

I didn't know what to say or do. I could hear the bedroom music. Then from all the way back in the corridor, a tall man in a black suit peeked around a corner near the elevator, waved, and loudly whispered to get my attention: "Pssst, Mr. Ingels. Pssst. Pssst."

I looked at Shirley and asked her to wait while I checked it out. I could sense my sweet evening starting to unsweeten. When I reached the end of the corridor, the man, with a thick Hungarian accent, said, "Mr. Ingels, your credit card has been declined. They say this number has been reported as stolen. We can't give you the room."

"But all my stuff is in there," I said. "I was in the room all day. That credit card is good. This has to be a mistake. Who can I call?" He said it was late Saturday night and there were no MasterCharge supervisors on duty. I was just out of luck. I glanced back down the hall, seeing my dream goddess standing there by the door. It made me crazy.

"Call the general manager," I said.

"He went home," said Mr. Suit and Tie.

"Call him at home," I demanded. "I'll meet you downstairs." Jogging the length of the carpet back to Shirley, I told her there was a tiny problem downstairs. When we reached the lobby, I placed Shirley far enough from the desk to miss the flak, but close enough to be recognized. The Hungarian, who turned out to be the assistant manager, was dialing the phone. I thought I'd make one more try. "Don't you see who that is over there?" I said, kind of pointing with my elbow. "That's Shirley Jones."

He looked at me. Then at her. And nothing. Absolutely nothing. I was flabbergasted. Then he handed me the phone and said, "His name is Mr. Krueger." This was the boss.

He had the brains. And he would know who we were. I took a deep breath and instantly prepared a barrage of my best stuff, made the "okay" sign to Shirley, and jumped right in, certain that our million-dollar evening was now saved.

"Mr. Krueger, this is Marty Ingels, from NBC. And I'm here with my fiancée, Shirley Jones, the movie star—*Oklahoma! Carousel*? You see, we're celebrating Shirley's twentieth anniversary in show business, and there is a special press party happening at the suite here—*60 Minutes*, Mike Wallace, *20/20*, *Entertainment Tonight*. And, ha-ha, they tell me here that there has been a computer goof-up at the MasterCharge office, and my credit card, ha-ha, comes up 'stolen.' And we have to have the suite tonight to prepare . . . so I'm sure you can let us . . ."

I was hitting him with everything but my disabled shrapnel-wounded-veteran number, but Mr. Krueger had other plans. As sure as I stood there, God had sent me Rudolf Hess. In the best black leather Gestapo accent I have heard, he took me apart piece by piece. "You know," he whined, "you actors are all alike. I haf seen you. I know you. You are always in trobble."

I couldn't believe it. I wanted to strangle the s.o.b., but I had one weak bullet left. "Mr. Krueger," I said, "you must realize that if you humiliate us publicly like this, I will own your hotel come Monday morning."

"Vunderful," he said, and I heard a click on the line.

I found myself looking again at the tall Hungarian. I peeked painfully over at Shirley, now leaning against a lobby pillar. I felt my hopes fading, fading. I was desperate. I beckoned to him to come closer over the counter. "What would it take," I asked, "to get me in that suite right now?"

"Two hundred and seventy-five dollars, cash," he said.

"I'll be right back," I said. I grabbed Shirley, forced the

best smile I could, and said, "Come on, we have a little errand to run." I needed $275 in ten minutes. It was close to ten o'clock, and I knew nobody in Beverly Hills with ready cash. I could smell the steaks burning.

The closest other hotel was the Beverly Wilshire, real snobby. It was a long shot. In the car with Shirley, I tried mightily to act the gay blade with everything under control. It wasn't easy. We reached the Beverly Wilshire. I slammed on the brakes, double-parked, and raced to the desk, totally unsure of what I was going to say.

There was a bright young redhead clerk, who burst into a big wide grin when he saw me. "Hello, Mr. Ingels," he said. " I haven't seen you since your uncle was here."

"My uncle?" I said.

"Yes, your uncle, the mayor of New York, Abe Beame." It was a gift from the heavens. My uncle *was* the mayor of New York, and, yes, he did stay at the Beverly Wilshire. And *voilà*, they were happy to cash my check for $275.

Back in the car, I was David Niven again, confident, secure, my big evening back on schedule. And not a second too soon. I knew Shirley was confused, with maybe a hundred questions on her mind, but I wasn't about to let her start asking any of them. We were back at the other hotel and I was standing tall at the desk now, this time flashing my pack of crisp new twenty-dollar bills.

Except that now my Hungarian friend in the black suit was nowhere in sight. Instead, there was a new guy, younger, who said the assistant manager had gone off duty. "Fine," I said, "here's your money, just give me the key to room 1408."

"I'm sorry," he said. "I spoke to Mr. Krueger, and he said not to accept your money."

This couldn't be happening. "*Not accept my money*?" I bellowed. "Cash?"

"No," he said. "Mr. Krueger said that he did not wish to do business with anyone carrying a stolen credit card."

I am not sure exactly what I did at that point. I do remember clearing the desk of all that registration crap and climbing over the counter, reaching for that little bastard's neck. In a flash, there were two burly security guards scrambling to get between us. By now I could only think of all my own property in that room.

I did manage to steer the older-looking guard off to one side. "Look, what's your name?" I asked.

"Lasky," he said.

"A *landsman*?" I asked (Jewish for being Jewish, a tribesman).

He nodded. America's only Jewish security cop, and I had him. There was still hope. I had about seven seconds of plasma left. I went through my entire NBC, *60 Minutes*, *Oklahoma!* routine, now adding my years of dedication to Israel. Praise God, it was working. He asked for the cash. He took it over to the young clerk, exchanged whispers, and was right back with the key. I was on track again.

I am purposely leaving out any descriptions of how my pure and patient date reacted through all this because, to tell the truth, I can't be certain what she was feeling inside. A range of expressions flashed across her face at various times. I was just thrilled that she somehow never, for a second, decided to throw in the towel.

But there we were, finally, in our gorgeous suite—more gorgeous than ever in my desperate eye, the jeweled lights of the city spread out there before us, music transfusing the air, and time at last suspended. Yes, the steaks were long gone, reduced to cinder, the wine was flat, and the ice in the bucket had melted. But my angel and I saw the sun rise together; for me, the most perfect night of my life.

To complete the circle, a check from the hotel arrived at my office the next day. It was a refund for the room, with a note of apology.

~~~~

Marty continued his relentless campaign to win the heart of his WASP princess. She was soon on location for a movie, filming scenes at different locations around Los Angeles every day. He rented a thirty-eight-foot motor home, and each morning at eleven he pulled into the parking lot of the Brown Derby, where the headwaiter would meet him and set the table for a candlelight lunch, which included their Cobb salad and an iced-down bottle of vintage champagne. The Cobb
~~~~

salad—Shirley had mentioned it was her favorite—consisted of lettuce, bacon, chicken or turkey, blue cheese, and onions, all finely chopped.

Using a copy of her itinerary he had sneaked from the production office at Universal, Marty drove to wherever Shirley was filming that day and waited in the motor home until the cast broke for lunch. He wore a silk smoking jacket and an ascot, had her favorite flowers on the table, and their own special song, "An Affair to Remember," repeating over and over on the tape deck. They danced and kissed and, finally, made love, which was even better than the Cobb salad. It was a glorious way to spend a parking-lot lunch hour, even if Marty did trip on the floorboards and leave half the cork floating in the bottle. He thought he was Cary Grant. She was falling in love with Woody Allen.

Curiously, he never called Shirley to arrange these noontime rendezvous. He would just show up, and somehow she was always there.

He pursued her with plainly outrageous acts, and at least one or two misdemeanors. At one point, Shirley was also dating a well-known producer, and Marty plotted a way to cut down the competition. He actually managed to pilfer a full set of his rival's medical X rays from his doctor's office, pieced it all together on a large board to form one life-sized skeleton, and had it delivered to Shirley's house complete with red arrows that indicated secretly developing conditions, such as ulcers, gout, sterility. A brief anonymous note advised her that "there wasn't much future in this guy."

"I thought he was an absolute maniac," said Shirley. "I had met a lot of people in my lifetime, but I thought, This is really one of a kind. I didn't return his phone calls at first. I didn't really feel like dating. I wasn't in the mood for it. The day that I decided to call, I happened to be in a very sad frame of mind, had spent an aimless day driving around, and I thought, Well, he ought to be good for a laugh. That was really what I thought. So I called him back, and he told me he had to get his notes. Of course, I started to laugh, and I never stopped. I guess the night I really fell in love with Marty was New Year's Eve [1976].

"We had been dating, but neither of us had committed to each other in any way. I had plans to join some friends for a

New Year's party, and I was going alone. I really felt I wanted to be alone, and Marty was not happy about that."

Marty: "She was going to Jimmy Cagney's house, and one of the promises I had made myself, down there on the floor, if I ever got up, was that I would be done with the games that people play to death. And this was my first real test. I said to her, 'Listen, there is no New Year's Eve for me without you. So I'm staying right here, at my desk, until you get in, *whenever* you get in.' And I stayed right there, waiting.

"By nine o'clock, I was a little stir-crazy, and I grabbed a pad and pencil and started writing. Wasn't sure why. By ten-fifteen, I had written what I thought was a beautiful poem, and I had my assignment for this night: Get this printed and framed before midnight. I found a print shop that was closed, but a sign on the door gave an emergency number. I called the owner at home and convinced him to get dressed and come back to the shop to work on my poem . . . and I stood over his shoulder and watched him hand-print it, letter by letter, line by line. When he finished, I asked him if he knew a framer who might do *him* a favor, and frame it by midnight. I'm sure he thought I was crazy or very rich. Either way, he wasn't going to refuse me.

"In no time I was at a framery, and had my New Year's package ready by twelve forty-five, just a little past my deadline. So I raced to Shirley's house and asked the maid to place my three-foot creation 'where the lady will see it the minute she gets in.' Then I went back to my apartment, to my desk and phone."

It was two A.M. when Shirley walked into her front door and saw the large package propped against the stairwell. "Inside was the most beautiful poem I had ever read," she said. "It was just lovely, and it made me cry. Before I could pick up the phone, it rang. Marty was on the line. 'Well,' he said, 'what do you think?'

"He can be so infuriating. I said, 'Why couldn't you let me call first? Of course it's wonderful and brilliant.' The words were very personal and moving.

"Of course, Marty is always trying to come up with these very original gifts. He would have boxes hand-carved from rare woods for people to keep their valuables in. He had one made for me as a Christmas gift, with my divorce papers from Jack inside. I nearly fell over; at the time, I thought it was in such terrible taste. In one way, it was irreverent, but in another direct and honest. And those are both sides of Marty."

By midyear they were lovers, but not yet living under the same roof. The courtship was complicated by the presence in the house of three boys who were not stupid or jaded or very impressed with Mama's suitor. Marty had to overcome a series of lesser hardships. In Beverly Hills, the police security system is aided by the fact that cars are not allowed to park on the street, anywhere, after 2:00 A.M. "In one year," said Marty, "I had four hundred dollars' worth of tickets, courting this lady, because I didn't want to get out of bed and move my car.

"She was constantly waking me out of these wonderful deep sleeps and telling me to move the car and, tired and groggy, I was constantly telling her to just 'sell it.' "

Shirley worried about doing the right thing. She worried about the boys. Finally, she consulted her lawyer. Says Marty, "I guess she must have asked him, at what exact point are you legally considered to have 'spent the night' with someone? Lawyers being lawyers, he looked up some obscure California statute and told her the exact cutoff was four fifty-three A.M., when the sun hits the horizon or the low tide rolls in, or whatever.

"Well, that became a series of Marx Brothers routines. She would shake me violently at precisely four-thirty and tell me, 'Marty, you have to leave now.' I asked her why, for crying out loud, and she would say that it was four-thirty, and in a few minutes the sun would soon be on the horizon and it would be light outside. I said, 'What am I, a fucking vampire?'

" 'The children are getting up for school,' she'd say. 'They'll see you.'

" 'No, they won't,' I would argue. 'They'll just go downstairs as they always do, have their breakfast and go.'

" 'No,' she'd say. 'They'll see your car outside.'

" 'I told you to sell it.'

"But there was no sense of humor where protecting the kids was concerned. So I would sneak downstairs, feeling my way with one shoe and one slipper and pajamas sticking out of everywhere, and drive my car, with the six parking tickets fluttering under the windshield wiper, around the block until I was sure the kids at least were up and having breakfast.

"Then I would go right back to the same parking space and ring the bell, as if I had come from my own apartment, standing there in this totally disheveled condition until Shaun, who was maybe fourteen, let me in.

"He would say, 'Hi, Ingels. How come you're wearing one slipper and your pajama top?' I'd say, 'Aw, I dressed real fast this morning. Uh, Shaun, is your mother home?'

" 'Yeah, she's upstairs.'

" 'Good. I've got to tell her something.' And I would go right back up the stairs and to bed again without missing a snore."

Marty disliked this charade, not only for the inconvenience, but because he felt it was hypocritical. But he reminded himself that Shirley had an obligation to the Cassidy boys, and to the fans of the Partridge family. He was, after all, in love with America's Mother.

With variations, mornings at the Cassidy home went on in this fashion until Shirley's divorce was final. It was not without bitterness. While Shirley and Marty were on a weekend trip, Jack showed up with a moving van and hauled off most of the furniture, including the bed and credenza from the master bedroom. Not unlike Dinah Shore's ex-husband, George Montgomery, Jack was good with his hands, a craftsman who in idle moments enjoyed finishing, restoring, or designing pieces of furniture.

"He took everything of value," noted Marty, "everything he felt was his because he had worked on it. He took the plants, all the antiques, some paintings. And Shirley showed no anger, as if none of it mattered. I was amazed. I said, 'The man has taken almost everything from you,' and I spent three weeks convincing her to change the locks. I was getting to know Shirley. Nothing of what Jack took was ever retrieved, of course. Later, the fire consumed it all."

Having worked his way into Shirley's embrace, Ingels gradually worked his way into her home, and into Jack Cassidy's closets.

Theirs was a clash of nature, culture, and birth. Not in a mean-spirited way, but almost from the start the romance was a combative one, this pairing of the sparkling blond singer-actress and the abrasive, inventive Brooklyn comic. A fine example was the Episode of the Teutonic Ski Instructor, as told first by Marty:

~~~~

I think I really began to understand Shirley the night she gave a dinner party at her home for a ski instructor. This was still in the days when I just didn't know what I was supposed to be for her; if I was going to win her and how; even a question in my own mind if I loved her or this was just another way to succeed.

My psychiatrist had told me that when I crashed, I gave up any expectation of ever being a star. I still wanted attention, so I figured I would get it through someone else. He saw Shirley as a great part of that, but at the same time he thought I was deeply convinced that I did not deserve her.

So one day she was planning a dinner for this fellow who had given her skiing lessons, and I would help greet the guests. I said, "Listen, for me to be the host of a party with a young, good-looking German ski instructor that you may or may not have had an affair with is not exactly my cup of tea."

Shirley gave me a glare and said, "Marty, stop it. Right now."

Against my better judgment, and against my natural feelings, I'm standing at the door when in walks this German Adonis, this Aryan god, lean, graceful, the blond hair, and I know this is going to be a wonderful evening. The producer Ross Hunter and his wife were there, several star couples, and a chic male fashion designer kissed Shirley and tossed me his topcoat.

As I'm hanging up the coat, I say to myself, "Ingels, you have got to get into a business and do your own thing."
~~~~

I'm convinced that the ski instructor and Shirley once had a big affair, and I'm walking around like a shmuck, passing him a tray of hors d'oeuvres. We sit down to dinner, and I am on Shirley's right—I'm not yet the man of the house—and the ski instructor is on her left. She was being gracious and enjoying herself, but I notice that she turns to say something to her guest of honor, and her head doesn't turn the other way for forty-five minutes.

We haven't exchanged a word in this time, and I'm fuming. They continue talking. Not lovey-dovey things, just talking, but it gets to the point where one of her friends looks at me, and in a gesture meant to be kind, mouths the words, "It's okay. She doesn't mean anything by it."

Now I know it is obvious to others at the table, and I can't wait to do my number. Finally, Shirley turns her head and says, "What do you think about that, Marty?" I suppose she thought I was overhearing whatever they were discussing.

I said, "What do I think about that? Is it time for me to come out of my cubbyhole? Is this my cue? Do I speak now?" At this point, I did what every man does with every woman when he feels he has been outraged. It's time to throw a little dirt in the air to see how it works. And if he really has been wronged, his woman will run after him and say, "I'm sorry, darling, I love you and I behaved shamelessly." This is what the woman does, it says here.

So that was my moment. I hadn't a qualm in my soul that it would work out as I imagined, and I did my Zachary Scott thing.

I took my napkin and flung it to the table and said, "Look, I've got an idea. You're having such a good time together and I missed my cue because it took you so long to get to me, why don't you two have a nice night and call me in a couple of weeks when it's time for me to talk."

I got up and started walking toward the door. There is a big mirror on the wall, and I'm able to see behind me as I walk toward it. I'm figuring I will get three steps, maybe four, maybe all the way to the bar before Shirley tackles me. In the mirror, I see her turn to the ski instructor and pick up the conversation right where they left off. And I'm heading for the door. I'm thinking, Ingels, where are you going to go? It's chilly out, and I'm not even dressed warmly.

Now I find myself outside, and I get in the car and drive around. I am not good at leaving for long periods. I have an unending need to resolve things. I came back to the house, walked in the door, sat down at the table, and started eating my dessert. I felt like a world-class idiot.

We frequently talk about that night. I have told her, "Shirley, I learned something important about you, that games don't work." That is why, in time, we got along so well. For me, instinctively, because of my breakdown, games were over. And Shirley just doesn't play them. She may love you, but she will let you go. She will let you walk.

Of course, it was the same way with Jack, and I questioned her: "Shirley, I know you're not from the school of running after your man and clinging to his pant leg as he drags you across the floor, screaming, 'Don't leave me,' but what the hell is wrong with opening up and saying, 'Don't do this. I love you?' "

She says she can't see the point in chasing someone who wants to leave. Would that we could all live by that code. I think we all feel that way intellectually, but there are people who cry, who suffer openly, who hang around on the sidewalk hoping to win someone back.

We would debate this back and forth. She would say to me, "Why are you so anxious?" And I would answer, "That's like telling a guy who is five-seven why aren't you tall?" I had a T-shirt made up that says, simply, BE 5-7. It's not easy for most of us to change our ways. She can.

~~~~

In the beginning, Shirley did not believe the relationship had any future:

^^^^

I never dreamed that it would end in anything, God knows, not marriage. We were at each other's throats all the
~~~~

time. We really did fight about everything. I think most of it, on his side, was insecurity. On my side, it was my need to be independent.

At that point in my life, I wasn't about to give an inch. And Marty was so insecure about me—little things frightened him, and his insecurity wound up in anger.

Take the night of the dinner party. First, the ski instructor wasn't a German or a Greek god. His name was Scott, not Hans or Helmut. He was from Seattle, Washington, and he was one of the teaching pros at Sun Valley. He was about thirty, very handsome and bright. My friend Betty and I spent about ten days skiing, and that's all there was. He came to Los Angeles on a visit, and I said, You'll have to come for dinner. I invited Betty and her husband and a few other couples, and Marty was my date.

This was still fairly early in our relationship, and I realized later that I was testing him. I thought, If he can't overcome my tests, I don't want him. That was a weak side of me. But the theory is, if he can accept the worst of you, he will love the best of you.

I wanted him to see all of me. I didn't want to go into another relationship where I had to walk on eggshells, never again. So at dinner I was leading the conversation to Scott, and it's true, we went on and on. I knew Marty was getting irritated, and I thought, Well, he needs to get to know the other people at the table.

It was so rude it was comical. He did none of those things you see in the movies. He pushed his chair back and announced, in effect, I can see I'm not wanted here and I'm leaving. I couldn't believe my ears. I mean, I looked at everyone, and they looked at me. Most of them didn't know Marty, and I couldn't understand why he was doing this, making a scene. So I let him go and went on talking to Scott, and he walked out. Ten minutes later, he was back, and I said, "Oh, nice of you to return." When we were alone, he was absolutely livid, and he grabbed me and said, "Shirley, you can't do this to me." I said, "I'm not doing anything to you. This is your problem, not mine."

We fought about it. He was very jealous. And Jack was never jealous, which, of course, wrecked me. Marty cannot handle any of his feelings with delicacy. They are always on the surface. He can't be subtle or tactful about anything. So whatever he feels, he has to display in some physical way because he can't keep it in.

vvvv

And so they turned their fragile love affair into a kind of tennis match, not always with strokes strong or sure. Marty's might go thudding into the net, but he was seldom hesitant:

~~~~

That's the other side of Shirley, the part that won't finish an argument. If we disagreed and she got tired of it, she would simply say good night and go upstairs to bed. And I would sleep on the couch and wake up with a headache and a crimp in my back. I was always waiting for that day when she would come down during the night and say, "Come to bed, honey, I'm sorry." She just isn't that kind of person. The only time she ever came down was on a Halloween night. We had fought over something, and apparently she had a bad dream, or thought she heard chains on the roof. I was sleeping on the floor, my place of security, and she came down and said, "Marty, would you come upstairs?"

I sat right up and beamed. "Aw, you love me, right?"

She said, "No, there's a ghost upstairs."

That's a part of Shirley that is elusive, and it fits into our peculiar puzzle. But the moment that I treasure, that was wonderful, was the first time she told me she loved me. Many times I had despaired. We were saying good night in the laundry room. It must have been one of those four o'clock in the morning times when we were outwitting the California judiciary.

I had my jacket over my arm and my socks in one hand, and the wet clothes were spinning in the dryer. She was edging me out the door, and she looked at me kind of funny and said, "I think I'm in love with you."

The next thing I remember was sliding behind the wheel of my car and tears pouring down my face. It was one of the
~~~~

great moments of my life. There have been few times that I cried out of joy—I'm a Jewish crisis person—but it happened, in the morning dark. I cried as if there were years of something built up inside of me. I started to hyperventilate and felt a little dizzy and had to pull the car over. Only years later did I tell Shirley that it was such a wonderful moment for me, I cried most of the way home.

~~~~

What long and twisting roads they had taken to find each other, out of their two different worlds.
~~~~

5

Keeping Up with the Joneses

IF BEAUTY IS ONLY SKIN-DEEP, does talent, like toughness, go all the way to the bone?

Shirley Mae Jones, of Smithton, Pennsylvania, was a tomboy with a voice three or four generations in the making. Her family owned the town brewery and the town hotel, and the Jones women, her aunts and great-aunts, had sung in the Methodist choir as long as anyone could remember. They were of Welsh stock, and music was in the blood.

She wasn't especially keen on beauty pageants, but if you are going to enter one, you want the judges to vote you pretty. And the judges always did, even the ones in the big city, Pittsburgh, an hour's drive away.

In many ways, it was a pastoral, idyllic childhood that Shirley Mae led. Her best friends were her cousin Joanne Jones, who was chubby with blond Shirley Temple curls, and a sweet, go-along-with-anything girl known as "Red."

Smithton in the late 1940s was a Norman Rockwell vision of America. A lazy, lovely town of less than five hundred, along the banks of the Allegheny River, with clean air and clean streets. It was west of Johnstown, where the great flood swept across the valley in 1899 and two thousand people drowned. You couldn't find Smithton on a map, and no one famous had been born there, but you could almost walk to Donora, the home of baseball great Stan Musial.

Everyone knew everyone else, and most of them seemed

to be named Jones. In the spring, the kids went swimming in Jacob's Creek, where the water was cold and the rapids were tricky. They had the run of the brewery, and Shirley played hide-and-seek in the beer vats and the ice lockers and gave the workers fits. It was a small brewery, sixty people, and they worried that the granddaughter of the founder would accidentally lock herself in the freezer one day, and the next morning she would be an ice sculpture.

But Shirley Mae Jones always seemed to know just how near the edge she could go, and of course that meant closer than anyone else. She was absolutely fearless.

In the summer, the girls went to a camp on Lake Erie, and it was there, the year Shirley was eleven, that an alert camp counselor realized the child had a gift. The counselor's name was Peggy Demler, and the first time she heard Shirley sing, the back of her neck tingled. Miss Demler played the piano at the camp musicals, and she knew a God-given voice when she heard one. It was untrained, but the timbre, the range, the clarity—no one could teach her these.

When she was four or five, Shirley could hear a song on the radio for the first time and repeat it note for note, lyric for lyric. She had accepted this not so much as a talent as a nice trick to amuse her father and aunts, her mother's sisters, Ina and Nell. They were single and pretty at a time when most of the unmarried and able-bodied men were at war. They worked in town, and as the years passed, they became handsome, respected matrons, very proud of their famous niece. They may have been her first fans.

^^^^

My aunts were always asking me to sing this or that. But Peggy Demler was the first person who seemed to take it seriously. At the time, she was the most beautiful girl I ever saw. She had natural platinum hair down to her shoulders. I was just in awe of her.

We would have little amateur shows in camp, and then a sort of open house for the parents every other weekend, and I would always get up and sing a solo, while Peggy played the piano. She was amazed that I was so polished at that age without having taken lessons. So for the eight weeks or whatever I was at camp, she really cultivated my voice. When I went home, she called my parents and said, "Your daughter has something special, a very rare talent. You *must* give her lessons."

That was when I became aware that there might be more here than singing for my family. My mother had me take piano lessons, and the counselor called again and urged her to arrange for singing classes. There were always people in my life urging me on, somehow, rather than me finding my own way. These things just happened, and Peggy was the first.

Mother was referred to the music critic for the *Pittsburgh Press*. He and his wife were supposed to be top voice coaches in the city. His name was Ralph Lewando, and I started studying with him when I was about twelve. We would drive into Pittsburgh twice a week for an hour's lesson, and then I would practice at home with the local pianist.

There was a hidden benefit in all this, because my mother didn't drive, and so my father, who wasn't home much, had to arrange to take time off from the brewery to drive us to Pittsburgh. On those days, after my lesson, I'd go to the movies with my father, while mother went shopping, and it was great because we got to see the first-run movies. Some nights we went to the Pittsburgh Playhouse, a dinner theater. My father was a sponsor, and we'd have great food and see a play, and I loved that.

It was patterned after the playhouses in New York and Pasadena, and they had classes there, and they would bring in a pro for one or two shows. The productions were quite good.

Pittsburgh was then a drab and backward place, but exciting changes were around the corner. The Mellons were about to pour in millions, and the renewal would follow to compensate for the devastating effects on the city of the coal mines and steel mills. But, then, in the late 1940s, they had the playhouse and Carnegie Tech, which was the leading drama school in the country at the time. Gene Kelly and a few others of his caliber had come out of Pittsburgh, but there was really not much culture, no ballet, no opera company that I can remember. They had vaudeville at the Old Nixon Theatre, and that was about it.

The image of the city was a true one: hard hats, a beer-and-a-shot kind of town, football and baseball and a general feeling of being losers. I remember as a twelve-year-old keeping a handkerchief to my mouth and nose most of the time, and by the time we left, the hankie would be black with soot.

Back in Smithton, one of the workers would get back from a day trip, which was like an adventure, and say to my father, "I come clean from Pittsburgh." And my father would say, "Well, you might have come from Pittsburgh, but you didn't come clean."

It was grimy and depressing, and on the drive home you'd see the mills going, and at night we passed the railroad, where they dumped the hot steel into the open cars, and they lighted the sky like the aurora borealis. About ten years later, they began the campaign to improve the air and rebuild the inner city, and today Pittsburgh is a lovely place.

Mr. Lewando was teaching me some opera, and some operetta, and I kept saying I wanted to sing musical comedy. Even then, that was what I wanted. He said, "We'll throw some of that in, but it's not good for you. I want you to learn technique first."

Soon I started to sing for the Lions Club, and the local amateur productions, and they would pay me ten or fifteen dollars a night to sing for them.

VVVV

More interesting than the early talent, the bars of the music that would make the woman, is the flip side: the spirited, stubborn, cold-tempered little girl who led her own parade. This is the one recurring theme in the memories of virtually anyone who knew Shirley Jones before she became this refined, stylish, graceful lady who helped define her musical era. When Marty Ingels teases her as "Perfect Shirley," he means it nonetheless. She was the only child of a doting, gentle father and a strict, strong-minded mother. Her friends think she inherited the reliance and leadership, without the ego and selfishness that are often the tax on only childhood. Her friend Red insisted, "She was the best-adjusted only child I ever saw." And yet her growing-up years were a fine mix of achievement and what might be called controlled rebellion.

^^^^

I was raised to be a "good little girl," and to act the way a well-bred young lady is supposed to act. All of that. So I figure there is a little demon inside there that likes to strike out. I think that is partly why I chose the kind of men I did. There is a basic rebel inside me, and it surfaced when I was a child. I was never a follower, never a follower of rules. The moment someone told me I had to do something, I went the other way. I am bored by the nine-to-five kind of man that society molds. I dated a boy in high school who went to West Point, and when I saw him there, as a regimented soldier, blindly obeying all the rules, at that moment I fell out of love.

When I was nine years old, I started wearing lipstick and makeup. It made my mother furious, and there were always spankings. My aunt Nellie handled it more wisely. She would take a tissue and say, "Now you have it smeared just a little," and she'd dab at my face, and what she was doing, of course, was wiping it off. In those days, nice ladies didn't take their nieces out in public with red mouths.

I don't know where I got that quality. My father was no rebel. He was in his way the black sheep of the family; a college dropout and kind of a playboy, all the things that his brothers were not.

Because of the way I looked, I got away with a lot of mischief that my girlfriends didn't. One of them had a sort of coarse appearance, but she was every inch a lady. I was the one who looked ladylike, when in fact I wasn't.

I was the first girl in town to wear a strapless dress to the prom. When I was sixteen, Red and I were out with our boyfriends, and I talked everybody into driving to Maryland to get married. We drove across the state line and were within ten miles of the justice of the peace's house before we turned back. He was a nice Italian boy from Pittsburgh. My parents would have killed me. They were not bigots, it was just the times and the smallness of the town. The phrase you always heard was "staying with your own kind." In those days, you didn't know what a WASP was, a White Anglo-Saxon Protestant. But you didn't marry boys whose name ended in a vowel.

And I smoked. My friends would wait for me while I had my singing lesson, and my teacher, who was very puritanical, made them put out their cigarettes. He would always say he knew he never had to worry about me. I was his protégée, and he was confident I wouldn't do anything that might harm my voice. By the end of the hour, I was dying for a cigarette. Red would giggle and say, "There goes your career."

It was all very 1950s, very tame by today's standards. I never did anything that I knew would cause my parents grief. But I had a knack of going right to the wire, and usually someone else would chicken out.

VVVV

She was five when she caught an adult lying to her for the first time. The unfortunate culprit was her beloved aunt Ina, the one who taught her to sing "God Bless America."

Shirley had a toothache, and she refused to see the dentist, whose office was on the second floor over the five-and-dime store. Aunt Ina recalls it painfully: "She had a lot of faith in me. I baby-sat with her a lot, and after her nap I'd dress her up and take her for a walk and people would just stop and look at her, she was such a beautiful child.

"So I told her I knew a secret entrance to the dime store, and her mother and I led her through a hall and up some steps, and when we opened the door, the dentist grabbed her and threw that gas bag over her face and put her right to sleep. And he pulled the tooth.

"The first thing she said when she was awake, she looked me right in the eye, this darling little five-year-old, and she said, '*Damn you, Aunt Ina.*' "

It was the kind of editorial comment that went to the core

of what would become Shirley's attitude. "She is very trusting," Aunt Ina said. "She can't stand deceit. She knows what she wants, she tells you what she thinks, and she expects people to be straight with her."

Understand, she was not a bomb-throwing radical, nor is there anything on the record to suggest that she sailed across the line and into hookers-on-Eighth-Avenue territory. Shirley's deviltry was of the foursquare kind: She followed her urges, accepting the risk that she might catch hell for them. And on occasion did.

She was nine the night she led the raid on the Smithton Fire Department, more or less. This was about as wild as the action ever got in Smithton, a town so small the head of the Mafia was rumored to be a Filipino.

There were the three of them, Joanne, Red, and Shirley. It was around seven o'clock at night, and they pushed the fire alarm. Actually, Shirley did the pushing, and all three ran like hell to the Jones Hotel a block away, which her grandfather owned and where Joanne lived in one of the eight apartments.

When Joanne's mother walked into the room a short time later, she asked why they were all hiding under the bed. She was not long in getting an answer. With the siren of its only wagon wailing, the Smithton Volunteer Fire Department pulled up to the front of the hotel, and its volunteer firemen raced into the lobby, asking a startled desk clerk where the fire was. It did not take long to check all the rooms.

"One of us squealed," recalled Shirley, many years later, sounding just a little less grim than Susan Hayward in the death-row classic *I Want to Live*. "I think Joanne told her mother. We were taken to the local constable's office—we didn't have a police department—and he gave us a big talking-to. All the parents came down, and everyone agreed on what a terrible thing it was. People were crying.

"I asked the constable, 'Are you going to put us in jail?'

"He said, 'Well, I could, you know. But this time I'm going to give you probation. For a full year. So you better watch your step, young ladies. I leave you in the custody of your parents, and I want you to report to me, once a month, for a year.'

"We called and went down to the station once or twice, and then everyone sort of forgot about it. No one could remember when there had been a fire in town, and I just wanted to see what would happen if I pulled the alarm. And I found out. I was always doing things like that, kid things, very tomboyish."

Even more out of character with her later elegant image is the fact that Shirley Jones was sort of a female Mike Tyson of her neighborhood. She was frequently getting into fights, and she usually instigated them. She fought with other girls who lived down the road in a section called the Hollow, and she fought with the boys who preferred to pick on girls who wouldn't fight back.

"They didn't think I could stand up to them, and I always did," she says. "Bloody noses, broken fingernails. With the girls, it always went right to the hair-pulling. On the ground, scratching, the whole thing. This happened a lot. I was always coming home with my dress ripped off. Even on Sunday, in my best clothes, dressed for church, we'd be rolling around in the dirt."

By her own admission, Shirley was a difficult child who too often provoked her mother's discipline, which Marge was never reluctant to administer.

No one banked Shirley's fires, she simply tempered them herself, redirecting her energy and her curiosity into a career that leaped far beyond her own ambitions. The contradictions in her nature would remain: She was as bold and confident as a lumberjack, and yet deliciously feminine. She could be calculating and logical and unconditionally romantic.

Her friend Red sheds additional light:

"In the second or third grade, Shirley would slap somebody at the drop of a hat. She had no use for a smart-ass. If we were playing marbles, if someone tried to play out of turn, she would just elbow them aside. If they were bigger, if they were boys, it didn't matter. She just took the consequences.

"And those were her instincts, not acts of temper. She left home at seventeen or eighteen, and we've always stayed in touch and she has changed less than anybody. Her parents did a damned good job. Her father was very dedicated to her. He would take her anyplace, nothing that involved Shirley was an inconvenience to him. I'd go with her sometimes on the drive to Pittsburgh, and he'd often say to her, you know, 'One day your name is going to be in lights.'

"Shirley would roll her eyes and just shake her head. She thought it was so corny, and she said to me, 'What the hell does he know? That's just a father talking.'

"Her mother had to be the disciplinarian, and her father just took her around and showed her off. So that wasn't a very fair trade-off. But daughters always clash with their moms. She kept gobs of lipstick and rouge in her purse, and the minute she left the house, the makeup went on like crazy. She took great care in how she looked, even at ten or eleven, and in our little circle was a rebel as far as fashions went.

"I mean, if bangs came in as the hot new hairstyle, it took four years for Smithton to get it. Shirley would be the first one to cut her hair, and no one else would try it. She was always different. Her mother objected to a lot of what she wanted to wear. Her mother wanted her to live in white blouses and cute gingham skirts, but that wasn't her style. Jewelry was her fetish. Mine, too, and it still is with both of us. Rings and bracelets and necklaces, layers of them. But she seemed to put it all together very well. She was able to manage it. On her, nothing looked cheap or gaudy.

"Where her singing was concerned, her mother had a lot of confidence in her. Marge was no stage mother, but she was very supportive. When she did light opera, her mother would write out the lyrics on cue cards, three by five, because it was a lot to memorize. She did it even if Shirley didn't need them. And she wanted her to be disciplined; if there was a party or a school activity, and Shirley had an engagement with one of the local clubs, the singing came first. We always had to wait around until she finished.

"Every guy who saw her went crazy. She didn't play the field. She always has been a one-man woman. Her first crush was the one who went to West Point, Lou Malone. And she visited him there and decided he was too straitlaced, just like that. He made the military his career and went on to become the assistant to the Surgeon General, not too shabby. And I'll tell you, the last time I saw him, if anyone asked, the man was still in love with her.

"Then she fell hard for Bill Bonini, the city boy from Pittsburgh, who was Italian and had a red convertible. He would drive back and forth—Smithton was a forty-mile drive—and some nights he put a hundred and twenty-five miles on that car.

"The night of my senior prom—I was a year ahead of Shirley—Bill was her date, and I was with my future husband, Roy. That was the night she wore a strapless gown and everyone else had on a high neck. We danced at the prom and we went out and necked and did all those wonderful things, and finally it was two in the morning.

"Bill's family owned a very nice restaurant in Pittsburgh, and it was his job to clean up after hours. It's two in the morning and we're parked in the convertible, and he said, 'I forgot to tell you, folks, but I have to clean the restaurant tonight.' He and Roy are in tuxedos, and we're in gowns, and I said, 'What the hell do you mean?' And he said, 'I have to go back to the restaurant and clean up, and you guys have to come back with me.'

"And Shirley piped up and said, 'Sure, we'll help you.' And, you know, it's scrub buckets and mops and Shirley said, 'Well, what the hell else do we have to do?' So that's what we did. We were in that restaurant until four in the morning, mopping floors in our gowns and tuxedos. I said, 'Boy, this is something I will always remember about my senior prom.'

"Once she made a commitment to you, her friendship was unfaltering. You could depend on her for anything. Anything. All during our years together, we never had an argument. There was no rivalry for boyfriends. She always went for the blonds, and I took the dark-haired ones.

"Shirley was never competitive in that way. The things she wanted just sort of fell into her lap. It's funny . . . I know Marty always comments on this . . . she is living the American Dream, but she was never caught up in it.

"We were teenagers in the late forties and early fifties, and there was a lot of lust going around, a lot of talk about sex, but there were all these taboos. Many people only married for sex back then, because it wasn't practiced before marriage. You have to keep in mind, we came from a small town, and we adhered to the strict codes of that time.

"So people did tend to marry young, and Roy and I were the other couple the night she almost eloped. We were going to a dance or a night spot, and Bill said, just a kind of flip remark, 'Why don't we run over the border [to Maryland] and get married?' And from the backseat, Shirley said, 'Yeah, why don't we? Both couples.'

"Roy and I did marry later, but neither one of us was ready for that kind of crazy commitment. Nobody said no, and we kept driving toward Maryland, and I was getting absolutely panicky. I thought, She's going to do it.

"Finally, Roy said, 'I don't know if we're ready for this. You know, our parents will kill us.' I jumped and said, 'That's right.'

"But Bill said, 'So? What the hell,' and Shirley said, 'If you two don't want to go through with it, you can just stand up for us.' And we kept driving. I asked Shirley if she was sure, and she said, 'Yes, yes, I want to do it.' And Bill was delighted, just out of his mind.

"We were almost there, and Roy said, 'Are you really sure about this? You're sixteen, and there'll be hell to pay.' We were maybe twenty minutes from where the justice of the peace was, and I looked at Shirley: 'Your mother's going to kill you, and your father will have a heart attack.' Bill kept saying, 'I don't care, it's okay with my parents.'

"I said, 'Yeah? What about hers? You're an Italian, and they don't even like you. They don't even like your name.'

"That kind of brought everyone down a little, because we started thinking about the reality of telling everyone's parents. Shirley says now she backed out because she knew Roy and I weren't ready, and she didn't want to get us in trouble. But, really, she was too levelheaded to go through with it. She finally said, 'I guess maybe we better not. You know, it's too much to face. My mother would have a cow.'

"The thing was, though, we didn't turn around until Shirley had the last say. If she had wanted to be stubborn, this is what would have happened: Her career would have gone down the drain, and by the time she was twenty-two, she would have been singing lullabyes to six bambinos."

On a dark country road in Maryland, the red convertible

made a U-turn and headed back for Smithton, and the big bubble of a world beyond it that was beckoning to Shirley Mae Jones.

It was Red who, indirectly, landed Shirley a spot in the Miss Pittsburgh Pageant for 1952. They were sunbathing at a swimming pool one day when a photographer was milling around, snapping pictures. They had no idea why, but Red suggested Shirley walk over and get in one of the shots. Shirley said she would if Red would. And her friend replied, "You're the one with the career. I'm going to be a secretary."

So the photographer clicked off a random shot of a pretty blonde, and Shirley received an invitation to compete in the contest to become Miss Pittsburgh. Ironically, Red wasn't there to see her friend crowned and her suggestion pay so rich a dividend. "I didn't think she could win. Not because she wasn't beautiful or talented enough. I thought she just lived too far from Pittsburgh. I thought, They're not going to pick some little hick from the country. As it turned out, that was why they sent out the photographers . . . to scout for pretty young things in the boondocks."

Shirley takes it from there:

^^^^

I was eighteen when I entered, in my last year in high school. The talent competition was supposed to be half of the judging, but the big thing was the bathing-suit competition. Even then, much more so today, they didn't want it to appear like a flesh market. But they crowned you wearing the bathing suit, not in a gown, and that was the picture they gave me and I still have today.

I was one of the youngest, if not the youngest, of twelve contestants. You had to be seventeen to enter. I won five hundred dollars and some jewelry, a charm bracelet, and a scholarship to the drama school at the Pittsburgh Playhouse. For me, that was the big one. You went to school in the daytime, and then at night you performed in their dinner theater. So you could put your acting to work if you were good enough. But first you had to go through an apprenticeship: painting the scenery, working the props. In class, you studied Shakespeare and did mime and took speech therapy and modern dance.

As Miss Pittsburgh, I made a few appearances across the country, and then I went on to the Miss Pennsylvania competition, where I was the runner-up. Finishing second really changed the direction of my life, because I decided to take advantage of a two-year college scholarship. I wanted to study drama, but I didn't want to commit myself to a four-year program. I had qualified for the National Honor Society, and my grades were fine, but I already knew what I wanted to do with my life.

Through the Pittsburgh Playhouse, I had access to most of the instructors at Carnegie Tech, and that was the best drama department in the country. Northwestern was next. So I planned to spend two years in Pittsburgh, taking classes at the Playhouse, and then two years of junior college at a small school in New Jersey.

VVVV

She lived in a sorority house near the Pitt campus, and those were exciting times. She had a roommate, got a taste of sorority life, and soaked up all the wonders of being away from home for the first time at eighteen.

But she never made it to New Jersey. Everyone kept telling her to go to New York, and so she borrowed four hundred dollars from her father and went. Within a week, she was auditioning for a part in the chorus of a new musical by Rodgers and Hammerstein called *South Pacific*.

What happened next is described elsewhere in these pages. Pure native talent brought her to New York, and it was quickly apparent that not even the Great White Way was going to change her, how she looked or how she thought.

Right away she discovered something she did not like: the Method acting principles derived from Stanislavsky, which had spread across the campuses from the Actors Studio in New York.

"I disliked it," she said. "I didn't like the way you were

treated, the way you were belittled. They tore you down, and everyone said that was to make you dig deep inside, and it would make you a better actor. I was so secure I wouldn't allow anybody to do that, to tear me down. So consequently I didn't like that kind of teaching. I preferred the approach of the late Bette Davis. She was waiting one day while a Method actor discussed with the director his motivation for taking off his shoe. They discussed the options, the camera angles, whether his mood was angry or thoughtful.

"Finally, Miss Davis cried out, 'Just drop it on the floor. It's only a goddam shoe.'"

Before the end of the decade, events beyond her control would subdue some of the rebel in Shirley. In 1958, at the height of her early success, her father, Paul Levinton Jones, died at the age of forty-nine from complications after surgery for lung cancer. In fact, he died of medical negligence, literally drowning from fluid that doctors failed to drain from his lungs.

One tragedy begat another and then another. After her father's death, for the first time that Shirley was aware, her mother began to drink. Marjorie Jones became an alcoholic, consuming awesome amounts of gin, and in a reversal of the often-tense relationship of the past, she became dependent on her only daughter. Shirley had to spend years dealing with doctors and nurses and hospitals, and watch the long, slow death of her mother.

"My father was in intensive care for five days," she recalled, "while no one diagnosed his problem. His had to have been a terrible death, and Mother was at his side. Until the day he died, I had never seen her take a drink.

"I was always away, never there, and her two sisters worked. She didn't have that many people around her. She and I wound up battling for years over her drinking problem. It was unfortunate that she was one of those women who had been taken care of all her life by men. Here she was left, a woman in her forties, and she knew nothing about how to go out and start over again.

"It amazed me because she was such a strong-willed lady, and as a kid she had worked in the five-and-dime. She came from a family where she had to work, but she had developed a pride, a sort of principle, that she was never going to work again. Someone would come along to take care of her. In fact, getting a job would have been the best thing that could happen to her. She could remake her life, meet new people. What she did was sit around and wait for some man to ask for her hand in marriage, like the spoiled southern ladies of Scarlett O'Hara's time, who felt that taking a job was beneath them.

"And that was her downfall. She married the first man who asked her. He owned a white Cadillac and a Rolls, a solid-gold pocket watch and a condominium in Florida. She always compared him to my father, wound up hating him, treated him like dirt, and turned their marriage into a true Virginia Woolf relationship. Her drinking moved up to another level, and so did his, and they played out their years in a wet and bitter fog."

6

The Red-Haired Stranger

LOOKING BACK, nothing good ever seemed to happen to the boy, Marty Ingerman, without a jolt or two of emotional pain. It was as if Mr. Pavlov was at the controls: "Smart kid. He knows how to work the lever. Let him have the candy, and then, whap, fifty volts of juice."

His was not a tidy, around-the-bases-and-into-home kind of childhood, growing up in the boroughs of New York. To begin with, there was the shadow of Arthur, the older brother whose birthday he shared—the ninth of March, five years apart.

One might understand a younger brother feeling inferior if he can't even have his own birthday. Their mother would bring out the cake, as he remembers it, with "Happy Birthday, Arthur" in icing at the top, and "Happy Birthday, Marty" squeezed into the remaining space, with his name curling over the side.

Arthur was an honors student, steady, dependable, clean-cut, a good athlete—at least, in Marty's mind. The funny thing is, the younger son might have been the better of the two at sports if he had tried. He wouldn't try. Arthur only had to be average for Marty to see himself as a zero.

Life is not a movie, we keep reminding ourselves, except that this case comes closer than most. The scripts might have been by Neil Simon or Rob Reiner . . . with subtitles by Kafka. As if to prepare himself for the television years still to come, the childhood of Marty Ingels had a pattern that was clearly episodic.

I. The Gym Class

Marty was ten or eleven, edging into puberty, the day he was undressing in the locker room and someone noticed for the first time that he had red pubic hair.

"This kid kept staring at me, I'll never forget it, and he's saying, 'Whazzis, whazzis?' This is an Italian-Jewish neighborhood, and it was like no one had seen red body hair. Suddenly, he says, 'Hold on, will you, hold on just a second. Hey, Tony! Bring the guys over here.' And I'm standing there like a schmuck, naked, and they're saying, 'Look at this, he's got red hair down there . . . no kidding . . . yeah . . . hey, Phil, c'mere, you gotta see this.'

"I have the whole frigging class around me. What it did was reinforce the feeling that I was different. Who am I? What kind of kid was I? Gee, even my pubic hair is funny. Who asked for this? I didn't ask for this."

Sammy Davis, Jr., got laughs with a gag about playing golf, and having a club member ask about his handicap. "I'm a one-eyed black Jew," replied Sammy, "and you have to ask what my handicap is?"

So here was ten-or-eleven-year-old Martin Ingerman, a klutzy redheaded Jewish kid with a voice like sandpaper. His hair would turn dark when he reached his mid-teens and had his growth spurt.

"I have a vivid memory," he says, "of when I was very little, and it snowed. My mother put the leggings on me, and a cap with flaps that came over your ears and buttoned under your chin, and only your eyes and nose and mouth stuck out. A guy drove by in a postal truck, and he yelled out the window, 'Hey, Red!' I couldn't get over it. How did he know I was a redhead, when nothing showed except my eyes, nose and mouth? That phrase stuck with me forever: 'Hey, Red!' It was as if I had been . . . found out."

He would come to regard these as the oddities of his life and he spent a disproportionate amount of his time trying to turn them to his advantage. "I was the only kid who had to put a T-shirt on to go swimming, in the summer, because I had red hair and pink skin and I was sensitive to the sun. Somebody would say, 'Let's jump in the water,' and they'd all rip off their T-shirts and I had to put mine on.

"The signs kept pointing to the fact that I wasn't quite the same as everyone else. So I tried to develop a theory. Take a scientist, conk him on the head, stick him in the middle of the jungle with his memory gone, and what would happen when he sees the monkeys swinging through the trees? There are thousands of them. He knows he isn't one of them, but he doesn't know he's superior, either. What does he think? He thinks, Look at those monkeys jumping around, and I'm standing here like a dummy. I can't do any of that. He doesn't know his capabilities. At best, if they taught him, he would learn to swing a little bit, but he'd be a lousy monkey.

"On the other hand, if he knew what he was, a scientist, he would get to the high ground, build a fence, and own all the monkeys. As I got older, I tried to explain this theory to the girls I dated, with mixed results. All I meant, really, was that being different didn't mean you had to be inferior. You could be a scientist in a world of monkeys."

II. The Pool

For most New York youngsters, day camp was where you learned to swim in that more innocent time, the 1940s; and where the cool blue water of a community pool provided an escape from the heat of a sweltering summer.

But not for Marty, whose fear kept him from learning to swim, who felt only waves of panic when his head was ducked repeatedly beneath the surface and he gagged on the water that tasted of chlorine and spilled out his nostrils.

He says simply, "I was in pain all the time. Perhaps it would have been great if we had had a Little League encounter group and sat around and talked to each other, but who knew back then?"

The swimming instructor was basically a decent man, he

thought, a family man, good-natured, not sadistic. It was his methods that scared the hell out of Marty. He belonged to the old school: Dunk 'em in the deep end, and if they don't drown, you've created a swimmer.

"The minute the bell rang and I knew it was swimming time, I used to hide under a bed. It was almost hysterical. As soon as the bell rang, everybody knew they [the counselors] would be chasing me, and when they found me, they'd drag me out. It would seem funny if it wasn't for the fact that I was so terrified of being visited upon. Some of the other kids fought it, too. They thought it was torture, but a funny kind of torture.

"It was the same thing every day. The guy would grab me around the stomach and—this was what he thought teaching was—he would paddle out to the deep end with me, and then we'd go 'one, two, three,' and he'd pull me under the water. He'd hold me there until I was out of breath; he could tell by the way I struggled. I guess this was supposed to get me familiar with the water. I don't want to think he was a sadist or anything, but he did that every day, for weeks.

"He was kind of like the Great Santini. Like a macho guy, not a bad human being, but everybody had to toe the mark and show that they could do it. Of course, we all lived for the grades and the results and the approval. There was an obstacle course, and you had to climb over a wall. He would be cheering me on—'Get up there, Ingerman, yah, great, keep going.' And he'd pat you on the head if you made it.

"In my case, it all went wrong because I came to think of him as my enemy, and my mother wouldn't listen, so I saw her as a part of this conspiracy against me. He lost respect for me. I hated myself anyway, so when he called me a pussy, I wasn't sure what he meant, but I didn't mind.

"I quit going. I would rather have rotted on the hot streets of New York than go back and face that drowning pool. A lot of years later, I tried to tell a psychiatrist about a little boy who felt so unworthy of being alive that he couldn't learn to swim, who felt they were basically trying to torture him, and he couldn't even relate this to his mother. I thought about the sadness and the tragedy of it, and I cried all day. The only thing that came out of it was, I never went back to that doctor."

III. The Speech

When Marty graduated from the eighth grade, he was chosen to deliver a speech about George Washington as part of the school's ceremonies. His selection was more than an honor; it was close to a vindication. He had qualified for nothing else—no scholastic awards, no sports medals, no citations for good conduct.

But he was to have his moment nonetheless. In his hand, he held a speech about the nation's first president, and his parents were there to hear him deliver it.

Finally, the principal rose and said, "Our graduation day speech will be delivered by Martin Ingerman," and Marty left his seat and began walking down the aisle, while his classmates and their guests applauded.

"I was on my way to the stage and I started to get nervous, and I realized that I wasn't going to be able to say 'Washington.' I kept walking with that piece of paper with the name 'Washington' on it ten thousand times, and I knew in my heart, I couldn't say it."

Marty did not have a speech impediment. What he had was a transmission problem, a form of brain lock. Sometimes he could not get a word to travel from his mind to his lips. This was one of those times.

"I looked out at the audience, petrified, the sweat pouring off me. And I started my speech: 'George Wa- Wa- Wa-'

"I couldn't say that simple bloody word, and people started coughing, squirming in their seats. The teachers were looking at each other. Nobody knew what to do. I couldn't say it. So what I did was read the speech, inserting the name of Abraham Lincoln. I could say 'Lincoln.' And I delivered the entire essay with Lincoln at Valley Forge and crossing the Delaware, and Lincoln chopping down the cherry tree, and Lincoln with the wooden teeth, and Lincoln as the father of our country.

"I did the whole thing that way, and nobody knew why, but they were hysterical, doubled over, laughing. It was my first comic appearance."

IV. The Book Reports

"I made up my own book reports, even the books, all the way through school. I never read anything, I didn't have the patience, and I always liked to write. So I would actually make up a plot and the characters and give it a title. The kids in my classes knew what I was doing, and they screamed each time I read one.

"English was my best subject, and I figured there were hundreds of thousands of novels out there, how could this one teacher have read them all? There were thirty-eight kids in our class, and there was no way she could verify every book that we reviewed.

"I'd come up with an interesting title, and the rest was easy because I had a fertile imagination. I'd stand up and say, my report is on *Oh, the Purple Sky*, by Paul Trail, and this is the story of a young man who grows up on a ranch in New Mexico, and everybody around me has their head in their armpit so the teacher won't hear them giggling.

"One day I gave a book report about a Jewish family that moves to the South and is met with prejudice. The story is about how each member of the family fights it in a different way. The father just goes out with his fists, he wants to kill everybody, and the mother cries and hides in the house and doesn't want to offend anybody. The daughter goes out and is loose with the other boys. The sixteen-year-old son overcomes it the best, just by his attitude, by being a human being, and knowing when to turn the other cheek and when not to, and it is really the study of a young boy who has it all over the grown-ups.

"And the teacher said, 'Yes, Martin, very well done. I read that book, and it was absolutely wonderful.' The more she went on about how enlightening the book was, the more the class screamed, and the teacher had no idea what was going on."

V. The Practical Joke

Marty was still in grade school when he paid a visit to a penny arcade and had a bad experience with a practical joke. "The jokes were kind of limited, maybe six or seven. One looked like a portable radio, with a little speaker and a red button in the center. A sign said, PRESS BUTTON TO HEAR FUNNY SOUND.

"Right. When you pressed the red button, a needle came through it and stuck you in the finger. So the funny sound was "*Ouch*!" I fell for it right away, and I thought, Great. My father was a funny person, everybody liked him, and he kept a drawer at home filled with tricks and games.

"Man, I was going to be popular. So I stopped the first person who walked by, a big guy, looked to be about six-foot-four, and I said, 'Hey, mister, you want to hear a funny sound? Look at this.'

"He said, 'Yeah, sure,' and he pressed the button and, oh, Christ, he took his fist and just hammered the top of my head. He said, 'Here, kid, how do you feel about that funny sound?' "

Marty accepted this reflex, this unexpected cruelty, for what it was: a reaction to his own lack of judgment. "And ever since," he said, "whenever I see a practical joke, I think about that day at the arcade.

"I don't enjoy a practical joke. This is my fear: You pull the squirting pen gag, let's say. He is sitting there in a nice, light-colored suit, and now there is black ink all over the front. Through the veil of friendship, and who knows how deep that goes, he cries out, during the minute he thinks it is real: 'You Jew bastard. You son of a bitch. You prick. I never liked you. Your sister sucks eggs. Your mother is a hooker. Not only that, I stole two thousand dollars from you . . .'

"Now he looks at his suit. 'Oh, it's drying up . . . hee-hee . . . you son of a gun, what a joke. . . .'

"And you're saying, 'Wait a minute. What happened to Jew bastard and my sister sucks eggs?' So the things that one might blurt out during a practical joke I consider dangerous, and the laugh, if there is one, doesn't justify the risk."

VI. The Gas Mask

His family and friends tease Ingels about being a compulsive shopper, and a notorious bargain hunter whose desk is always cluttered with mail-order catalogs, who will go to extraordinary lengths to get a "good deal." This vignette is the kind that reveals the boy inside the man:

"I was walking down Thirty-fourth Street once on my way to see my uncle, who was a dentist. I passed a hardware store with all these wonderful surplus things, and a big cardboard sign that said, GAS MASKS, 98 CENTS. There was something absolutely irresistible about that sign.

"First of all, how many times do you see a gas mask on sale for any amount of money? No twelve-year-old would fail to stop and look at such a sign. Now I didn't have any money, except the money I got to ride the subway. But I scraped up the money, and I figured I would walk home the rest of the week.

"I walked in the hardware store and said to the owner, 'Uh, I'd like one of those gas masks,' and I couldn't wait to get it home. I thought I had done something terrific.

"I burst into the house and I shouted, 'Ma, look what I got,' and I put it on, with the goggles and the long funnel that hung down from your nose. I looked like the Elephant Man. You can't hear my voice through the mask, and I'm squealing, 'Isn't this terrific?'

"And my mother says, 'What is that thing?'

"I'm bouncing around, excited. 'It's a gas mask. See, when the gas was sprayed, they wore it like this and they ran and—'

"She sputtered, 'What . . . what . . . what the hell did you need a gas mask for?'

"And I said, 'Ma, where can you find a gas mask for ninety-eight cents?' She left the room and complained for days, and her reaction devastated me. I thought this was like a valuable artifact, and she had no sensitivity to my fascination with gas masks. To her, I had just thrown away ninety-eight cents."

VII. The Bar Mitzvah

The year he turned thirteen, Marty studied for his bar mitzvah, the rite of passage for young Jewish males:

~~~~

You're supposed to go to Hebrew school every day, and study the Torah and learn enough Hebrew to read or chant part of the services from the Torah.

I don't know where I went or what I did when I was supposed to be studying Hebrew, but the week before my bar mitzvah I faced a crisis. I had written my speech, in which you declare, "Today I am a man," but I told the Hebrew teacher there was no way I could read from the Torah. I couldn't do it. What was I going to do? It was the next Saturday, my family would be there, I didn't want to embarrass them.

The Hebrew teacher was young, a good guy, and he could see I was desperate. He said, "Look, this is what we will do. Later tonight, after the synagogue is closed, we'll sneak into the chapel and take out the Torah. I'll type out everything in phonetics—'Sha-mah, Yis-roel, ah-do-noy elo-hey-nu'—and we will slip it inside for you to read."

This was a scary, even sacrilegious, thing to do, and to this day I don't know why he would go that far to help me. At the time of your bar mitzvah, two rabbis lead the young boy who is growing into manhood to the tabernacle. They open the doors and from behind a curtain remove the Torah, which is said to have been handed down from God, and they slip off the heavy satin covering, which is elaborately embroidered. And they unroll the scroll until they reach the appropriate portion for that week's prayers.

What we did, we took the phonetic script and Scotch-taped it onto this sacred parchment from God, rolled it back, and returned it to the ark.
~~~~

The morning of my bar mitzvah, wearing the prayer shawl (the tallith) and the skullcap (the yarmulke), I sat on the stage with the rabbis and the cantor and my father and the president of the congregation. It is a long, solemn morning, a three-and-a-half-hour service. I walked to the podium and gave my speech. People are crying and smiling at me. Then came the big moment, and the rabbi said something to the effect that "Marty, today you celebrate your commitment to the Jewish faith and its traditions by reading directly from the Torah." He recited a little history, and then the rabbis and the cantor go to the great door, and pull back the curtain, and gently remove this ancient Torah that the hands of ordinary men never touch. The rabbi begins chanting, and I'm waiting for them to get to my place in the scroll.

Then they moved aside so I would be in position to read the prayers from the scroll. Suddenly, a piece of loose-leaf paper came into view, and I began to chant. The rabbis looked at each other and then at me, and then at the paper Scotch-taped to the Torah, and I just went right on. They glared at me, stepped on my foot, gave me a little kick, trying to indicate their displeasure. But they didn't want to ruin the ceremony and, in circumstances somewhat strained, I was bar mitzvahed.

When it was over, I kept my distance from the rabbis, but I felt exuberant.

VIII. My Bodyguard

Growing up, one of my best friends was Tony Debias, an Italian who lived over a bar in a neighborhood so rough that longshoremen went there in pairs.

I dreaded going to Tony's apartment, because it meant passing the front door of the bar, and climbing the stairs, maybe stepping over a drunk or a wino. To me, bars were places where people were out of control. The words that came to mind were *punch, stab, kill.*

Tony lived alone with his mother, who was a very old-fashioned, almost imbalanced woman from the old country. He was tough, and in the natural order of things he ran with other tough guys. That was not the company he wanted, however. He was sensitive, loved to draw and had a talent for it. The test for Tony was whether or not his environment would sink him. He was the perfect example of a young man who wanted to reach out and break away from the squalor and despair around him.

He survived in a world of bums because he wasn't one of them. He happened to be big and muscular, and everyone was afraid of Tony, even though he had a nature gentler than mine. We were like the pair in the movie *My Bodyguard*, in which an unlikely friendship develops between a small, more cerebral kid and the brute who protects him from the school bullies. Tony introduced me as his friend, and so anybody who wanted to push me around knew they had to deal with him. He was, in fact, my bodyguard.

No one knew why we liked each other, but we had a very soft, trusting friendship. We developed our own language, words we would say to each other that no one else knew. Tony would say, "Don't give me 'humils,'" which was short for humiliation. He had a fear of being embarrassed. If anyone really put him down, I believe Tony was capable of hurting them in a major way.

When we first discovered girls, he disliked his hair, which was kinky, and constantly worked at trying to straighten it. He went to sleep with a hair net, which was a secret I promised to keep, and I did.

We fit nowhere—not him with my Jewish friends, certainly not me with his street toughs. My mother despised him, the sideburns, the look, all those implications. My father, God love him, just felt something good about Tony and refused to judge him.

Each of us saw something in the other's life we needed. The best part were the times we had, just me and him, not on his turf and not on mine, but on those excursions out there in the world. The movies, the subways, the libraries, searching and watching and laughing.

But, damnit, he never did get the chance to catch the tide and ride it out of that mindless squalor. On a trip east, on an absolute odyssey to locate him, I found Tony working as a short-order chef in a restaurant-bar on Staten Island. Shirley and I drove across the bridge (the first time for me) and met with him in a dark booth in the back of the bar. He was wearing a greasy T-shirt and an apron and a floppy chef's hat, but the face looked exactly the same. He was warm and sweet and almost speechless around Shirley. There was no mention of his art or his music or any of that . . . he had survived, period.

As we drove away, I had a sad, sinking feeling that I couldn't shake, as if somehow I should have taken him with me. If not then, all those years ago back there on Lincoln Place.

IX. The Gang

It was Groucho Marx who came up with the classic line, "I wouldn't belong to a club that would have me as a member." When and where I grew up, there were always clubs, and I always wanted to belong to one of them. I never did. There were sports clubs, scholastic clubs, glee clubs, stamp clubs, Spanish clubs. None would have me.

Ultimately, I joined a gang because I had a need to belong. I became the court jester and made everybody laugh—partly as a way of staying alive. Or at least not getting beat up.

At one point, my goal was to organize all the other misfits and form our own club. I invited them to meetings, where I more or less took charge as the acting president. I would construct minutes of the meetings, and keep careful records and official-looking books. I always had a thing about structure. I imposed a system of fines: twenty-five cents for spitting on the floor, fifty cents for breaking something.

The problem was that these were not people who wanted to be organized. They would sit there and ask "Whaddya doin'?" They would come and go, mostly go.

There was something unspeakably sad in my inability to at least bring together the dropouts and rejects and castoffs. I wanted so badly to be part of a group that I once went out and made up my own club jacket. I had LINCOLN STREET BOYS lettered across the back of it, a tough-sounding name. Of course, there were no Lincoln Street Boys. A club jacket was valued according to how many other guys wore it. So if you jumped on a character wearing a jacket that said, THE TOOMBS, or THE VIPERS, eighty or ninety guys wearing jackets would fall out of the sky and spread you across the pavement like apple butter.

I had a nice jacket, it was reversible, but it was one of a kind. Technically, if I got jumped or beat up or killed, they wiped out the whole club.

X. Melvin

In a strange way, a big part of my childhood was a handicapped boy named Melvin, who was, sadly, born with a severe case of Down's syndrome. He had bulging frog's eyes and a long neck twice the size of a normal person's. His head was large and tilted to one side, and he leaned in that direction when he walked. He wasn't able to close his mouth, and he talked like Charles Laughton in *The Hunchback of Notre Dame*.

"Melvin the Mongoloid" was how the kids referred to him. Between their innocence and their cruelty, the way kids can be, everyone made fun of him and everyone enjoyed him. No one was afraid of him, except me. I would run into my house to avoid him. Not the other kids. If he was walking down a street, the cry would go up, "Hey, here comes Melvin," and maybe someone would walk along and mimic him. If there was a softball game going on, he was invited to play: "C'mon, Melvin, hit the ball."

The more sensitive kids liked him and were nice to him. Some felt a kind of love for him. No one ever heard Melvin complain or talk about how difficult his life must have been. I'm not sure that I can explain exactly how he fit in, but he did. He wasn't part of any group, but unlike me, he was accepted. He belonged to the neighborhood.

~~~~

XI. The Graduate

When his family moved a third time, Marty no longer had his own space and slept on a cot in the living room.
~~~~

After two years at Erasmus High in Brooklyn, he spent a third year and part of a fourth at Forest Hills.

Those dislocations were not to blame for his difficulties in school. He was simply an indifferent student. There was nothing memorable about his high school years, except by association. The star of the baseball team at Erasmus was a left-handed pitcher named Sandy Koufax.

On graduation day, Marty was breezing through the halls in his gown when the principal stopped him. Politely, the principal said, "Excuse me. What are you doing?"

"Nothing," said Marty. "I was just trying on my gown."

The principal asked him to step inside his office. He closed the door and said, "Martin, you are not graduating. Didn't you know that?"

He honestly didn't know. I mean, if he had been paying that much attention, he might not have failed a couple of courses. "Wait a minute," said Marty, "that can't be right. Why wouldn't I graduate?"

The principal slid a folder containing his grades across the desk. He would not graduate with his class. He would have to repeat the second half of his senior year.

"When I went back to school the next semester," he said, "I couldn't cut it. I just didn't care. I had to figure out another way to finish school."

He found one. The New York *Daily News* ran a contest in which readers were invited to submit captions to baby pictures taken by a photographer named Constance Bannister. "I was good at that," says Marty. "Every day I sent in some captions. I sent in one under a baby with its cheeks puffed out that said, 'Say, Doc, tell me when to exhale.' I won first prize that week, five hundred dollars. I gave it to a teacher who tutored me in mechanical drawing, the only course where I knew I could get the credits I needed to pass. So my ticket out of school was that contest in the *Daily News*."

The patriarch of his family was his mother's brother, Irving Crown—a grand name for a dentist. When Arthur graduated from high school, Uncle Irving tossed a party for him and at the end of the evening handed him an envelope marked "The Irving Crown Scholarship." Inside was a blank check. Arthur was headed for the Ivy League, his expenses paid.

Marty graduated at midterm, without the fanfare, without the party. Still, he looked forward to receiving his envelope. He sent off for brochures from Miami University and Tulane and Vanderbilt, rich men's schools, and he showed them to his uncle. He was wise enough not to humor his nephew or mislead him. "Marty," said Uncle Irving, "you're not going to college. You don't belong there, and it isn't what you want. Tell me, what can you do? What would you be?"

"Well," said Marty, "if I can't go to college, then I want to be an actor."

"An actor," said Uncle Irving, not mustering much enthusiasm. "Well, let's see if we can find you a place."

XII. The Usher

At eighteen, Marty had what he later believed was his first nervous breakdown. He stayed in his parents' apartment for most of six months, refusing to go anywhere or see anyone. Then, as suddenly as he slipped into solitude, he was out again, out of the house and into the stream of city life.

He had an earnestness that led people to befriend him. One, an agent named Stan Friedman, arranged a job for him in a seamy movie house in a poor neighborhood. As Marty described it:

~~~~

The Brooklyn Bridge empties out onto Delancey Street, or did the last time I looked, in the lowest part of New York. The Palestine Theater was a block off Delancey, and I went to work there as an usher.

We showed American movies with Spanish subtitles. I was grateful for the job and never thought to ask about the guy I replaced. Later, I found out he was recovering from a knife wound in the abdomen.

I worked in the balcony, absolutely the worst place. I
~~~~

was issued a blue uniform, and right away I did whatever I could to make it resemble a policeman's. The management said I could wear a gun, but I couldn't buy any ammunition until I got a license. So I actually bought a pistol, and kept it unloaded in a holster. I don't know what I would have done if any of the customers had actually caused real trouble. I guess I would have asked them to check back on January 8. That was when I'd have my license and could buy bullets.

You had to be a certain age to sit in the balcony, and my job basically was to chase off the kids who were underage. This required a fairly limited Spanish vocabulary, actually one word, *abajo*, which meant, "downstairs." That was about all I ever said to anyone for the months I worked there, *abajo*.

Mainly, I enjoyed being this semi-police character, but getting home at night was always a thrill. I rode the subway at two or three o'clock in the morning, from Brooklyn to Queens, where we had moved. For anyone who looked like a cop, the subway was just about the worst place you could be. Ladies would sit next to me to get away from rapists, and I would whisper to them, "Look, I don't have bullets yet. Don't make me crazy. You'll get us both killed. Come back in January."

Then I would always run into real cops, and they would call out, "Hey, buddy, what station you from?" I had on a badge I bought in a toy store and a gun with no bullets, and I tried very hard to avoid these encounters. When all else failed, I replied with mumbles or double-talk or a wisecrack.

I alternated between working in the balcony and handling the front door for private dances on nights when no movie was playing. My assignment was to make sure no one tried to crash the dance. Now we are not talking about Park Avenue or Beverly Hills. This was the pits, "Hell's Kitchen," where killings were an almost nightly event. People stabbed and shot each other for cutting in line.

A part of me was frightened, but I also experienced something new. I enjoyed being me. I loved the authority.

~~~~
~~~~

XIII. Honor Thy Father

Jack Ingerman was a short, round, humble man, well liked by all accounts, easy with people and quick to take a joke. He owned an automotive repair shop in Jamaica, New York, worked hard at it, and hoped the business would someday provide the nice living he wanted for his wife and sons. A heart attack changed his plans.

This is not, however, the way Marty Ingels remembers his father, which is a pity, because among the aunts and uncles and cousins Jack was a favorite. It is hard for Marty to think of his father without unresolved surges of sadness, of regret, of guilt and emptiness. He sees his father the way he was after he lost the shop and his physical powers. Marty was torn by the idea that other people felt sorry for Jack Ingerman, a proud man who allowed his family to accept the financial help of a rich brother-in-law.

Shirley Jones has an interesting theory about her husband's feelings, and his memory of his father. She doesn't believe a small child makes a distinction between success and failure. She believes Marty acquired from others the idea that his father was one of society's losers. Nevertheless, he was to grow up knowing only a family in need and a father too weak to turn it around. Marty's uncle Abe Beame (then the New York City comptroller and soon to be mayor) was a constant hope for the Ingermans.

Marty was seven when Jack collapsed. There was no clear point when he knew that his father, at family gatherings, was the poorest man in the room. He did not want to see him in an undignified job, and yet it didn't seem to bother his father. It wasn't shame that Marty felt, so much as a need to protect Jack Ingerman from realizing he was an unsuccessful person:

XIV. The Peddler

~~~~

My recollection of my father, in the early days, was that of a sturdy man good with his hands, who did a lot of heavy lifting around his garage. After his heart attack, he was someone else. Near the end of his life, he was a weak little man who dreaded weekends because you could never find a doctor on a weekend. Of course, he died on a weekend, on his way to a hospital.

I remember our relatives sitting around and talking about how to help Jack. My uncle Abe Beame was in politics most of his life, and he finally got Jack a license to operate a street concession, a snack bar. In New York, you see them on every corner, silver wagons with an umbrella, selling hot dogs, ice cream, soda pop, cigarettes, chewing gum, the works.

My father didn't land one of the choice locations, Madison Square Garden or Central Park or one of the big museums. His space was in a tiny park next to a cemetery on Long Island, and on the weekends Arthur and I were supposed to help him.

I hated everything about it. I hated seeing my father make penny change and slap mustard on chili dogs for all the dreary people. I even hated his cheerful, polite ways, his joking with the kids. Most of all, I was scared. I knew all about street gangs. I was terrified that someone would confront my father and I'd have to defend him.

You would think it would be fun for a kid to be with his father in the park, in the open air, selling refreshments from a wagon. I couldn't stand it. I never sold a thing, not a nickel's worth, and worst of all I stopped going.

I came to detest getting up on a Sunday morning, and laying out all our paraphernalia for the wagon: our hats and aprons, the belts and change-makers, all those rolls of nickels and dimes. Arthur stuck it out, as always. I was the family heel, but at least I would never see that dark and dingy park again.
~~~~

The last job my father had was working for a company that operated a chain of restaurants in city-owned sites, libraries, parks, museums. His job took him from one restaurant to another, checking the inventory, the service, helping out at the register if it happened to be lunch time. I dropped by the Museum of Fine Arts one day to visit him. There was a long line of buffet foods in the cafeteria, and an unending stream of people sliding their trays along the metal railing. At the register, ringing everyone up, was my father. He was laughing, and the customers loved him. I stood in back and watched before he noticed me. I left there with an ache inside me, and to this day I don't know why.

I would be the first to concede that this is not a normal reaction. A young kid looks up and sees his father standing behind a cash register, to him that is an authority figure; that is the boss.

All these years later, I can drive anywhere and see something poignant, an elderly newspaper vendor standing on a corner, in the cold—especially the ones who are out there at two in the morning—making something like three cents on each paper he sells, and I want to offer them a few dollars and tell them to go home. I get a flashback to the pain I felt for my father.

I am angry with myself that I didn't know my father better or talk to him more. The irony is, I demanded more love from my mother, and when it was offered by my father, I saw it as weakness. When I was very young, he worked long hours, and later I didn't reach out to him. I didn't know how to go to him—or anyone else. He would have been available to me. He loved kids, and he loved me. When my mother said I wasn't getting my allowance because I misbehaved, he was the one who stuck ten dollars in my pocket.

Then there was the night the police came. Two gangs had rumbled, as we called it, and someone wound up with a fractured skull. There were a lot of dark-haired Jewish and Italian teenagers in jackets, and when the cops asked the neighbors for descriptions, all anyone remembered was this one kid with a mop of red hair. Everyone knew the Ingerman boy, so two cops were in our living room when I got home.

My mother was wringing her hands. "My God, what has he done now?" she cried out.

One of the officers said, "Well, your son fractured some kid's skull."

With that, my mother threw herself onto the couch, screamed, and said, "I knew something like this would happen."

These were dispiriting times. I was not doing well in school, hanging out with people my mother disapproved of, wearing my hair long and my slacks pegged at the bottoms. I was not a conformist, but I hesitate to say this was my form of rebellion. I simply dressed and acted like the other non-conformists.

My father stood up and walked over to them. As frightened as he always was of the system—and this was a man who lumped the police and the Internal Revenue Service and the phone company in the same bag—his voice sounded like a trumpet. "Officer, that is impossible," he said. "You can tell me anything else, but I know my son. I know the things he can do and the things he cannot do. And there is no way on earth that he could ever hurt anybody. He did not do what you accuse him of. Whatever happened out there, he had nothing to do with it." He was right.

I still had to make an appearance in juvenile court before the charges were dropped. All the big Italian kids were there, sitting on their mamas' laps. In the waiting room, I walked over to my mother for support. "Don't come near me," she sobbed, true to the Jewish Mother syndrome. "When this is over, I'm sending you to reform school."

~~~~

XV. The Car

Near the end of his only season on network TV, when he was riding as high as he would ride, Marty called his mother in New York. Idly, he asked, "How's Dad?"

And Minnie said, "Oh, he's the same. You know, he's having heart troubles and the other thing." The "other thing" was called emphysema, a condition in which the lungs be-
~~~~

come congested with fluid. It is an exhausting illness, in which exercise becomes impossible, walking is difficult, and breathing is an effort.

Marty asked if they went anywhere, and she said, "No, you know your father. He hates to give up his parking space, and he worries about the car breaking down."

"What kind of car does he have now?"

"The same one, the '58 Chevy."

When he put the phone down, Marty felt a heaviness that was new even to him. He felt ill. How could he have been so blind? "I thought, I'm not a cheap guy, and yet my folks had zilch and I was so single-minded I had done nothing for them.

"I said to Jean, 'My father doesn't even have a decent car.' We were planning a trip to New York, and I knew what I was going to do. I had a few extra bucks in the bank. This is one of the times when having money makes you feel good.

"The morning after we arrived in New York, I went to the first Chevrolet dealership I could find. My father was very conservative. He didn't even think the automatic shift was going to last. He wouldn't drive a car unless it was solid black.

"I asked the salesman if they had a black Chevy with a standard shift in stock somewhere. He said he thought they had one left. I told him to bring it out. The car was brand new. The sticker price was six thousand, five hundred dollars, big money at the time. I wrote a check for six thousand dollars, told him to shine it up and have the car ready in an hour.

"I got the keys and drove it straight to where my parents lived. I went upstairs, and there was my father, sitting in his underwear, spreading cream cheese on his bagel. I told him to put his pants on, I wanted him to come with me for a ride. I had something to show him. There was no exchange of affection. But I had planned how I would do it.

"We went downstairs and I talked him into the car and we drove around for miles. Every once in a while, he would say, 'Gee, what a nice car.' Then I drove him home. When I walked him back upstairs and said good-bye, I took the keys out of my pocket. 'Oh, by the way, these are for you.' I handed them to him. 'It's your car.' In my whole life, I had never seen that look, that glow, on his face. I had a cab waiting downstairs, and I took that look with me.

"Of course, for the next two weeks all he did was drive around New York telling his friends that Marty had bought him a car. And a few nights before Jean and I were to leave, my mother called, and she was yelling, beside herself. He was having an attack, coughing, couldn't breathe. I said, 'Come on, Ma, you've been through this before. Call the doctor and get him a cab, and we'll meet you at the hospital.'

"With his two-week-old car at the curb, he hobbled into a taxi holding on to his wife's arm. The driver got lost on the way to the hospital, and my father died in the cab on the way there. When we arrived, the police were taking the personal effects out of his pockets, and an intern was filling out the death certificate.

"I felt so helpless when he died, and in a way that feeling never left me. For my mother, I had anger, and I don't know why. I wanted to indict her for things she did, but she was a nice lady who just didn't understand me. Nothing so wrong.

"Then there was the funeral. The Jewish thing is, you dress up and the next morning he's in the ground and it happens so fast you haven't got it through your head yet that anyone is dead. It was an open casket, and we were all sitting there, the whole family, in the first two rows. I kept looking over at the coffin, with my father inside, and I had this idea, this plan: after everybody left, I was going to close the door and I needed to talk to him. I wasn't sure what, only that I had so much to say, and this strong urge to say it. I waited an eternity for everyone to leave. Finally, they were gone, getting into their cars, and I walked over to the casket and I stood there.

"I studied his face and his hair and the funny suit he always wore. I couldn't help but think about all the lunch lines and the museum folk and the skinny ghetto kids with ice-cream money who had lost their friend. Suddenly, an unstoppable wave of pain welled up in my chest and I could feel the tears on my face and I was about to make my peace with the father I had never told how much I loved.

"It was going to be a very important moment for me, but sadly my brother didn't let me have it. Not deliberately. I was about to say something, and Arthur walked in, frowning: 'What are you doing here? Come on. We have to go. Everybody is waiting.' So he dragged me away, and the words went unsaid. If I had known then what I know now, I would have said, 'Hey, I need some time with my father, twenty minutes. I'll meet you.' But it was a wacky thing, then, to want to talk to a corpse. I suppose it still is."

XVI. Arthur

When both were what society thinks of as middle-aged men, Arthur Ingerman, the New York dentist, offered his analysis of his younger brother's conflicts:

"Marty did indeed hate the world for what it had done to our father. He programmed himself to go out there and beat the system that had caused this damage, and be able to say, as he had with that new Chevy, 'Here, Dad, this is for you.' He was prepared to break the rules along the way. I could almost hear him, as he skipped school and swiped the car keys and broke curfew: 'Forgive me, Dad. I gotta do this. But trust me. I got a plan. And I'll be back with all the stuff you were denied.'

"And this was what he did. But Pop played on him the rottenest trick of all. He died. That was what I saw on Marty's face in the funeral chapel. Even now, I think the last of my brother's unrest could be stilled by two simple acts of forgiveness—one to himself, for not having been a 'good' kid, and one to his father, for having died a foot from Marty's finish line."

7

Shirley: On Stage and Screen

A FUNNY THING HAPPENED to Shirley Jones on her way to college. She stopped off in New York for a final summer holiday, and one thing led to another, as things often do.

First, she called to say hello to a friend she had known at the Pittsburgh Playhouse, Kenny Welch, who was now teaching in New York. He took her around to see Gus Shirmer, the agent, whose company was casting a couple of plays for summer stock.

No one had anything in particular in mind, least of all Shirley, but Gus sent her over to the Broadway Theater, at Fifty-second and Broadway, where an open audition was being held. Three or four Rodgers and Hammerstein musicals were running at the time, including *South Pacific* and *The King and I,* and every few weeks people dropped out of the chorus and had to be replaced.

The wings were packed with singers and dancers, nearly a hundred of them, professionals, who had at least two advantages over Shirley: They knew where to stand and what to do. Not that it mattered. She was eighteen, and classes started in two weeks; she had nothing to lose and no idea what to expect. Hers would be a triumph of the uncluttered mind.

So Shirley Jones stood in line with Kenny Welch, a thin folder of music under her arm, and waited to be discovered.

It was going to take damned near forever, two hours at least, but the wait would be worthwhile.

^^^^

It was interesting listening to everybody sing. I learned from that, waiting in the wings. It was my first audition. If they liked the person, they would ask them to sing another song. If they didn't, they broke in after a few notes and said, "Thank you very much." There were too many people waiting to engage in idle politeness.

Finally, my turn came. There had been no time to prepare, but Kenny had coached me in the time we had and accompanied me on the piano. I sang "The Best Things in Life Are Free," and when I finished someone said, "That's lovely. Where are you from and what have you done?"

I wasn't sure how to answer. In high school, I had been in all the singing contests. Somehow I didn't think that was what they wanted to hear.

Gently, the voice said, "Have you ever been in a show?"

I said, "No. I just got to town. I haven't done anything." I was acutely aware at that moment of the singers who had preceded me, rattling off the choruses they had been in, the small parts they had played. I was intimidated. I thought I could sing—I knew I could sing—but I was not a pro.

As I soon learned, I was talking to John Fernley, the casting director. After I said I hadn't done any shows, he said, "Do you have something else prepared?"

"Oh, yes, I do," I said, eagerly.

"Well, sing what you have."

I sang "Lover," in a very high soprano key, and then, to my surprise, he asked me to do a third song. I was hoping he would. Kenny Welch had written a special number for me, which is a big no-no at an audition. You're not supposed to do original material. They want to hear something familiar so they can judge the kind of singer you are. But I wanted to do Kenny's song, which was called "My Very First Kiss." It was very young, very ingenue, very much the way I was and the way I looked, a lovely little song.

When I finished, John Fernley said, "Well, Miss Jones,

I'm very impressed." He said there was someone else he wanted to hear me sing, who was across the street rehearsing an orchestra, and did I mind waiting while he called him?

I assured him I wouldn't mind in the least. He explained to the rest of the people in line that he was going to need some time, and he suggested they check back another day. Not very much later, Mr. Fernley greeted his guest, there was some shifting of seats in the front rows, and I sang the same three songs.

"You're just lovely, young lady," the man said, from his seat. "You have a beautiful voice. My partner is at home, and I would like to have him hear you. Can you wait a while longer? If I can reach him, it will take him about twenty-five minutes to get here."

I hesitated, then said, "Well, no, that's fine. But . . . who are you?"

"I'm Richard Rodgers," he said.

Gasp.

Behind me, Kenny coughed politely and said, "Shirley, I hate to do this to you, but I have a plane to catch. I can't stay."

Richard Rodgers overheard him. "That's all right," he said, "I have a full orchestra across the street at the St. James. You can sing with the orchestra."

"But I've never sung with an orchestra," I said.

That didn't seem to upset him. "Do you know the score of *Oklahoma!*?"

"I know the music," I said, "but I don't know the words or anything."

"That's fine. I have a copy of the score I'll give you, and you can sing with the orchestra for Mr. Hammerstein."

I took a deep breath and said, nervously, "All right." Kenny kissed me good-bye, the rest of the auditions were canceled, and Richard Rodgers led me across the street to the St. James Theatre. There I was, with a full City Center Orchestra onstage, and we had a few minutes to rehearse before Oscar Hammerstein arrived.

They sat together, Rodgers and Hammerstein, with their casting director. I stood there with that thick score in front of me, just shaking, my knees feeling weak, shaking all over, and I sang: "Oh, What a Beautiful Mornin'," "Oklahoma," and "People Will Say We're in Love."

These were enchanted songs, and the richness of the orchestra made them soar. Now I faced a series of quick questions: Was this going to be my career? Did I intend to stay in New York? Would I promise not to go running back to Smithton? Yes, yes, yes.

They huddled among themselves, then Mr. Hammerstein said, "Miss Jones, we've decided, if it is all right with you, we have a spot for you in the chorus of *South Pacific.* One of the girls is leaving, and we'll sign your contract in the morning. You can observe the show for the next three days. I'll give you the script. Learn the role, and you can go in next Wednesday and do the matinee."

vvvv

She tries to recall this encounter as it happened, without giving it too much or too little meaning. At the time, she could scarcely believe it. These things don't happen that way. The understudy doesn't really go on and save the show when the leading lady falls ill; the second-string quarterback doesn't come off the bench to throw the winning pass.

But it happened that way once. A nameless singer from a nowhere town walked in off the street, auditioned for the most famous songwriting team on Broadway, and signed a contract, all in twenty-four hours.

The process was more significant than Shirley knew. *South Pacific* was a perfect show for a newcomer, because it had no chorus line. Every member of the cast had dialogue, and in the idiom of the theater, it called for a white contract. Those in the chorus, in the background—no speaking parts—sign pink contracts. Shirley was to be paid $120 a week—in 1953, money an heiress could live on.

What she had no way of knowing was the fact that Dick Rodgers and Oscar Hammerstein had other plans for her. They were casting the motion-picture version of *Oklahoma!*, and Shirley was their long-shot candidate for the role of Laurey. From the moment each of them saw her, they thought, Well, she certainly *looks* like Laurey. She was as green as young corn, and they saw that, too. They had tested most of the starlets in Hollywood in the most publicized talent hunt since *Gone With the Wind*. With the film at least a year away from production, they had time to groom her.

Since she was twelve, Shirley had studied and sung the music of these legendary composers. It would not be stretching the point to say she had been preparing for this part most of her life. The role would be everything she dreamed. The system would be everything she detested.

^^^^

After *South Pacific* closed, I had a featured role for the last month of what was perhaps the least successful of the Rodgers and Hammerstein shows, *Me and Juliet*. It was a play within a play, neither of which worked very well.

I wasn't concerned then, or later, with matters out of my control, and that included the box office. I was studying, learning, reading scenes with an acting coach and rehearsing numbers with a vocal coach. There is a myth, I suppose related to my age, that I kind of glided in, and everything came to me on silken wings. Well, making things look easy can be mighty hard work. I cared about the craft, and all day, every day, I worked at it. I could never, ever, sit back and sail through a script or a score on some kind of automatic pilot.

What was unusual in my case, I suppose, was this facade of calm everyone saw. In truth, I had my bouts of nerves, but never churned with it, never lost sleep or my lunch, never felt panicky. I know many of the finest actors do. Even Jane Fonda talks about it, how she has to throw up before every performance. For whatever reason, my butterflies are short-lived. By the time I have said the first words or sung the first notes, I have forgotten about whatever is out there—the audience or the camera.

If only I could have adapted as easily to the strange and arbitrary and dictatorial ways of Hollywood, and the system the bosses used to keep their actors in line. It was my luck, good or bad, to come along at the very end of the so-called

Big Studio system, the era of the star-makers, the last of the years when *glamour* was the operative word. This was especially true of Metro-Goldwyn-Mayer, the studio famous for its lavish musical productions.

I do not exactly celebrate the passing of that era. I was glad to be able to get a glimpse of it, of the world the Bette Davises and the Greer Garsons traveled in. I came along when the studio would still send a limousine to the set to drive you to lunch—half a block away.

When I flew to Hollywood to test for *Oklahoma!* in 1954, I was struck by the sharpness of the distinction between stage and film actors. It was as if two schools, two camps, were joined (at best) in an uneasy truce. To the movie crews, I had come from "the stage," but it had not been my career, my mission in life. I measured my time in months, just long enough to round off some rough edges. I was still flexible, not hung up on technique, soft clay ready to be molded. The director who did my test said, "I can't believe you're coming from the stage. You treat the camera as you would another person." Stage actors tended to overact. I had no problem bringing myself down, mentally, to the level of the camera. I loved the feeling of holding a thought and having it show on the screen. I loved close-ups.

I was too naive to be awed. This was the first experiment with Todd-AO, the wide screen, the predecessor of Cinerama. Strangely enough, I liked what I saw. Most actors avoid seeing themselves on screen, hate whatever is there, are made miserable by it. I had never seen myself on such a scale, as if anyone had, nor heard myself in that quality of sound. I am stuck with this positive attitude about life in general, this Pollyanna side of me. I loved it all. Everything excited me.

That is, everything except the business end of it. By that, I include the attempts to manipulate you. I had a director who said I couldn't eat when I wanted to eat; a producer who told me what actor to be seen with. I had orders to get to sleep at eight o'clock. I was eighteen, and I hated restrictions.

Fred Zinnemann was the director, part of Hollywood's New Guard. He had directed Gary Cooper in *High Noon*, and had scored big in 1953 with *From Here to Eternity*, whose blockbuster cast included Montgomery Clift, Burt Lancaster, Frank Sinatra, and Ernest Borgnine. He was very Svengali in his feelings about me, possessive, as were Rodgers and Hammerstein. They believed in the star system, and I was, no modest way to put this, their baby. I had a fierce dislike for what I saw coming.

Of all things, it began with a complaint over a slice of cherry pie. I had put on a few pounds, and I suppose it showed in the rushes. Someone had actually reported to Zinnemann that they had seen me putting away the cherry pie. He came to me and suggested I cut out desserts.

I was aghast. "You mean I can't—"

"You're going to have to go on a diet."

Having been raised entirely on home-cooked meals, I literally did not know what a diet meant, or what calories were. I said, "I thought that was what you liked about me, the fact that I was corn-fed."

He said, "Well, yes, but you're getting a little bit too corn-fed."

Then Oscar Hammerstein sat down with me one day at lunch, and said, "Shirley, you've put on a pound or two, my dear. It looks as if Gloria Grahame is sending you care packages." This was his way of telling me that other actresses were jealous, and wanted my part, and I had better watch myself.

All of which, in the circular way that Hollywood works, led to my first scandal. Of course I understood I could not appear fat on the screen, but it did not occur to anyone to tell me what weight to lose and how to lose it. So I stopped eating, dropped ten pounds very fast, and passed out while we were filming the country bath scene, which was shot in ice-cold water in a pond on the back lot at MGM.

I had gone days without any nutrition, no vitamins, and I simply fainted. They pulled me out of the water, revived me on the bank, and put me in the studio's infirmary. Then the rumors started that "maybe she was pregnant." In those days, if a woman fainted in Hollywood, this was the only answer that made sense.

Finally, my hairdresser, bless her, had a fit. "Is everyone

crazy around here?" she said. "That little girl hasn't been out of anyone's sight since she got here. She's as pure as the snow on a Christmas roof. The poor thing hasn't eaten in a week, and no wonder she fainted. Now let's stop that nonsense." I mean, she really stood up for me.

Not surprisingly, I got along very well with the crew, and felt much closer to the technicians than the cast. Again, it was probably my small-town upbringing. I have found most actors too self-involved for my taste, and here I was much younger than everyone else. I had no pals my own age, we were up at four-thirty every morning, worked seven days a week, and on location in Arizona had to contend with torrents of rain that threw us behind schedule.

I admired Gordon MacRae, Eddie Albert, and Gene Nelson, but didn't know them. Everyone else was running off to nightclubs or playing poker on the set or doing all the things that so-called grown-ups do, and I was really alone. On location, loneliness was a problem for nearly everyone, meaning that I had to fend off some of the fellows. I wasn't accustomed to that, either.

Charlotte Greenwood, who played Aunt Eller, the marvelous old lady who did the high kicks, took me under her wing, but otherwise I really hung out with the crew. At the end of the picture, they gave me a lovely gold charm, a disk at the end of a chain, and it said, SHIRLEY JONES, BLESS YOUR BONES. YOUR CREW. It was a sweet moment.

I had a battle with myself about whether this was a life I truly wanted. It was marvelous, the first crack out of the box to get a role like Laurey in *Oklahoma!* But then to be catapulted into a giant motion picture, where a great deal of money was at stake, and to be swept off for seven months to a desolate little town in Arizona called Nogales, was not my idea of a fairy tale.

I wanted to understand how the movie business worked, how the people who ran it thought, and I should have known from the start that this would be a losing effort. In the beginning, Richard Rodgers wanted to change my name. He said they felt that Jones was too common, and I needed a name that sounded more like an actress. It was that MGM thinking: You had to be Lana Turner, Miss Lamour, or Miss Lamarr if you wanted to be glamorous. And I said no. I refused to let them change my name. I had gotten that far with it, and there was nothing wrong with being a Jones, or even a Shirley. They finally dropped it.

I was not going to let them do to me what they did to Rita Hayworth. They changed her hairline, gave her a new set of teeth, fixed her nose, her ears, her jaw. There was more cosmetic surgery done in those days than anyone imagined.

I let them lighten my hair and remove a little peach fuzz from my upper lip with hot wax, and still get angry when I think about it. The procedure was painful. They smeared on the hot wax, froze it with ice cubes for thirty minutes, then ripped it off. Later, what had been peach fuzz began to grow back as dark whiskers, and in the end I needed electrolysis to eliminate what had not been a problem in the first place.

At one point, someone noticed a space between two of my teeth, and wanted to send me to have all my teeth capped. I refused, and told them to change the lighting.

I will never understand about the making of motion pictures, because they never seem to learn from their mistakes. The producers spent so many millions for the wrong reasons. They chose to film *Oklahoma!* in Nogales because they wanted to capture the beautiful cumulus clouds that were the area's claim to fame. So they chose the rainy season.

It would rain for certain lengths of time over a period of five or six days, flooding what they called arroyos, or gulleys, and washing out the old, shaky bridges that had been built for burros and donkeys and wooden carts. There was no drainage at all. The water would just keep rising until the bridges were wiped out.

Of course, there were fifty limousines on call down there, one for everybody, the director and the producers and the stars and the important visitors from Los Angeles, taking them back and forth to the airport at Tucson or wherever.

We must have lost twenty limousines that season. The bridge would collapse, or the limo would just slide right into the gulley. The driver and the passengers usually had enough warning to leap out—no one was drowned or injured—but they lost tens of thousands of dollars in camera equipment, and precious days of film footage that had to be reshot.

It was absolute lunacy. Between rains, the drivers would

be outside waxing and polishing the limousines. MGM had planted a cornfield, built a farmhouse and a smokehouse and a barn. They planted an apple orchard. In order to avoid telephone wires and anything that looked modern, they had to create this farm two hours from where we stayed. So every day, before dawn, we had to climb into one of the limousines and drive to the location, two hours there and two hours back at night. Then they had to ship the film from Nogales to either Tucson or Phoenix, so it could be processed in Hollywood.

As soon as we finished filming, I was sent out on a national tour to promote the picture—a year before it opened. I don't believe that had ever been done. I was interviewed by every major newspaper in the country, every magazine from *Newsweek* to *The New Yorker*. After the initial excitement wore off, the trip depressed me more than the rainy days in Nogales. I was the Cinderella Girl; and the dullest interview anyone ever had. From a hotel room or a restaurant table, New York and Chicago look the same as Oklahoma City.

I had lunch with a reporter at Sardi's, and she greeted me with, "Shirley Jones. At least you could have changed your name. I mean, what could be so simple, Shirley Jones from Smithton, Pennsylvania."

I said, "Well, I wanted to change it to Shirley Smith from Jonestown, but they wouldn't let me."

In New York, I had lunch with a reporter from *The New Yorker* at "21," and the man in charge of publicity for the picture, Nick Pachukis, came along to see that everything went smoothly. He was sweet, even held my hand while this sophisticated Madison Avenue type lobbed his questions at me. After the interview, the reporter went back to his office and called Nick. "She may be the Cinderella Girl," he said, "but she's dull as dishwater. I don't need this kind of aggravation. What can anyone write about her? So she's in a movie. She hasn't done anything. Her life is about as interesting as wallpaper."

I had been told to be positive; that was my position, and no one was going to pry me loose from it. This was the first movie Rodgers and Hammerstein had done. They wanted me to talk about how wonderful it was, which it was, and how they planted the corn a year in advance, and how grateful I was to land this plum part. I laid it on. I wasn't there to tell people what a rotten time I had on location.

My favorite press reaction was Hedda Hopper's, after the movie finally came out. "She's a one-time Charlie," said Hedda. "She's pretty and she sings well, but it's a one-picture deal for this girl. She's never going to work again."

At least I had learned a tiny bit about the inner workings of the publicity monster. I had sort of signed up with Louella Parsons, and if there was any news about me, the studio leaked it to her. At that time, you had to choose, one or the other. Whichever one you chose, you were on the enemies list of the other. So I picked Louella, partly because I felt she did a little less sniping, at least in public. Hedda had a very nasty tongue, and she kind of frightened me. Basically, Louella was nicer to me, but it was a little like choosing which vein you wanted the doctor to open.

vvvv

There was nothing about Shirley's manner or her attitude that stamped the phrase "vestal virgin" across her forehead. Still, many a Hollywood male, even respectable ones, were mightily attracted to her wholesomeness.

The first was Richard Rodgers himself, in a scene Shirley handled deftly and with sensitivity.

Rodgers kept an office at MGM during the production of *Oklahoma!* One day, during costume fittings, he sent word for Shirley to stop by when she finished.

She had not yet met Jack Cassidy, had no time for dates, and wasn't involved with anyone in particular. Rodgers was fiftyish, younger than his partner, not as well liked, but regarded by many as a genius.

He began by reminding Shirley how thrilled she should be to have landed her part in the movie. "Yes, Mr. Rodgers," she said. "I'm excited. I'm very happy about it."

He nodded, punched his intercom, and instructed his secretary that he did not wish to be disturbed. Then he walked across the room and locked the door. Instead of returning to his swivel chair, he sat on the edge of the desk and put his hand lightly on Shirley's shoulder. "You know," he said, "we should become closer, you and I. I'm a very understanding man. If you ever need to talk, or want to share any personal things, you can come to me. You're a very beautiful girl."

A warning light was flashing inside her head. Do it now, she thought. Stop it now, or you're going to have to deal with it later.

"You're not in love with anyone, are you?" it occurred to Rodgers to ask.

"As a matter of fact," she said, "I am."

"Engaged?"

"Not really, but I hope to be, soon."

"Oh, you'll get over that," he assured her. "You should talk to me about these things, let me help take care of you."

Shirley decided to make her move. "You're very kind, Mr. Rodgers," she said, then adding the fateful words: "I will always think of you as I would my father. And I appreciate your very fatherly advice."

Rodgers eased himself off the desk and dropped into his chair. "Well," he said, "if you're in love, I guess there's nothing much we can do about that." Shirley started to say how much she respected him, and he raised his hand and smiled weakly. "Thanks for stopping by," he said.

She was still single when she was signed to co-star in *Carousel* opposite Frank Sinatra, but she was not quite unattached, having fallen in love with Cassidy. The movie was to be shot in the picturesque Maine fishing village of Boothbay Harbor.

She knew all about Sinatra's reputation as a ladies' man, but they had spent several weeks in preproduction at Twentieth Century–Fox, recording the sound track, and she had no reason to feel uncomfortable about him. Then, after work one day, a member of his entourage walked over and said, "Listen, Frank wants to see you in his dressing room for a few minutes. He wants to talk to you about the picture."

This is my leading man, she thought. How can I say no? She knew the reputation. Who didn't? Sinatra was then in the midst of a comeback from his voice problems of the early

1950s and the turbulence of his Ava Gardner period. He had his triumph in *From Here to Eternity* behind him, in a non-singing role, and his Mia Farrow period just ahead of him.

Shirley knocked on his dressing-room door and heard the familiar voice call out, "Come in." She walked into a typical dressing room—a couch, a piano, a couple of chairs, and a small bar, well stocked. From the bathroom, the voice said, "Fix yourself a drink and have a seat. I'll be right out."

When the door opened, Sinatra emerged bare-chested, a towel draped around his neck, his slacks worn as he always wore them, a little above the waist, giving the impression that he was missing part of his abdomen.

Shirley felt there was a bit of a performance being staged. Not wanting to make herself too visibly at home, she sat on the arm of a chair and sipped her drink.

Frank wandered around the room, not talking, not taking his eyes off her. Finally, he said, "I think this is going to be a terrific picture. How about you?"

She agreed.

Sinatra began to sort of circle the chair, as if they had reached an understanding. "I think we ought to rehearse together as much as we can," he said, "and really make the best movie we can."

Shirley couldn't argue with that, either.

"So, would you like to have dinner with me tonight?"

"I can't," she said. "I'd love to another time. I really look forward to working with you, and I know it's going to be a great movie. But I've got to go now." And she left.

Two weeks before the shooting was to start at Boothbay Harbor, Shirley was on the set, rehearsing a scene, when a black limousine pulled up, and a man in a dark suit got out. He spoke briefly to the producer, Henry Ephron, got back into the limo, and drove off. Shirley looked at Henry, and his face was white, with tears lining his cheeks. She had never seen a man cry before. To no one in particular, he said, "I've got to get to a phone. We just lost our leading man."

Incredibly, Frank Sinatra had pulled out on the day filming was to start. The story he gave to the press was that he didn't know the picture was to be done in CinemaScope, which was then a double process, requiring scenes to be shot twice. He said he had signed to do one picture, not two, and he wanted his salary doubled. Others thought he had got cold feet because he was still not confident his voice was strong enough to carry him. His part called for an operatic voice. In the prerecording stage, he had crooned his part of the music.

It was Shirley who suggested to the producers that they call Gordon MacRae, who had the baritone voice, the confidence, and a reliable nature. He quickly accepted, and Shirley was delighted to be reunited with her friend Curly from *Oklahoma!*

"If you see Gordon in a movie," she said, "you know exactly what kind of person he is. Very midwestern, direct, wide open. The first time I met him, he said, 'You know, I've got four kids'—like it was the biggest news in town—'and I'm going to have another one in a few months.' That was Gordon. He was up front about everything. His wife, Sheila, was there, and in fact their son Bruce was born during the filming of *Oklahoma!* Gordon was never an acclaimed actor, but he loved to sing, and he was very good as Curly."

No one, least of all Shirley, ever thought Sinatra lost interest in *Carousel* because his leading lady didn't leap into his arms. Shirley later appeared with Frank on two of his television specials, and changed her opinion of him completely.

"I had heard all the stories," she said, "the chart on the wall of the famous women he had conquered, the rumors of his connections with the mob. But once I was married to Jack, we became friends. He seemed to really like and respect me. Part of it was the Italian honor thing, not hitting on a married woman. He knew I was very much in love with my husband.

"Strangely enough, the first time I appeared on his show, we sang 'If I Loved You,' from *Carousel*, as a duet. He was in every sense a gentleman, totally giving and warm. We bumped into him one night after Jack had recovered from a burst appendix, had been in a life-and-death situation for hours. Frank rushed over and hugged Jack and said, 'I'm glad you're well and out of the hospital. If you need anything, money, anything, let me know.'

"Frank wasn't aware that he was Jack's idol. Jack wanted to be like him, sing like him, have that kind of legend. There are all kinds of stories about how generous Sinatra has been to people over the years. He almost wanted you to be obligated to him. Loyalty was his obsession. Whatever he did, he kept his reasons to himself. I never did learn why he really walked out of *Carousel*."

The performance that provided her career breakthrough was the prostitute, Lulu Bains, in the movie *Elmer Gantry*, opposite Burt Lancaster. It was the picture that established Shirley as an actress, rather than a singer-slash-actress. The part came to her over the objection of the person who had the power to withhold it. As Shirley tells it:

^^^^

I had played an alcoholic in a *Playhouse 90* production opposite Red Skelton, and Burt happened to see me in it. He fought to get me an interview with the director, Richard Brooks, who had his mind set on Piper Laurie. He thought of me, as many did, as "the musical lady." Even though I had by then done a few serious roles on television, it was a hard label to shed.

Brooks couldn't really visualize me in the role. Yet the girl wasn't supposed to look like a hooker. Her image was a country girl who had gone wrong, so they didn't want someone who looked as if she had mattress burns on her back. So physically I think I could pass.

Burt did persuade Richard Brooks to meet with me. I was doing a show with Jack at the Fairmount in San Francisco, and I flew back to Los Angeles on a Saturday. I wore a very tight dress, so they could at least see there was a figure in there. I'll never forget that interview. Brooks spent the entire hour, hour and a half, sprawled on a couch, his face turned away from me, sucking on a pipe, looking sort of gruff. Burt and Bernie Smith, the producer, asked most of the questions. Brooks did very little talking. He just sprawled there, rather quiet, at one point raising up to ask, "What makes you think you could play this kind of a role?"

I said, "I'm an actress. I'd be able to act it."

He said, "All right, here, step outside and read this, and then I want to hear what you think of it." He handed me the sides of the script for my part, which is how he worked. No one ever got a complete script. He would give an actor his lines, and that was it. He didn't believe anyone but the director needed to read the entire script.

I knew the story, had read the novel by Sinclair Lewis. So I stepped into the hallway and read the part of Lulu Bains, which took about thirty minutes, and walked back in. I thought Brooks was going to ask me to read, to audition for him. All he said was, "Do you think you can play this part?"

I said, "Yes, I'd love to play this role. It's a wonderful part. It's so beautifully written." Of course, he had written the screenplay. He looked terribly unhappy as I handed back the script, and I had no idea what to do about it. This was different from any interview I ever had. I hadn't read. I hadn't done anything. No one asked me about a test. Brooks was afraid to gamble on me—he wanted an actress—but he didn't want to go through a tedious series of testing people, and I think he wanted to satisfy Lancaster. The next thing I knew, I had the part.

The first day of shooting was to be my biggest challenge, because it involved the hardest scene in the picture. This was the scene in the whorehouse, where all the girls are sitting around and I utter the famous line that shocked audiences forever:

"He took me behind the pulpit and *rammed* the fear of God into me so hard and so fast I never heard my old man's footsteps."

That was the line, which just sent audiences of that time gasping. And that was the very first scene I had to shoot, in my slip and the stockings and the raw sexuality. To my astonishment, Brooks offered me no direction other than to say, "Let's see how you do it."

To my disbelief, I was on my own. I was for one of the few times in my life a nervous wreck. I came home that night and went to Jack, literally in tears. "That man hates me," I said. "He actually hates me, and I don't know why. He's just mad that I'm doing the character. Obviously, someone talked him into it. He didn't give me an ounce of direction. This is just going to be an agonizing experience, I know it."

The next day was a light one, with very little involving my character, and I returned home still feeling dejected. That night the rushes of the first day's shooting came in, and around ten o'clock my phone rang:

"Shirley, this is Richard Brooks."

"Yes?"

"May I apologize to you?"

That caught me off guard. I said, "What for?"

"I just saw the dailies of the scene you did, and it is brilliant. You're going to be just wonderful in this picture. I must tell you, I didn't want you for the part. You must have guessed that. I was talked into it, resented it, and took out my indecision on you. A nasty thing to do, and I must apologize, because you may wind up being the best thing in the picture."

Those words made my day, and the days still to come. Richard Brooks was a tough customer, a director who took no guff from anyone. Crews hated him. He wouldn't let anyone read a newspaper on his set, or play cards. He was tough on the crew, the extras, the actors. I have seen him rip an actor to ribbons in front of everybody and send him fleeing in tears. You had to be on your toes with him, because he showed no mercy to anyone if he felt you were not doing your job.

I was fortunate because Burt Lancaster had adopted me. Two weeks before we started shooting, he called, and we would meet on the set and work out our scenes. I had read that first scene with Burt, but not for Richard Brooks, and he would encourage me, pacify me, nurture me. "Relax, take your time, you're doing fine," he kept reassuring me. We would talk about the characters, what they meant to each other, and because I had no script to go by, he would tell me basically what they had shot, what the story was, where my character was. No one ever had a more timely helping hand.

Brooks was very specific about how I was supposed to

look. He knew exactly what impression he wanted Lulu Bains to give. I was mildly self-conscious, but it was not as though I were uncovered. I had stockings with garters, and in 1957 that was a sexy, very risqué scene. I really got right into it, once I started on the character. I have found in my own experience that the parts hardest to play are the ones closest to the bone, to your own self-image. The extremes, the hookers and the murderesses, the characters nowhere near you (you hope) are the easiest to explore, to develop the color and depth and variation.

Elmer Gantry turned out to be a high point for me, because a musical person has a harder time than anyone—including a comic—to break out of the mold. The singers of that era seldom went on to anything else after the musicals faded away. I mean, look at the Jane Powells and the Kathryn Graysons, all those lovely and talented people who starred at MGM who had no place to go.

I knew the danger of it happening to me. I went to the head of Twentieth Century–Fox after *Carousel*, and wanted to know why I had been bypassed for several interesting roles. "They weren't a musical," he said, very carefully, as if I were hard of hearing. "You're a musical person."

I continued to be turned down for serious parts, no matter how much I insisted on being treated like an actress. The studio's idea of consoling me was the role of the leading lady in *April Love*, another musical, with Pat Boone.

I don't recall ever discussing, much less arguing about, how much money was involved. I was earning five hundred dollars a week by the end of the fifties, a fortune, fabulous money for someone who came out of a chorus. I wanted to act. I didn't miss the singing.

Before and after *Gantry*, I did a string of comedies, including *The Courtship of Eddie's Father*, with Glenn Ford, *A Ticklish Affair*, with Gig Young, and my favorite, *Bedtime Story*, with David Niven and Marlon Brando. I wasn't thrilled with the idea of doing comedy. The studios usually referred to them as "sophisticated comedies." Too often they were neither.

I had reached the end of a five-picture deal with Twentieth Century–Fox, when we filmed *Never Steal Anything*

Small. The year was 1958, and I was early in my pregnancy with Shaun. This is the only way I can remember certain pictures, by which baby was born, or which child turned what age. The movie was a clinker, but it gave me a chance to work with Jimmy Cagney. Jack's idols were Sinatra and Cagney, and I worked with both, a reflection of my luck and his lack of it. He never worked with either of them.

Never Steal started out as a musical, with a score written by Rudolf Friml, whose father had written so many popular operettas, including *Rose Marie*. Cagney played the part of a gang boss, leading a union strike and trying to steal me away from Roger Smith. It was his film debut for Roger, the husband of Ann-Margret.

The picture simply did not work. The music was ludicrous, coming out of situations where Cagney's gang hijacked a shipment of watches, and then everyone would break into song. They finally cut most of the music, leaving in a number or two, and it still turned out to be a bad hash.

The differences in our ages kept Cagney uptight through much of the filming. I was in my twenties; he was in his fifties. He kept telling the director, "You know, I really feel rather uncomfortable about this, kissing her ear and all. My God, she's a baby." We adjusted the characters so that I thought of him as a father, and he was seen as the older man struggling with his feelings.

Jack adored giving parties, and we invited the Cagneys to one of them. We rolled up the living room rug, and someone played the piano while Jimmy tap-danced for us, all over the house. He was fantastic to watch. He was small, about the size of Michael J. Fox among today's stars, and his wife, Billie, was even tinier. But she was a feisty woman who taught Cagney all he knew about dancing, so he said. She had been a hoofer on Broadway.

What he really loved was holding court, telling stories that brought out the Irish pixie in him. People would sit there and listen for hours as he talked about the glory days at Warner Bros., palling about with Pat O'Brien and Errol Flynn; making gangster movies with Humphrey Bogart and Edward G. Robinson. He held you in the palm of his hand every minute, which was his way, I suspect, of keeping people at a distance. He wanted you to see Cagney the film star, Cagney the prankster, Cagney the storyteller. But rarely did he allow you to know Cagney the man. This was a very private person. When you read articles about Ronald Reagan in the 1980s, I think you picked up a sense of the same mechanism.

vvvv

Casting against type has a certain risky appeal. Shirley found herself playing a madam in a wonderfully funny western co-starring James Stewart and Henry Fonda, *The Cheyenne Social Club*. She enjoyed watching the easy camaraderie between the two aging, still-brilliant actors.

Her descriptions of them do not vary in any important ways from the accepted ones. Fonda was polite, shy, and remote. Stewart was just as you find him on the screen, slow-paced, kind, absentminded. His stories charmed Shirley, especially the one about the birth of his twin daughters.

"He was so excited about being the father of twins, he said, he couldn't wait to bring them home. The day he drove to the hospital to pick them up, he exceeded the speed limit, which was unusual for him. He parked the car and raced to the room to help bring down his wife and babies. He helped them down to the lobby, wheeled his wife out to the sidewalk, said he would be right back, and went off to bring his car around. Then Jimmy climbed into the car and drove home, while his wife waited in the wheelchair, holding the babies. Jimmy gave you the impression of being a little befuddled. His wife said he did those things all the time."

Shirley's memories of Glenn Ford are less innocent. They worked together in two pictures, and would have made a third if romance had not interfered—his, not theirs.

She accepted the part of the leading lady in *A Pocketful of Miracles*, one of the last films of the great director Frank Capra. Then it developed that Ford wanted Hope Lange, with whom he had fallen in love, in the role. He refused to do the picture without her. The William Morris Agency asked Shirley to bow out gracefully; at the time, the agency represented both her and Ford.

She hated losing the chance to work with Capra, whose credits included such classics as *It's a Wonderful Life* and *Mr. Smith Goes to Washington*. She hasn't many regrets about her career, but that was one of them.

^^^^

If I had known then what I would know later, I would have fought to keep the part, but at the time the rule was not to make waves.

Glenn was still courting Hope Lange when he and I signed to make *The Courtship of Eddie's Father*. The three of us had become friendly. Hope was not as smitten with Glenn as he was with her. He called me when the affair hit a bump, asking me to talk to Hope and remind her of his virtues.

We invited him to dinner one night, Jack and I, and he cried during most of the meal because Hope had dumped him. Not long after, Glenn got it into his head that I was what he always wanted. This notion was encouraged, if not actually invented, by Peter Hurkos, a psychic well known for his work on several kidnap and murder cases.

Glenn was deeply involved in the occult and psychic phenomena, and consulted Peter with such frequency that he kept a spare bedroom for him in his home. Our first day on the set, Glenn took me aside and said, "Well, you're not going to believe this."

I said, "Believe what?"

"Peter Hurkos predicted that you and I will be married by April."

"Glenn, I'm already married."

"I know," he said, "but something is going to happen, you'll be free, and we'll marry in April."

I smiled and said, "That's all very nice of you, but I just don't see how that will happen." I never believed he really cared for me, or that I was what he wanted, but he had to go along with his faith in Peter Hurkos, and in the stars.

I can say with certainty that he was picking up no vibrations from me. I respected Glenn Ford as one of the finest actors of his time. He had a quality on film, a naturalness, that was remarkable, and it made working with him a pleasure. Much like Jimmy Stewart, he brought his own nuances to a character. Whatever he said sounded as if he had just thought of it, as if he had never looked at a script. That is a marvelous quality to have.

We finished the film, and he was at loose ends, still looking for his fantasy lady, still believing that fate had plans for him in April. I had told Jack about the prophesy, and even though he had his own interest in the occult, he thought Glenn more than passing strange. April came and went, quietly.

On New Year's Eve, Glenn invited us to a party at the new home he had built on property behind the Beverly Hills Hotel. He also had a new lady friend he wanted us to meet.

The plan for the evening was to stop by Glenn's, then continue to a party given annually by Charles Lederer, who had directed the picture in which I played opposite Jimmy Cagney. This was one of Hollywood's galas, a black-tie affair with a thousand guests and an orchestra under a huge tent on the front lawn. Then many of the guests would close out the evening by returning to Glenn's home.

Jack proceeded to get roaring drunk, and at midnight he stayed [at Lederer's] and I left. I seldom enjoy large parties, and Jack wasn't keen on seeing more of Glenn, but he said he would be along shortly. By two o'clock in the morning, the Ford party was down to perhaps a dozen people, still keeping the bar jumping. I was bored and tired and wanted nothing more to drink. What I wanted was a place to lie down until Jack arrived. I wandered upstairs and found what looked to be a spare bedroom. I curled up on top of the covers in my strapless evening gown, with a long, flowing cape attached to it. I wrapped the cape around me, and promptly fell asleep.

Jack never did return. When I woke up, my eyes were looking right at a clock on the wall, and it was seven-thirty in the morning. I looked beside me, and there was Glenn Ford, also on top of the covers, stripped to the waist, but still wearing his slacks, and his arms across his chest.

His eyes were open. I felt the kind of embarrassment one feels when you walk into a bedroom, or a bathroom, that is already occupied. "Where's Jack?" I asked.

Glenn jumped up and said, "That's what I'd like to know. How could you be married to that son of a bitch?" He was livid that Jack had not come back for me, had left me alone, and to complicate matters, I had wound up sleeping in Glenn Ford's bed.

Now I knew how Goldilocks must have felt. I said, "I am awfully sorry. I didn't realize this was your . . ."

"I haven't slept a wink all night," he said. "I didn't know what to do. I didn't want you to think I would take advantage of you under the situation. I'm a gentleman, after all, and that is more than I can say for your husband."

I said, "Glenn, I don't know what to say. I'm so sorry about this. I don't know where he is. Obviously, he was very drunk when I left him at the Lederers' party. Let me try to call him."

I started to get up, and Ford said, "No, I'll call." He dialed the Lederers, and to my amazement Jack was still there, singing with the band and having a hot time. When he came to the phone, Glenn gave him a blast:

"I'd like you to know," he said, "that your wife is here and in my bed."

And that was all that had to be said. Jack sobered up instantly and said, "I'll be right there." He had just completely forgotten that I ever left. Fifteen minutes later, the doorbell rang. Glenn answered the door and said, "I want you to know that I was a perfect gentleman, and not out of any respect for you."

He didn't let him off the hook at all. Jack said, "Which is what I would expect of you, of course," and he made some joke about it to clear the air. It was either that or come to blows.

We were never again to have any close contact with Glenn Ford, although there would be a baffling confrontation at a party a year later. Glenn walked up to Jack and said, "How dare you! I heard what you called me, a necrophiliac. That's the worst thing anybody can be called, and it's a damned lie. I ought to sue you for slander."

Jack had no idea what he was babbling about; he wasn't even certain he knew what a necrophiliac was. I whispered to him, "That's someone who has sex with a dead person."

Glenn left the party, and as he went out the door, he

could be heard muttering, "Nobody gets away with calling me a necrophiliac." Months later, he found out that his informant was wrong. He called and apologized. It wasn't Jack who made the remark, if indeed anyone had.

Of all the actors I have known, Glenn Ford may have been the least like his image. On the screen, he was everyone's guy next door, or in his westerns, a believable hero. In person, you would describe him as almost ineffectual.

vvvv

She entertained twice in the White House, for presidents Eisenhower and Johnson; she brought to an end the 1988 Republican convention, with a rich and powerful version of "God Bless America," as thousands, including George Bush, joined her in the final chorus. So her "political" career has spanned four decades.

For all her eternal, down-home, Middle-America appeal, Shirley always had a modern streak. In the eighties, the movies she made dealt with serious and even tragic themes. *Last Cry for Help* was about the growing problem of teenage suicide. She won an Emmy nomination for her role in the drama *And There Were Times, Dear,* which tackled the dilemma of Alzheimer's disease.

In the seventies, she appeared undressed in two of her movies, both times with the same leading man. That may be no big deal today, when nudity is commonplace on the big and small screens and the stage, and gaining on America's beaches. Still, Shirley came out of a generation that believed there were limits to what one did in the name of art.

And so this is how she tested her limits.

^^^^

Fortunately, I've had only two nude scenes in films, and in each one my leading man was Lloyd Bridges. So I didn't have to work up the courage to take my clothes off in front of a second stranger.

The first time was in the television movie based on Maxwell Anderson's play *Silent Night, Lonely Night*, which is just about my favorite story. It had been done in New York by Henry Fonda and Barbara Bel Geddes in the original cast.

Briefly, it is the story of a chance encounter, of a couple who meet on a bus going to Amherst in the winter, on Christmas Eve. She wants to visit her son in school. He needs to visit his wife in a mental hospital.

Her husband is having an affair. His wife doesn't recognize him. They find they are both registered at the same small inn, and their pain brings them together for a fleeting moment.

In one scene, as they begin to reach out to each other, the man talks about growing up in Amherst, and his first affair—with the town groupie, inside the high school gym, at night. As he tells the story, she begins to daydream, and imagines herself in the young girl's position.

The director, Danny Petrie, came to me and said, "Shirley, in this particular sequence, how do you feel about taking off your clothes?"

I said, "I don't know. This is a television movie. How can you get away with that?"

He said, "No, it won't run that way on TV. They're going to distribute it as a motion picture and, you know, what we would see is the top, briefly, and then the back of you."

Again, I said, "I don't know. I'm really not sure," which was perhaps an understatement. Danny, a fine director, said to think about it. The decision was up to me. "Keep in mind," he said, "this is the way you would dream it, and it is perfectly legitimate in this particular scene."

He added that he would clear the set, and the camera work would be discreet. I called Jack and asked him what he thought. Jack said, "Why not? If it's part of the picture and not thrown in for shock. You're an actress," and so forth.

I made up my mind to do it, although I was still unclear how I would. First of all, I had three lines to say while I stood there naked. I thought, I'll never get the words out; I won't remember what to say. My face is going to be crimson.

They did clear the set, and Lloyd could not have been sweeter. He said, "Don't worry, we'll get through this. Please don't feel self-conscious."

I managed. I had to walk out of the locker room in the gym, holding a towel under my arms. Then, as the girl in the dreams twenty years earlier, I spoke his name, and dropped the towel. What the audience saw was my backside, as he came toward me, and toward the camera, and we embraced and kissed. That was the scene. We broke for lunch, and I did not try to hide my relief at having it over.

Actually, they did have a photographer on the set. When I found out about it, I had Danny find him and turn over all the photos and negatives to me.

That was my first nude scene, and then a few years later along came a film called *The Happy Ending*, directed by Richard Brooks. I play a woman who has been kept for nine years by a millionaire, and we have not seen each other for a while. I am in a penthouse apartment in Acapulco, and he is going to meet me there. The way the scene was written, he walks in and we kiss.

Brooks said, "I don't know how you feel about this, Shirley, but I'd like you to undress in front of the camera. Take the dress off, down to your bra and panties, and then discard the bra."

I said, "Are you kidding? No problem." And it did strike me as funny, because the millionaire, of course, was played by Lloyd Bridges. We had become good friends, and I called him by the name his friends use, Bud. I assured Richard Brooks, "Bud has already seen me, so we might as well do it."

That was the beginning and the end of my nudity in films. Two pictures, two scenes, years apart, the same leading man. I can't imagine what the odds are on that.

Elmer Gantry would turn out to be the one pure drama of my career in motion pictures. I craved a chance to play the roles that were so stylishly done by the Greer Garsons and the Deborah Kerrs, the mature love stories. So that part of my career has been unfulfilled.

No doubt I did not help my cause by turning down other film offers in which I was to play a prostitute. I was grateful to Burt Lancaster for his kindness and to Richard Brooks, however reluctant, for the chance to appear in *Elmer Gantry*—the role rewarded me with an Oscar, and I cherish it.

But that's Hollywood. I had to battle to stop being typed as "the musical lady," and then I had to say no to the producers who wanted to type me as a hooker.

8

Laughing All the Way

One of the problems with being funny is that it usually takes a while to learn that you can make money from it. And, of course, some people take longer than others.

By the time Marty Ingerman graduated from high school, half a semester behind his class, one thing was certain: He could make people laugh. Even in unexpected places—the army, for example—Marty could turn some fairly serious business into a joke. The country was between wars in 1955, out of Korea and not yet drawn into the quagmire of Vietnam, which was good, because Marty didn't sign up because he was mad at anybody.

~~~~

I read in the paper that they were forming a special-services unit downtown for the army reserves. This meant that you went to weekly meetings and at some point you put in six months of active duty. So I joined, and it may have been the best decision I could have made. Every Wednesday night I rode the subway to Fifty-third Street in Manhattan, in full uniform, and sat around with a lot of guys, reading *Variety* and looking for acting jobs. There were actually a few agents and assistant directors in the unit, and once in a while they made a meeting.

We didn't drill. We had lectures, and workshops on how
~~~~

to stock a library or stage a show. Every soldier is assigned an MOS (military occupational specialty). In every company, there might be a dozen communications men, twenty cooks, eight clerks, and the rest infantrymen. My MOS was for a master of ceremonies. In an entire division, there might be two of those.

In case of war, I would have been one of the very few American military men trained to stand up and say, "A funny thing happened to me on my way to the front." It was just as well. I wasn't looking to shoot and kill anyone.

When I decided to serve my six months of active duty, my luck held. I was stationed on Governor's Island. It isn't often you can pinpoint the time or place when your life made a permanent turn. This was mine.

Although I was headed for a post in special services, I had to take basic training the same as everyone else. Of course, we were assigned to a sergeant who hated me. He was a skinny black, five-foot-five at the most, about the size of Sammy Davis, Jr., and the army was all he knew or ever wanted to know. He called me Bendix, because he thought I sounded like the actor William Bendix. He felt an obligation to lean on me, because I was the kind of guy who would cut up in ranks.

It was always: "*Bendix!* Drop down and give me twenty!" With whatever load was on my back, a full pack and rifle, I did the push-ups. I began to get good at it, and he had to keep raising the number. I was just about the strongest guy in the company, because I had worked my way up to about two hundred push-ups at a time.

He rode me in other ways. My hair was still reddish-brown, and I had a light beard and tried to get away without shaving. I can't count the times he made me stand in front of the company and dry shave—no water or lather. I ripped the hell out of my face and bled all over the place, but I wouldn't give in to him. No one else could see how funny this was. I had an image of myself as a weak, frightened person. The sergeant was turning me into a macho guy.

I didn't know that he lived in a room in the back of the barracks, but one day I bumped into him in the latrine. We were standing at the urinal together, and he said, without looking up, "Bendix, there are three kind of people I hate—white people, recruits, and guys who are taller than me." Of course, I was all three. "But you know something, Bendix? If you'd get your ass in gear, you could be a damned fine soldier."

I was flattered and surprised and instinctively turned, almost peeing on his shoe. He was right, of course. I loved the flag-waving, glory part of the army. The first chance I had, I went to an army-navy store and loaded up on all the trimmings. I didn't even rate a stripe at the time. The army had just changed from summer khaki to winter greens, and they were really schlocky-looking. My taste ran more to the marine dress uniform with the white belt, or the paratrooper insignia.

So I bought about a dozen medals, braid, shoulder patches, epaulets, and captain's bars. I kept it in a duffel bag in my locker, and when we were granted a weekend leave, the bag went with me. I ducked into a rest room and upgraded my uniform before getting on the subway. I pinned on my ribbons and decorations, including a Syngman Rhee medal from South Korea—I had no idea what it represented. Enlisted men saluted me. On the subway, civilians gave me their seats.

I even tucked my pants into the tops of my boots. For that one, I got jumped and beaten up by three real paratroopers. They impressed on me the fact that you didn't tuck in your pants unless you were airborne, and my phony patches gave me away. From then on, I toned down my act.

One day in the mess hall, a woman sat down next to me during lunch. Three thousand soldiers are in there, and some of them hadn't been close to a girl in four months. This one says, "You know, you have a cute face." I'm trying to concentrate on my tray. "Lady, please," I said, "leave me alone. I don't want any trouble." See, they make you feel that anything you do is wrong. For all I knew, she was a spy.

She was, in fact, something even more exotic: She was a casting person for the television show *Name That Tune*, and she was checking out army camps in the area for possible contestants. She wanted, she said, a typical young American soldier. And to make a short story terse, I was invited to test for the show.

The test consisted of listening to seventy or eighty songs, a few notes of them, and writing down the titles you recognized. Once you were accepted, they tested you each week, and of course they kept a record of what you knew or didn't know. Like most of the quiz shows of that period, this one was fixed, but in an interesting way, one hard to detect or prove.

As long as the audience seemed to like you, the producers picked the songs from the list that you knew. The first time I appeared, I won a few bucks, tossed off a quip or two, and apparently they received some letters. They brought me back for another week and another.

And suddenly, I was a celebrity. At that time, there were very few channels, and you only had to appear on television a few times to become a star. Ed Sullivan was the host of the country's most important variety show, and no one knew what made it work. Sullivan was a former New York newspaper columnist, a man without wit or charm. "He does nothing," someone decided was the key, "but he does it better than anyone else."

More letters came in. The army was getting nervous about my popularity. At the base, the commanding officer called me in and suggested that I not forget my duty to the army. It would be unfortunate if I left some unfavorable impressions. Translated into civilian-speak, I knew this meant, One wrong word and we kill you.

Name That Tune would become a showcase for several ambitious young entertainers. During the same time I was on, Leslie Uggams and Pat Rooney were contestants. It was for each of us our introduction to show business. It was the first time I had heard applause from an audience that had the option of being critical.

I didn't figure out the system until the day one of the production people stopped me just before the curtain was ready to go up. "Hey, Ingerman," he said, "I need to see you for a moment." I said, "But it's almost time to go on." He said this wouldn't take long.

He led me to a small room and said, "We have a minute or two, and I just want to give you a quick test. Do you recognize this?" And he hummed a few notes, "The stars at night . . ."

"Yeah, that's 'Deep in the Heart of Texas.'"

"Fine. And this? Dum-dee-dum and dum-dee-dum . . ."

"Yeah, that's 'Mairzy Doats.'"

"Okay, that's all. Just wanted to see if you're cool."

I thought that was strange. A few minutes later, I took my place on the stage, and after a little chatter the announcer said, "And now, Private Ingerman, for two thousand dollars, name that tune!"

The few notes were not all that difficult to identify. The songs were "Mairzy Doats" and "Deep in the Heart of Texas." Now I knew. They liked the voice and the expressive face, and they wanted to keep me going. In no time, I won six thousand dollars and bought a brand-new car, which I drove onto the ferry and into the base at Governor's Island. The guards would salute me as I passed through the main gate.

So my army experience was actually the beginning of my finding shortcuts, a way of getting around channels, as much by instinct as by being a hustler.

If anyone wanted to research my past for character insights, I suppose they would find one or two in that brief army hitch. I consider myself a physically passive person. In my whole life, I have had three fights. In business, in school, on the street, I knew when to back off and how to win with words. I love words. They have the power to move people, to change minds, change history. If I had been a more serious student, less emotional, I would have made a fine lawyer.

One of my three encounters came while I was pulling KP duty. A tall, gangling southerner kept hassling me: "You Brooklyn boys think youah tough, huh, Ingerman? Lemee see y'all make a muscle." I had tried telling him to back off and leave me alone. He kept it up—"Hey, tough guy"—and, as a guy who thought of himself as an ex-member of a gang, I knew I could only let him push me so far.

He had the advantage in size and reach. I didn't want to fight him, but felt I had no choice. My immediate concern was not to be humiliated, so I said, "Why don't you and I settle this behind the mess hall. That way your friends won't have to watch you get whipped." He just smirked at that.

So we went behind the mess hall. He took off his hat and removed his watch, and then he charged me. I'm not a hitter. I wince at the idea of hitting a person in the face. But I was strong from all the push-ups, and when he came at me, I shoved him hard. With his momentum, his feet flew out and he went down on his ass. He got up and leaped at me again. I dodged a punch or two, and again I wrapped my arms around his chest, like a wrestler, and threw him. This time he went flying toward the garbage cans, rolled over, and scattered them. It sounded like a train wreck.

He was groggy getting up, and the cockiness was gone. I'm thinking, I'm kicking the shit out of this guy without throwing a punch, and *no one is seeing it happen.* So I keep pushing and slinging him down, but now I maneuver him toward the front of the mess hall, where the other recruits were hanging around. What they saw was the southern kid on the ground, his uniform torn, trailing flecks of garbage, his face dirty and flushed. With their own eyes, they had seen the evidence: Ingerman made mush of this mean-eyed southern redneck.

Nobody gets away with much during basic training, but I did. I found out rehearsals were being held for a camp play. I tried out, got the part, and was excused from all work details. That meant no duties, including KP (kitchen police) that would involve my missing rehearsals.

That should have satisfied me, but I looked in the army manual to see how they defined what a detail was. In the manual, making your bed and shining your shoes were also listed under "details."

So I said to hell with it. From then on, I slept in. The first morning my bunkmates tried to get me up, I read the manual to them and went back to bed. When they appealed to the sergeant, he checked the manual, and, livid but helpless, he ordered my buddies to take turns making my bed, shining my shoes, and policing my area for inspections.

Now I had a weekly gig on national television, a new car, and no duties. Needless to say, I was the most hated guy in the barracks, and my buddies spent part of each day inventing new things they would do to me when the play ended. They were going to kick the crap out of me, it went without saying. But it was also decided that I would go into the grease pit for a month. The pit was where all the grease from the kitchen went every night, after everyone ate and the stoves and ovens were cleaned. Someone had to go into the pit and feel around for utensils and things that got lost in there.

There certainly may have been a cleaner and more efficient method of doing this, but efficiency wasn't the point.

Wouldn't you know it? The week before the play closed, I was transferred off the base. I have always hated emotional partings, so I drove away without saying good-bye to the fellows. I felt they would understand.

After his stint in the army, an agent shortened his name to Ingels, and for the next two years Marty served his apprenticeship in show business. He did summer stock for thirty weeks at the Allenberg Playhouse, in Pennsylvania, where he built sets and drove a truck and earned his Equity card. He had one scene as a sailor in a production of *The Caine Mutiny*, and the first time he walked onto a stage, the audience laughed. One critic noted in his review, "Marty Ingels did three minutes and wiped out the show." Of course, that was not the memory of summer stock that stayed with him. . . .

It was kind of lonely. I was very woman-oriented, and I never could get the girls I wanted because I was always a lowly little *putz* in those places. I sawed wood, painted, hammered nails. My big thing was the truck, which picked everyone up and dropped them off. I finagled that job because no one else wanted it. Driving people around gave me a purpose.

After a party, there are always two people who need a ride and everybody is hiding out, pretending they don't know it. I'm the one who volunteers. "Oh, you want to go to the airport? I'll take you." Driving was my security when I began to get my anxiety attacks, jumping in a car, knowing I had that mobility.

In 1958, I made my national debut as a comic on *The*

Steve Allen Show. I walked into the offices talking about a speeding ticket a cop gave me on my way into the city, and they booked me before I did any of my material.

This was live television, and I could never memorize a joke. Even when I worked nightclubs, I had pieces of paper pasted on stools, the floor, the piano. On *The Steve Allen Show,* I did a bit about calling a baby-sitter that I wrote with my agent, and one based on being in the army reserves.

They actually mailed out a form letter instructing us what to do in case we were mobilized after an attack. The problem was, you had hundreds of reservists in each city, how do you get them together? So the army asked the colonel to telephone two majors, and each major called three captains, and the captains called four lieutenants, until you had the corporals calling the privates, and each private had to call a list of ten buddies. It was like a pyramid letter, and if it worked in a few minutes, you had hundreds of thousands of guys heading for the docks or to the airport.

I tried to imagine how this would work. I could see myself on the floor, dialing the phone, knowing how important it was I reach Private Marcus Schwartz and tell him about the emergency.

"Hello, Mrs. Schwartz? This is Martin Ingels. Yes, fine, fine. Is Marcus home? No, no, it's okay. Just take a message for me. Write down on a piece of paper that Ingels called. There's a war. Yeah, w-a-r. Have him meet me at the shipyard at nine o'clock. Yeah, a sports jacket would be nice."

I went on in that vein, and Steve Allen howled. Years later, I would bump into him, and he would greet me with, "There's a war," and he'd break up again.

If I had followed my instincts, who knows? I was terrific in offices, but onstage I was only as good as the words I stole. That was my great mistake. I didn't have the courage to tell stories out of my own life. If I had, I would have preceded Bill Cosby and the others who did it, Richard Pryor, by ten years, because I had the clown quality you need.

Then, and later, people would urge me before a show to tell a story I had told at a party. I'd say, "Oh, no, that's my life." People would tell me my life was funny, my very essence was funny, talking about a lamp was funny. I didn't

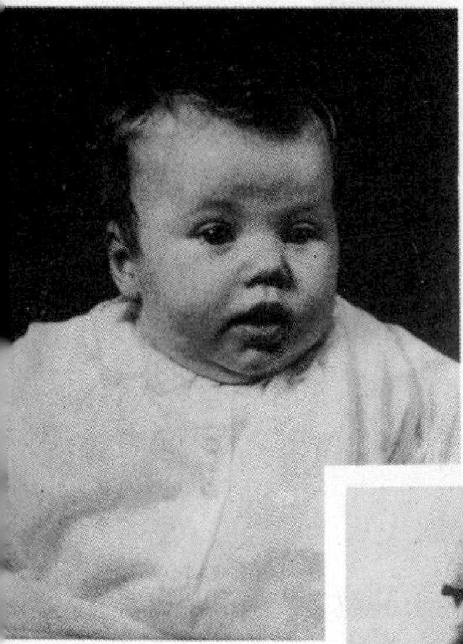

August 8, 1934. Shirley's first professional picture at six months.

Six years old. Shirley's first-grade picture. She hated bows, but briefly yielded to her mother's penchant for them.

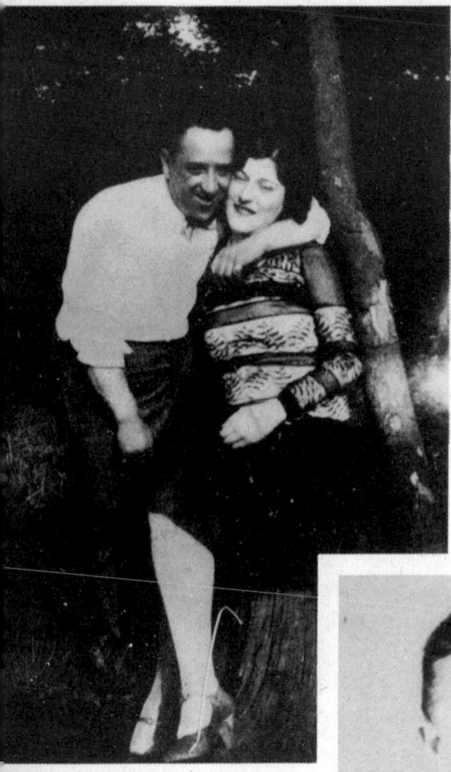

June 1927, Prospect Park, Brooklyn, New York. The only existing picture of Marty's Mom and Pop's courtship days (perhaps the only courtship *moment*).

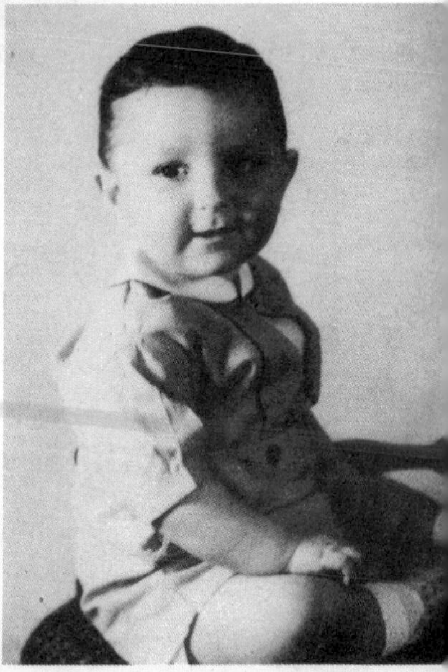

Marty at six months

Marty's family,
September 1938

The Joneses.
Pop, Shirley
at seventeen,
and Mom.

Marty at seven with his "perfect" older brother, Arthur

1951. Miss Pittsburgh, who prevailed over eleven finalists. Nobody knows where the trophy is now.

New York, 1953. Richard odgers *(left)* and Oscar Hammerstein II with Shirley. She was the only performer the two Broadway geniuses ever put under personal contract.

"People Will Say We're in Love" from *Oklahoma!* Shirley always felt Gordon MacRae had the most beautiful voice in America.

Universal Studios, 1956. Shirley's "make her a Hollywood glamour girl" period. It didn't work.

This was either *Midsummer Night's Dream* (Pasadena Playhouse, 1958) or a party at Alan Carr's house.

Shirley's Academy Award prostitute, Lulu Baines, in *Elmer Gantry* (with Burt Lancaster), 1960. *Gantry* was very daring for its time.

Marty and Burt Reynolds in Germany, 1961, when Burt saved Marty from a Munich lynch mob. At one point they talked about doing a nightclub act together.

Shirley accepted the Oscar saying, "This is the happiest day of my career." *Not* "the happiest day of my *life*"!

Shirley at twenty-nine, married to Jack and playing the Playboy Club in Lake Geneva, Wisconsin. The bunny outfit was a joke.

I'm Dickens, He's Fenster, ABC-TV, 1963. Thirty-nine segments and off. Marty with John Astin and Emmaline Henry, John's wife on the show.

COURTESY OF GENE TRINDL

The Cassidy clan, 1963. Shirley was twenty-nine here, Jack thirty-six, Shaun four. This was six-week-old Patrick's first professional photo.

Marty's marriage to Jean, 1963. "Everything in this picture is gone from my life except the goddamn cowlick."

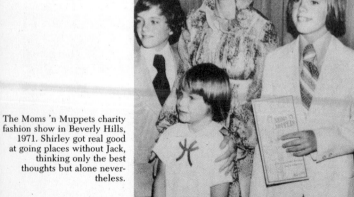

The Moms 'n Muppets charity fashion show in Beverly Hills, 1971. Shirley got real good at going places without Jack, thinking only the best thoughts but alone nevertheless.

The Unholy Three. Shaun (rigid and somber and old before his time), Pat (rambunctious and impulsive and full of the devil), and Ryan (introspective and ultrasensitive, even troubled), here seen praying he would not be brutally assaulted from either side.

The early days of Ingels Inc. in his bedroom office. Marty was his only employee.

1971. *The Partridge Family:* Susan Dey, David Cassidy, Suzanne Crough, Danny Bonaduce, and Brian Forster.

December 18, 1974. Their first date. Rare longer-hair period for Shirley.

1976. Marty's mother has the earrings; his uncle has the money. This is the only picture of Shirley where she actually *looks* Jewish.

Christmas. It's been suggested that Marty was guilty of a little courtship "overkill" at holiday time.

November 13, 1977. Frog wins princess.

It said on the invitation to this 1978 premier that the dress was "funk." Shirley does not appear to be very happy with it.

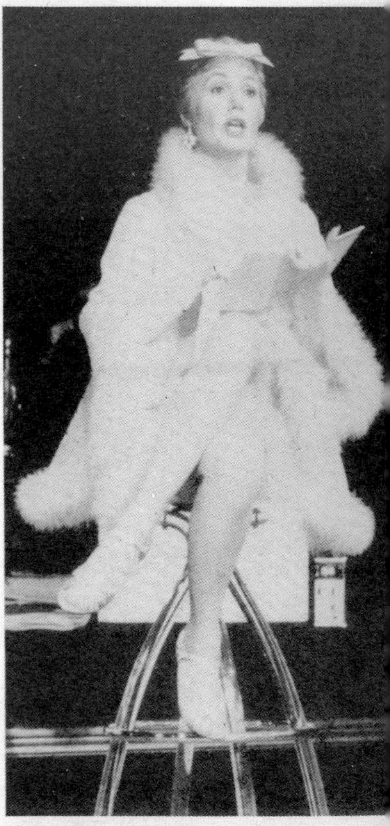

Before her decision to concentrate on symphony concerts, Shirley did a brief waltz-around with a nightclub act. She hated it.

In 1983 a new generation of Saturday-morning kids fell in love with Marty's voice as Pac-Man.

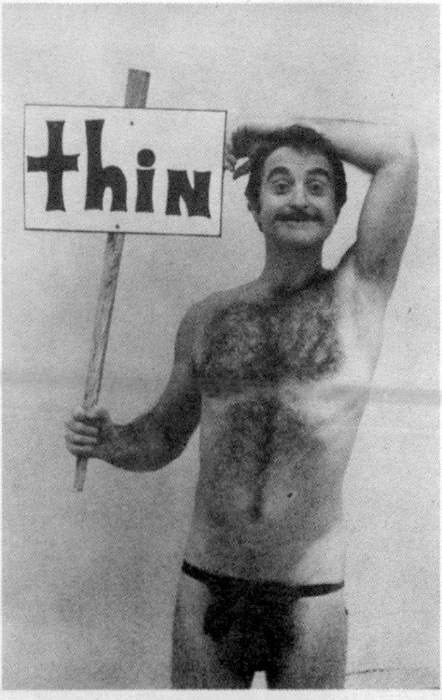

When Shirley was on the road, Marty sent regular update pictures of everything happening at home.

COURTESY OF MICHAEL LESHNOV

Together on the John Davidson talk show. Marty, self-conscious about being "Mr. Jones," is seen overcompensating.

A brief 1985 birthday reunion with "Perfect" Arthur. He always had that perfect gentile nose.

This promotion merger (Wayne and the Cancer Foundation) put Ingels Inc. on the map, even though it was a public service project and no money changed hands.

COURTESY OF STAN ADAMS & ASSOCIATES

Marty with the intimidating Orson Welles. Marty ate more than Welles did.

This shoot with Zsa Zsa was for a California wine and took a day and a half. It only seemed like thirteen years.

Shirley's surprise fiftieth birthday bash at The Bistro, one of Marty's most ambitious endeavors. Every step was a production.

Patrick's 1987 wedding. *From left:* Shaun, Patrick, Shirley, Marty, David, and Ryan.

After Marty's crash, he promised himself that he would never again wear a suit and tie to an office.

Marty and Tony,
after thirty-nine years

Rehearsal for one of Shirley's full symphony concerts

"Mom, I'd like you to meet a friend of mine."

get it. A trumpet player knows when he is on; he picks up his trumpet and plays. I thought there had to be a line in there somewhere between performing and not performing.

The Steve Allen spot was a hit, and I carried a kinescope of the show with me when I made the rounds. During that time, I auditioned for a part in a Broadway musical, *Kelly*, which turned out to be one of the most famous flops in show-business history. It closed after one night with a million-dollar loss.

The show was backed by Sam Levine, a Jewish immigrant, a rotund, funny little man who had produced *Hercules* and would go on to become one of the top film distributors in the world. A week before opening night, during dress rehearsals, I heard that Sam Levine was going to be in the theater. I had one song in the show, a group number with several other comics. I was convinced that the song would make me the next Danny Kaye.

I figured Levine would single me out . . . "Get me that kid! The one who reminds me of Danny Kaye. He's a natural." We were running through the whole show. The theater was dark and empty, but I could make out four or five people somewhere in the middle.

Then came the time to do my scene, my song, and I danced out with the other comics, most of them veterans, like Jessie White. I'm young and full of myself—I can hear Sam's words in my ear, "Get me that kid!" At one point, I step out of the group, do a leap and slide on my knees across the stage. The crew turned on a backlight, and I could just distinguish the figures in the audience. I picked out Sam Levine, sitting next to his wife, who is wearing the biggest fur coat I have seen in my life.

Sam is fast asleep, his head bent over and buried in his wife's coat. You cannot see his head. It is in the fur, gone. In the emptiness of the theater, I could hear the muffled sound of his snoring. All of my fantasies crumbled.

~~~~

When *Kelly* folded after opening night, Marty auditioned for a producer named Monte Prosser, who was preparing a
~~~~

revue for Las Vegas headlined by Jane Kean and Tim Herbert. They gave him a six-minute set, and Ingels knew he was in the right place this time. Las Vegas was right around the corner from Los Angeles.

~~~~

So, there I was in big-time Las Vegas, squeezed in between a hundred minutes of sketches and boobs and music and boobs and dancing and more boobs. We were eight long weeks in rehearsals. And opening night, like much of my life, should have been wonderful and exciting were it not for the paralyzing anxiety. (I had a migraine headache for most of my stay there.)

But the show went on, and it was my cue for my six-minute babysitter telephone routine. When I hit the stage, I was stopped right off by the continual clanging and rattling of glasses and plates and silverware. And the whole tipsy audience primed by the first raucous, bawdy, R-rated part of the show. Now here was this unknown comic, stuck in with six light minutes of sweet, family Bob Newhart–Sid Caesar TV-type material.

I was on and off and back in my dressing room in what seemed like seconds, my face white and sweating. I was like a guy who had come out of an operation. I had to ask somebody, "Is it over? Was I out there?" I couldn't be sure.

I was still standing there, feeling stricken, when Monte Prosser walked up. "Marty," he said, "the show is running long and we have to do some cutting. We're taking out your number."

It hit me like a cannon shell. All those weeks of working and dreaming and it was over in ten minutes. I had a bunch of valid arguments for him: it was opening night; it was noisy; I was nervous; but I could get none of it out. I was just too broken and humiliated to say a word.

Losing my co-star spot didn't mean I was out of the show. (I was kept to do all my other chores.) What it did mean was that I was out of the co-star's *Accommodations*. I was actually moved from my first-class room in the main part of the hotel to the back-end barracks where the chorus guys bunked.
~~~~

For the show, I was now another chorus boy in the line and in the sketches. One night, Buddy Hackett came backstage and said to me, "You know, you got a good comic face, kid. Why don't you do something up front?"

"Forget it," I said. "I tried that."

But what to do now? Go home? Not go home? Go somewhere else? Another migraine.

One night the whole cast went to catch Don Rickles, who was the lounge act at the Sahara. He wasn't a star yet, but he was the rage of the Vegas in-crowd. And, of course, he tore everyone apart. When he saw us, he started in on our show. (It was called *Sketchbook*.)

It hadn't occurred to me that he would even know my name. But he saw me and said: "And then there's Ingels. Cute face. Does his nice safe little cutesy-pootsy telephone bit. Hey, kid. Try this for a while. Stand up here in one for an hour and a half where they can reach up and grab ya'. *That's* show business." Everybody was laughing. And I made like I was too. But I wasn't. Rickles was too on target. And then some. I didn't even have that safe little cutesy-pootsy telephone bit anymore.

The only thing that kept me going was a fling I had with Jane Kean, totally unexpected and without calculation. We happened to be seated next to each other one day at lunch, and I am in awe of her. She's the star of the show, and I'm a chorus boy. The Kean sisters were big on the nightclub circuit, a favorite at the Copacabana in New York. They were the Dean Martin and Jerry Lewis of the ladies.

We began talking and laughing and having a good time. She seemed to need to talk to someone, and God knows, I needed to hear someone laugh. It was almost as much an accomplishment for me as hearing it from an audience. That's how insecure you get. Before I would go on the Carson or the Merv Griffin shows, I always told a joke to one of the grips. "Hey, did you hear the one about—" If the guy was pulling wires or something and says, "Hey, I ain't got the time," I would be deflated. If you got a laugh backstage, you were primed. Which is why actors have an entourage trailing behind them, people who whisper in their ear how wonderful and terrific they are.

I walked Jane back to her cottage, and standing at the door, I wasn't sure what to do. So I bent over and kissed her on the cheek, and that was it. The next night, we found ourselves at the same table again. When dinner was over and everyone had disappeared, we strolled back to her room, and this time I gave her a longer kiss. Three, four, five nights go by, and finally I decided it was time to move on from a plain, friendly kiss, and I planted one on her. Then I said, "Can I come in?"

She was a few years older than I was and, I could tell, a little troubled about appearances. "I wouldn't want anyone to know we're fooling around," she said. She was, after all, the star. She was also a little lonely. In the entire show, two of the guys were straight, and I think I was one of them.

"I understand," I said. "I'll get up and leave before it gets light."

We went to bed, and it was by far the highlight of my Las Vegas trip. I couldn't decide at the time whether it was exciting to me because she was the star of the show, or because she was a woman.

It was a sweet affair, and, parenthetically, she is one of the nice human beings. For four years, she played Art Carney's wife, Trixie, on *The Honeymooners*.

The romance ended the morning a room-service waiter brought in breakfast and opened the closet for some reason, and found me standing there naked. I said, "Can I check your coat?" He dropped the tray and ran out of the room, and Jane stopped speaking to me.

Best of times, worst of times. The revue was to run seven weeks, and halfway through it Tim Herbert quit to accept an offer to appear in *Flower Drum Song* in London. I thought to myself, What a perfect opportunity. I knew every one of his sketches.

I was with MCA at the time, and rather than go directly to Prosser, I figured I would be professional and let the agency represent me. I called New York, and they gave me the name of the fellow who ran their Las Vegas office. It took me a week to track him down on the phone.

I told him who I was and what I wanted. I told him about the opening in the show, and that they were auditioning comics from all over, and that I knew all the routines. He asked me what the bits were like, and I did the show for him. "That's interesting," he said. "I'll get back to you."

I felt good about having my business handled by an agent with a company as big as MCA. This fellow was going to be one of the best known in the industry, because after his divorce he moved in with Neil Simon's brother, Danny. The two of them became the models for the characters in the movie and television series *The Odd Couple*.

Two days later, I learned that the agent had flown in his younger brother, a comedian, from New York, and signed him to a contract with Monte Prosser to replace Tim Herbert. I stayed in the chorus.

In a way, it served me right. I had dropped a really decent agent who helped me get started, a big, blubbery guy who was good-natured and honest. He was in a field where these qualities are not always desirable, and I bought the line that was big then with MCA: If you go anywhere in the world and need help, we're there. London, Berlin, Chicago, Memphis, anywhere.

I left Las Vegas, talking a chorus girl into driving me to Hollywood and dropping me off at Hollywood and Vine. It was two o'clock in the morning, and I had eighty dollars in my pocket and the return portion of my airline ticket that Monte Prosser had bought as part of the original deal. I checked into a cheap hotel a block from the freeway, and the next day I unpacked my typewriter and my address books and started making calls. I worked up a pretty good mad and placed one to the MCA offices in New York. Each time the secretaries referred me to another agent who couldn't take the call, I grew madder.

Finally, I called back and said, "Who is the president of MCA?" And the answer was, "Mr. Chasen." I said, "Fine, ring his office. It's an emergency."

The secretary put me through, and I told him my name, which was unfamiliar to him, as it was to so many others. Even as these words are written, I wonder what it was that made me able to do this, a guy who lacked the courage to go on a stage and do his own material?

I said, "Look, I know it means nothing to you who I am.

I'm a client, a young comic from New York, who was sold a bill of goods, who was told that when I go anywhere, you guys are going to take care of me. And I went to Las Vegas and I have a shot at the star's part in a show, so I call your agent, and he gets the part for his brother. Now I'm in Los Angeles, with a couple of days to look around, and I'm thinking I should see a casting director. If I do, you know what they'll say? They'll say I need a New York agent.

"Now let me tell you this. When I hang up this phone, you're not going to know the difference, and I'm not going to remember that I called, but I'll feel better because I told you that this is the way your agency treats some of the young talent in America. And what happens is, if you treat everybody like you treat me, when the young talent grows up, there won't be an MCA, because no one forgets how it feels to be stepped on. If you treat all the unknowns like this, that will be the end of your company, because the future tells itself."

He made no effort to interrupt me, and when I finished, this Mr. Chasen said, "Would you do me a favor? I have someone sitting here. I'd like to put you on the speaker box, and I'd like you to repeat what you just told me."

I went through the whole speech, again, and he said, "Just a moment, I have someone who wants to talk to you."

He cut off the speaker box, and a familiar voice said over the phone, "Hello, Marty, this is Tony Curtis." Now, in my world, Tony Curtis was a folk hero. When I hung out on the street, everybody wanted to be Tony Curtis, with the hair and the smile and especially with Janet Leigh. I said, "Yeah, sure, you're Tony Curtis, and I'm Mahatma Gandhi."

He laughed and said, "No, no, trust me. This is Tony Curtis. Now I don't know who you are or what you are. But I heard this conversation, and I want you to know that you have got something. You stay in the business. They [MCA] will see you now. And I want you to know that anytime you need anything and it isn't happening, call me. You won't need me long, because you have what it takes. Anybody who would call here and lay out Chasen like you did, and damned rightfully, has something special. I don't know if you're talented. I don't know if you're funny. But I do know you have guts, and I'm telling you to stick it out."

(A few years later, when my television series was canceled, Tony Curtis was the first one to call. He offered me a part in a movie he was making, *Wild and Wonderful*. Not surprisingly, I count him as a friend.)

~~~~

Ingels stayed in Hollywood. Less than a month later, he was sitting in a pancake house at four in the morning with a showgirl. His back was to the door, and she looked past him and said, "Guess who just came in? Carl Reiner and Sheldon Leonard and their wives."

Marty picks up the story:

~~~~

At that time, and for years to come, Reiner and Leonard ruled television. They were the kings of situation comedy, the producers of Danny Thomas, Andy Griffith, Dick Van Dyke, *The Joey Bishop Show*, all of them.

To myself, I thought, What do I do? How do I get to them? I couldn't pass up that kind of challenge. I borrowed five dollars from the girl, and I asked our waiter to send over the fellow who had their table. I said, "Look, I'll give you five bucks just to let me serve the dessert." Deal.

I went in the kitchen, picked up the tray with their dessert order, and balanced it on my shoulder. Then I did my number. "Hey! Are you really gonna eat that?" The wives discovered they had a new waiter and they were amused, accustomed as they were to having their husbands hit on by would-be actors and comics. Reiner took one look and said, "Don't say a word. Here's my card. Come see me tomorrow morning."

The next day there happened to be an opening on *The Dick Van Dyke Show*, the role of an old army buddy who was trying to save him from Mary Tyler Moore. I had twenty-two lines on the show, and I wanted so much for the people to like me that I wanted to do something special for them.

I went to a cabinetmaker and I had him custom-make a coffee wagon, with an electric grill in the center and hooks all around the sides. I had the names of everyone in the cast inscribed on cups and hung them on the hooks. Then I covered it with wrapping paper and wheeled it onto the set the last day of my little stint, my twenty-two lines, and I gave them this hand-crafted coffee wagon. They all said, "Oh, isn't that nice," and I was not smart enough then to pick up the undercurrent of, "What the fuck is this kid doing this for? What does he want from us?"

It was so spontaneous and so harmless that I would believe for a dozen years, mistakenly, that I had done something nice. By then, I had gotten to the lip of stardom, fallen off, lost my series, and worked a little when I wasn't sick or in withdrawal.

Somehow I found another agent, Roy Silver, and he is calling around trying to find me a spot on a show. Everyone turns him down, and while part of me is relieved, I don't know why. I can't understand what I did wrong that no one in the whole industry will hire me.

"They say you did crazy things," said Roy, trying to put it delicately.

I said, "Hey, did I ever hurt anybody? What did I do that was so bad?"

"I'll give you an example," he said. "I talked to the people from Danny Thomas's office. They remembered when you were on *The Dick Van Dyke Show*. They said you did something nutty with coffee cups."

I said, "Yeah, I did something with coffee cups. I mean, it depends on what you mean by nutty."

Roy said, "Well, tell me, what did you do?"

For a moment, I was actually tongue-tied. Then I said, "You know, this sounds like we are talking about a guy who machine-gunned everybody in a building. All I did was have a coffee wagon built for the cast with their names on the cups."

"Well, they thought it was weird, and they don't want you."

I said, "Roy, wait a minute. I gave them a gift. Explain it to me. What was so wrong?"

And, of course, he gets right to the heart of it. "All they saw was this ambitious young *putz* from New York. He gets a few lines, and here he comes with a gift for people he barely knows, and it is way out of proportion. They can't figure it out, and that makes people nervous."

I said, "Why, Roy, why does this backfire on me? Why should it keep me from working? I know communists and child molesters who are working all over town. I give somebody a bunch of coffee cups, and I'm blacklisted. How do they explain that?"

Of course, that disillusionment had not yet sunk in, not in 1961. I was still testing myself then, and some of the days were actually good ones. While I waited for something wonderful to come out of the patronage of Jerry Lewis, Roy kept calling in favors, asking his friends if they had anything for me.

The lowest rung on the acting ladder were the parts on the courtroom shows: *Night Court, Day Court, Divorce Court.* You did a character for scale. One of Roy's friends said, "As luck would have it, we're doing a trial about a murder at a circus, and we need a clown. You say your guy is a comic?"

"Yeah, he's really funny. And he needs a break."

I went down to audition for the part, and there are fourteen midgets in the room. Every person in the room is a midget. No one thought to tell Roy that the part was written for a midget. I sat down and waited to be called. I read for the part and was hired on the spot. They liked my voice so much they decided to rewrite the character.

Even though I needed the job, it just killed me when I heard the casting director step into the waiting room and say, "Okay, the role has been filled, you can leave now."

All I could think about was what those poor souls must have been saying to themselves: Every nineteen years, a part comes up for a midget, and what happens, a guy six-foot-one gets it.

The random, whimsical quality of the business never lets us down.

~~~~

Marty rounded up all the Hollywood phone books and began making his contact lists. He was starting all over. But then, he was good at that. It was the stuff that happened
~~~~

further on that always shot him down. He was almost broke. And his air return ticket home would be good only nine more days. He had to make hay.

He started making the rounds.

It wasn't easy in Hollywood. Not like New York, where actors did that all the time. And he had no agent here. No one to set up appointments. And no car. And no money.

The studio accesses were almost impossible. Had to have a "reason" to get in. And Ingels got stopped at the gate every time.

It was Thursday. Three days before his plane. One studio left, Paramount. This one wasn't gonna beat him. He arrived at the Melrose Gate at 11:45 sharp, with a tray and a small apron under his coat, and went directly to the Movietime Restaurant right across the street. He bought eight coffees to go, put the apron on and the coffees on the tray, and waited for the 12:00 buzzer. It was the lunch-hour madhouse. And he slipped right in, waving and smiling all the way.

The names on the office doors were unfamiliar to Marty. He wasn't exactly sure who did what. But one door, right at the end of the corridor, he knew right off. It said JERRY LEWIS PRODUCTIONS. Marty loved Jerry Lewis. He walked right in.

"I'd like to see Mr. Lewis," he said.

"I'm sorry," said the lady at the desk. "Mr. Lewis is very busy. Why don't you call, and I'll make an appointment for you next week."

Marty took a long deep breath. This one polished off the last office in the last studio on his crumpled list. He took it out of his pocket and tore it in half.

"Well," he said, "I guess it's back to New York and dental school."

The secretary looked at him. His eyes were wet. "A dentist?"

"Yeah," said Marty. "A dentist. My brother is a dentist. I have an uncle who is a dentist. I can't get in to see anybody out here, so I might as well become a dentist."

Whether it was the voice, or the face, or the idea of sparing the country the burden of one more dentist, the lady said, "Look, there's something about you. I've never done this before, but I think he might like you. I'm going to get you four minutes with Jerry, and that's it. You're on your own."

With that, she walked Marty down the hall, opened a door, and gently pushed him inside. He learned later that her name was Rita Dillon. She eventually became a producer on her own, and for a long time after that meeting Ingels sent her flowers.

The office of Jerry Lewis looked to be roughly the size of a football field, but what it lacked in intimacy, it made up by being ostentatious. There was a gold-plated desk set and gold picture frames and elaborate hanging plants. This is what happened next, as Marty recalls it:

~~~~

And there was Jerry Lewis. I thought I had four minutes to tell my story, so I started racing, and the faster I talked, the harder he laughed. "What are you looking for?" he finally asked.

I said, "I don't know. I just couldn't get in to see anybody, and we just wound up here."

He said, "Hold it a minute." He pressed a button, told Rita he didn't want any calls, pressed another button, and said, "Bill, come in here, I want you to meet someone."

In no time, there were nine or ten people in the room, and then we all went to a stage and they sat me down in front of a camera and started shooting. Just like that, I was getting a screen test. All this time, Jerry Lewis is saying how great this was going to be.

If this sounds silly and absurd, it's only because it was. When I returned to my room that night, I shut the door behind me, jumped in the air, and clicked my heels. I had no clue as to what was going on, but it had to be an improvement over my recent luck.

At three o'clock in the morning, the phone rang, and it was Jerry Lewis. He told me to get a cab and come to his house. He never used to sleep. He was in the room where he kept his sound system, and for kicks he played back the tape he had just made of our phone conversation. We talked
~~~~

two or three hours, and when I finally went to bed, it was nearly dawn. I form quick impressions of people and rarely change them, a sometimes costly habit. I had little doubt that Jerry Lewis was bananas. It looked as if I had found a soul brother.

Lewis had come a long way from his early fame as the spastic comic in his act with Dean Martin, to the star of his own movies and television specials, and his annual role as Earth Father to the nation's handicapped children, producer-host of a telethon that raises millions of dollars.

Jerry loved to discover people, and he also liked to tinker with you for a while. A day or two later, he called to invite me to drop by the studio and join him while they viewed my screen test. It was funny, and when the reel ended, Jerry jumped on a chair and said, "Ingerman"—I had told him my real name—"you are going to be in the fucking movies." Then he said, "Let me see that plane ticket you carry around with you."

I handed him the ticket, which was now well wrinkled from being handled. With grand aplomb, he tore the ticket into shreds and tossed them in the air. "Kid, you're in the movies," he repeated.

I signed a contract to appear in Jerry's next film, *The Ladies' Man*, guaranteed a thousand dollars a week. The word went around that Jerry Lewis had a protégé, and I helped it along by taking ads in the trade papers. There was only one thing wrong. I went to the studio every day for eight weeks, I was getting paid, but I had nothing to do. They kept postponing the picture.

Meanwhile, another offer came along, a small part in a film to be shot on location in Germany called *Armored Command*. Jerry was right. I was going to be in the movies. An otherwise forgettable film, it was a trivia buff's dream. Tina Louise had the female lead, and Howard Keel starred in his first nonsinging part. The producers hoped the picture would be a breakthrough for Howard, which turned out to be an overly optimistic goal.

The movie did, however, introduce to theater audiences two young actors who were then, or would soon appear, in a TV series. Burt Reynolds was the second banana on a series that starred Steve McQueen as a tugboat captain. Earl Holliman was an unknown who would enjoy a long run with Angie Dickinson as the stars of *Police Woman*.

Even then, Burt was on his second or third career. The series was canceled after a season, or less, but Burt never doubted himself. He loves being around comics, and we hit it off the first hour we met, in a little Bavarian town near Munich. We were both playing soldiers, and neither of us was aware then of the tension between the townsfolk and the American military.

No one bothered to tell us what was off-limits, not that Burt would have cared. If ever there was anyone who is what you expected him to be, it is Burt Reynolds. He is all the things you see on the screen: macho, tender, honest, screw-the-system. He was hungry to be a star back then, and had his own definition of what that meant. "Jimmy Stewart," he would say. "Boring. Robert Mitchum. Boring. Kirk Douglas. Boring."

I mean, he saw himself as a leader of all men. He wore a wrist band and carried a cane and laughed like a maniac. He also had a sense of gallantry. He was sleeping with a pretty little *fräulein*—we all were—there were some hectic farewells our last night in Germany. A huge press conference had been planned, with entertainment writers from all over Europe invited. I was primed, even had my own glossies ready to distribute. When I asked Burt if he wanted to walk over to the interview area, he said, "Naw, I'm going to see the girl. It's my last night, and I think I owe it to her."

Now I am quite sure he didn't do so because he needed to get laid—I doubt they had missed a night. He had made a commitment to her. I think that says something about the person he is.

In our investigation of the local night life, we met some college kids, the cerebral German types, and they invited us to a dance at a beer garden up in the mountains. We were unaware that the week before a very bad fight had broken out, and a German had been stabbed by an American soldier. The war in Vietnam was getting nasty, and the soldiers at the camp had been told to avoid this club.

None of us knew this until later. That night we were all

there, Burt, Howard Keel, Earl Holliman, and everyone but me goes his own way, either to the bar or the dance floor. Then they started to play a traditional German polka, and I jump out and do my Red-Buttons-hopping-around imitation.

At that point, a Bavarian who appeared to be eight feet tall grabbed my arm, and spoke to me in German, a language I have no knowledge of, and I understood every word he said: "Hey, asshole, what do you think you are doing? Are you trying to make fun of us?"

I tried gracefully to disengage myself from his arm, but he simply dragged me out to the middle of the floor, and he stood there and made an announcement. Later, I was told that he said, "The clown is now going to clown for everybody. Okay, clown."

I am just making an assumption, of course, that when he said "clown" he was referring to me. Here I was, a Jew, in the middle of a town called something like *Schmittmueller*, in Germany, I can't speak the language, and my prospects are none too bright. And they owe us one from the fight the previous week. If you throw in the last world war, they might feel they owed us two.

Now events took a really unexpected turn. One of the German college boys walks over to my host, in an effort, I assume, to reason with him and calm things down. Well, the student gets right into the spirit of negotiation; the big guy chops him in the mouth and he goes down with a big, swooping crash. And someone said, "Get out of here . . . quick!"

We drew an instant crowd around us: three or four of the college boys, some local toughs, and the owner of the dance hall, who is pleading with everyone in German to stay cool and unheated and not to bleed on his linens. At which point, my captor responded by breaking a beer bottle across the table.

This is going to sound like an outtake from a bad Errol Flynn movie, but at that moment Burt Reynolds jumped off the balcony—he and the others had found seats at a cozy little bar up there—and landed between me and the German. And he said to him, I swear an oath these were his exact words: "Why don't you take me? I'm much better at this than him. Come on. Take me."

It was incredible, exactly the kind of thing you read about, usually in cheap fiction, but rarely see. I can't describe the admiration I felt at that moment for Burt. For one thing, I was moving too fast, which was the part that upset him, I regret to say. I figured that he had things under control, so I followed the German kid out the door, ran to a cab, and returned to the hotel—without knowing that the other actors were all still in there and in trouble. It turned out that a real brawl broke out, the security people sealed off the doors, and the police arrived and shut the place down.

I went to my room, and was having a snack when Burt, Howard, and Earl returned, with a police escort, their shirts ripped and torn and stained with blood—their own, the very worst kind. I honestly didn't know or suspect a thing, and when Reynolds walked into the room, I said lightly, "Hell, Burt, the least you could have done was call me and let me know that everything was okay."

At that, he grabbed me with both hands by the shirt collar, ran me right up against the wall, and lifted me off the ground. "You son of a bitch," he said, "if I didn't love you so much, I'd kill you. Where were you? We needed all the help we could get."

"The way you blew in there," I said, "I figured you had everything going fine. I thought it was over." As it turned out, the American actors had to retreat to the kitchen, and the owner hid them in the meat freezer until the police came.

Burt Reynolds really is as tough and fearless as the characters he usually plays. I don't know if he actually saved my life, but it was not the sort of situation where you wanted to hang around and find out. He forgave me for bailing out, but he got mad at me again when I gave the story to a fan magazine.

~~~~

Marty returned to Hollywood, as he had expected, in time for the final weeks of shooting on the Jerry Lewis production of *The Ladies Man.* He was on the set the day they filmed what was apparently intended to be the last scene. He heard Lewis announce, "That's it, everybody, thanks,
~~~~

that's a wrap." There was an awkward moment as people brushed past him, before Ingels spoke up:

~~~~

I said, "Uh, Jerry—what about, um . . ."

Lewis looked at me blankly, then his face seemed to light up. He raised one hand and quieted the room. "Hold it," he said. "Everybody. Sorry. Not yet, not yet."

He went back into his office with his writers, and ten minutes later they came out laughing, with a scene they had written for me. I was a baseball announcer, standing in a locker room, giving the day's scores. Then I said, "Now here's a word from our sponsor, Lotsa Shave." And I began to describe how you pressed the top of the can and how wonderful and soothing the product was, and as I talked, the can wouldn't shut off. It's everywhere, it's filling up the room, I'm in it up to my chin, and I'm saying, "and now back to the game."

They filmed it, and Jerry said it was hysterical.

I got my invitation to the premiere and bought a tuxedo to wear when I arrived with my date. We walked into the theater with the opening-night crowd, and I'm watching the picture, and watching, waiting for the scene, and it's nearly over. My mind is spinning: Could he have done that without telling me, cut my scene from the movie? Sure enough, the music comes up and the picture ends. It was a joke! He had me do a little scene for the cameras that he and the writers knew would never be used, and that was what he found so funny, so hilarious.

I turned to my date and said, "How do we get out of this theater? I can't face anybody." I mean, I had taken out ads plugging my part in the film. I never heard directly from Jerry Lewis again. Years later I saw him, and nodded or waved across a room, but by then it didn't matter. In a way, I was good at using one thing to promote another. The ads had planted the idea that I appeared in his movie, and to this day many people believe I did.

In the 1980s, a brilliant but almost unnoticed film called *The King of Comedy* was loosely based on our relationship,
~~~~

or so critics speculated. It starred Robert De Niro as an obsessed young comic, and Lewis as the superstar he revered and pursued. Introduced in the film was a funny and quirky comedienne named Sandra Bernhard.

By late 1963, I was up for my own series. So whatever attention I attracted because of Jerry, even indirectly, may have paid off.

The story of my being his protégé had a life of its own. For years, it would be hard for me to sort out my feelings about him. I think he liked me when I was the klutz from Brooklyn with the clothes too big and the hair too long. In the daytime, when he was Jerry Lewis, he didn't have any protégés, only himself. At night, when he was lonely and couldn't sleep and needed company, he would call and we would sit and talk for hours. I saw the human being, the one the camera didn't see.

Jerry taught me about insecurity, what little I hadn't already learned on my own. Insecurity can rule your life. Not long after I met him, when I was borrowing money to meet the payments on a car and writing hot checks to survive, I had to ask Jerry for a few dollars one day for gas to get home. We were in his dressing room with his friends all around him, and Jerry decided to make a production out of it. I went along.

"Are you kidding me, Marty? You don't have two dollars for gas?"

"Nope, I don't have two dollars."

"Somebody give this fuckin' kid two dollars for gas." And as he is saying this, he takes out a roll of bills that would choke a buffalo, all hundred-dollar bills, and he peels off one. "Here," he says, "take the two dollars out of this. Get enough gas to last the rest of your life."

I had seen a hundred-dollar bill before, but for Jerry's benefit I acted as if I hadn't. I snapped it in my hand, rolled over on the floor, got up, and said, "Uh, Jerry, I don't have change for a hundred."

"Hey! He doesn't have change." Everyone laughed.

To tell the truth, I wasn't sure if Jerry expected me to pay him back or not. Then one day, we were alone in his dressing room and he was in one of his morose and reflective and philosophical moods. He said, "You know, you'd be surprised how much money goes out of here as loans to people, and never comes back. It isn't a loan if it comes from a movie star. Everybody feels they have to pay the doctor, the mortgage company, the grocer. But nobody ever pays me back." And I figured that was probably true, because I knew I hadn't paid him back.

I wanted to make myself special to Jerry. So I decided to be the first person ever to repay one of his loans. I had just made a deposit of eighty-five dollars to open a checking account—at the Bank of America on Sunset Boulevard. I wanted the first check, Number 101, to go to Jerry. Now I had a dilemma. I wanted to give the money and endear myself to him, but on the other hand I needed what was left of the hundred. Question: How could I let him know the thought was there, while the money stayed with me? Then it came to me. I wrote the check, went to a specialty shop, and had it perma-plaqued. I wrote a note at the top—"Now you can't say that no one ever paid you back"—and dated it, July 1961. They put a gold border around the check, and I had the package gift wrapped and delivered. Then I forgot about it. It cost me twenty-six dollars, so I figured I made a profit of seventy-four dollars.

I forgot about it. Didn't even deduct it from my check stub. Would you believe it? He cashed my plaque. Two months later, I looked inside the envelope containing my bank statement, and found a second envelope in there. When checks are destroyed, I later learned, they come in a separate envelope. Inside was the check, chipped or peeled off from the plastic and then pieced together with Scotch tape.

I looked on the back, and it had been cashed in the luncheonette on the Paramount lot. I figured it out. Jerry Lewis had eaten there one day and left my plaque with the waitress as a tip. I didn't know if he had one-upped me or not. My cheapness, my devious act, had been out of desperation. His was just for the sport of it.

I had not gone through a really bleak period yet, a really rotten time. I was young and impatient and just thought I had. Seven weeks in Las Vegas and a month in Hollywood, and I still hadn't made the world forget Red Skelton. Would this torture never cease?

My theory of Hollywood was that the best place to meet a movie star was in the street. You lived in your neighborhood, and they lived in theirs. You ate in your kind of restaurant, and they ate in theirs. But everybody had to drive in the same damned streets. So my fantasy was, one day I would drive up to a street light and see a movie star and maybe a director in the next lane, and I'd say, "Hi." They would be instantly taken with my face, my curly hair, my smile, and the way I said, "Hi," and yell out the window, "We want you."

If you believe enough in something like that, it happens. Maybe it only happens to the dreamers who never stop dreaming, and I was one of those. The events that led to my role in a new sitcom began with my bumping into someone on the street.

~~~~
~~~~

and he nodded and said, "Let's go in and talk, I want to tell you about a new comedy series I'm working on."

I didn't realize then that he was dazzled by Jean. Many years later, he confided that his hand was on her knee under the table the whole time he was telling me how talented I was. But he was working on an idea for a show, which he then was calling *The Worker.* He had John Astin lined up for one of the two main characters, and he set up a meeting for us with Tom Moore, then the president of ABC, the third-rated network. Before he moved to ABC, Tom Moore sold cemetery plots for Forest Lawn.

We met in a cottage on the grounds of the Beverly Hills Hotel, and I saw right off that there was no proposal, no outline. Stern was selling this idea verbally, off the top of his head, which in those days was not uncommon.

Finally, he rubbed his hands and said, "Why don't we do a little improvisation?" Astin and I had been introduced only minutes before, and now we were going to improvise a scene in order to sell a show to a network president. Lenny said, "Okay, this is the premise: Marty and John are in the house to do an estimate for a remodeling job for a lady," and he motioned to a script girl who was there to take notes. "Mona, you're the lady. Okay, guys, take it from there."

John was a serious, straight-looking guy and I was the goofy type, so I thought right off the balance would be good. But improvisation was much more his bag than mine, and John started right in: "Well, let's see, we'll knock out this wall and I think we should put an aluminum cover here, over the fireplace, and we'll have to take up the carpet. . . ."

My mind is blank, my mouth is dry, and I am nervous as hell. I said, "Excuse me a second, would you have a soft drink around here?" The script girl didn't know if I was serious or getting into the scene, but she said, "The kitchen is the door on your right." I walked into a tiny room with a kitchenette and took out a Coke and there is no bottle opener. I can't get the cap off, so I yell out, "Is there a can opener in here?" John is still babbling away in the other room, I can hear him, and no one answered. So I started pounding the bottle on the edge of the kitchen counter, trying to snap off the cap.

And in the living room, Moore and Stern are roaring. For some reason, they think we have hit on a really hilarious gag; these two carpenters are going to redo the entire house and one of them can't figure out how to open a bottle. John is knocking out walls and I'm in the kitchen, banging away with a Coke bottle. Based on that moment of what they thought was improvisation, the contracts were signed and the show, *I'm Dickens, He's Fenster*, went on the air in 1963. I was never to enjoy any of it, you understand, but I had made the turn, I had made it to network television.

~~~~

The early, difficult signs of his mental disorders were becoming more frequent. He did not yet know about such words as manic or phobic; nor did a great many other people. He was anxious, hyper, given to bouts of dizziness and nausea, but as always with Marty, it was sometimes hard to tell what was irrational and what passed for his normal antic behavior.

He was never embarrassed or reluctant to pursue a movie star. Sure enough, almost as in his fantasy, he pulled up to a red light one day and saw Burt Lancaster behind the wheel of the car next to his. He rolled down the window and caught Burt's eye; he was thinking, who knows, they might make a movie together one day.

"I'm Marty Ingels," he said. "You don't know me, but I was wondering, you've never made a comedy, and it happens . . ." Before he could finish the sentence, the light changed, and the car pulled away. And Marty decided to follow him. Tires squealing, he went after him. Two or three cars moved in between them, and he was blocked in his effort to pull alongside. Marty kept up the chase for eleven miles, through Bel Air and Westwood, racing across a freeway. Finally, they hit a stoplight at the beach, and Marty suddenly realized they were in Malibu and he was hopelessly lost. He rolled down his window, leaned over and said, "Uh, Mr. Lancaster, could . . ."

Mildly irritated, but curious, Lancaster snapped, "What do you want?"

"Uh . . . could you tell me how to get back to Sunset Boulevard?"
~~~~

Both laughed. Years later, Ingels, Inc., would book Burt Lancaster for a television appearance.

Another incident with a famous star did not have so benign an ending. Marty's car was involved in an accident, a fender scraping, with a car that happened to be driven by Raquel Welch. "I didn't know who it was," he said, "I just jumped out of my car and started screaming.

"Then she jumped out of hers and belted me right in the mouth. Knocked me halfway across the hood of the car. And, of course, the next day I contacted everybody and threatened to sue. Her husband called back and said, 'Look, you don't want to do this,' and I realized what an idiot I would appear to be if the story got out. Everybody would be on her side."

That was one of his hang-ups, fearing that in any situation involving another person, Marty would be the less liked. You could make a graph of his complexes, and this one would be a straight line leading back to his brother, Arthur. But there it was.

~~~~

I have always oversold myself. I gave gifts they didn't want, sometimes out of gifts I didn't need. I did it to say thank you or to win them over, and I couldn't understand why people began to not like me. I couldn't see how my pushiness drove them away.

I used any excuse to pick an argument with John Astin, an extraordinarily nice man, patient, not easily offended. I felt a powerful pressure to outdo him. There were two of us, so this had to be a competition. Keep in mind that John chose not to compete. He was an actor who did comedy, not a comic. If I established that I was the funnier man, in the end I lost everybody on the set.

There was one weekly segment where the carpenters elected John as their new foreman, and he would be the one who had to do the firing. So he arrives home feeling sad, and he complains to his wife, "My first chore as the foreman, and I got to fire people."

She says, "Well, somebody has to do it. Don't take it personal."
~~~~

He says, "I got to fire Arch." That's me, Archie Fenster.

"You can't fire Arch," she says, stunned, "he's your best friend. What are you going to do?"

Now in the script he said, "Look, I'll just have to do it. I'll fire him the next time I see him." The doorbell rings. He's walking to the door as he says the line, he opens the door, and there I am. He says, "Hi, Arch." The script says he closes the door, then walks away. His wife asks, "Who was it?" And he answers, "Nobody."

Understand, we are rehearsing and I'm watching him play the scene and waiting for my moment. He says, "I'll fire him the next time I see him," and he opens the door and there I am. He says nothing and closes the door. Now I wave my arms and interrupt the scene. "Wait, John," I said. "You did it the wrong way."

To begin with, no actor does that to another on the set in front of the director and crew. But it was an honest reaction, I was overcome with my own impulse, and just blurted it out. Of course, everyone in the company thought I was a crude and inconsiderate ass. John said sharply, "What do you mean, it's wrong?"

I said, "Well, you shouldn't leave the door so fast. Stay near the door for a moment. Look"—I was so sure of my comedic instinct that I didn't think about winning the battle and losing the war—"I'll show it to you both ways. The way you did it and the way you ought to do it. Watch. Ready?" I run through the sequence and say, "It was wrong, because there was too much space between you and the door, and too little time to look at Arch.

"Let me show you how to really do it. And I stepped into his character: 'Okay, I'll tell him the next time I see him.' (Softly.) 'Hi . . . oh.' (Blocking the door . . . holding it.) 'Who was it?' (Keeps the door from opening, closes it.) 'It was nobody.' There," I said. "That's my way of doing. That's Milton Berle's way. There are other ways. Jack Lemmon would have a different way."

John was a truthful actor, took pride in it. I made such a thing out of this little bit of business that the whole crew was going, "Aw, Jesus Christ, Ingels, not again."

By the end of the first season, five months of rehearsals and taping, using three cameras, John was still the laid-back person he had been at the start. I was a driven wreck.

It became a running joke on the set, how if anyone wandered in who looked like a press person, I went all the way. Took them to lunch, sat with them on breaks, kept them laughing. So in the papers the items were always Fenster this and Fenster that, and there was almost nothing about the John Astin character.

One day we were rehearsing, and my disabilities had begun to surface. I didn't understand them, of course, but my need to succeed was so intense my blood pressure was elevated. I passed out once or twice on the set. (Later, a psychiatrist told me I had lost my "gauges," which was an interesting way of putting it.) This may sound like a variation of an old gag, but I couldn't tell when I was having fun. Even after I married Shirley, I'd come home and have to ask, in dead seriousness, "Did I have a good time?"

I wasn't sure of the difference between what was mean and what was acceptable because people could get away with it.

I kept in a closet a briefcase containing blue index cards, with jokes written on them. Jewish jokes, dirty jokes, clean jokes. I would take them to parties, and if the conversation lagged, I'd whip out a card. I was that insecure.

So this day in rehearsals was the day John very quietly paid me back for all the times I showed him up in the press. We rehearsed all morning, and the stands were empty except for a white-haired man in his sixties, dressed in a suit. I wondered who he was. In the men's room, I asked John, and he said, "Well, I'd rather not tell you."

I said, "What do you mean? I'm your partner. It's fifty-fifty. You've got to tell me."

He said, "Well, he's the TV editor from *Time* magazine."

"*Time* magazine," I said, trying to be nonchalant. "Oh."

Now Astin knew me well enough to know this was an invitation I couldn't resist. Immediately, I reappeared with my bow tie on, a nose that lit up, two hand grenades. I was suddenly playing to this audience of one, and everybody in the company could see what I was doing. I sauntered over and started a conversation. I said something like, "I don't know who you are, but you seem like a nice person. I'm gonna take you to lunch."

I bought his lunch, and when I returned to the set, Emmaline Henry, who played John's wife on the show, walked up to the white-haired man and said, "Honey, rehearsals are almost over. I'll be right with you and we can leave."

My eyebrows almost fell off. "What do you mean, honey?" I said. "How do you know this man?"

She smiled and said, "I ought to know him, Marty. He's my grandfather from South Carolina. He's spending a two-week vacation here." So I had spent the better part of my day entertaining Emmaline's grandpa. John was hysterical.

At the end of the season, the series was canceled, and for me the pressure was off. How I learned that we would not be renewed tells you all anyone needs to know about the heart of Hollywood.

The show had been produced at Desilu Studios, where it was always one big happy family. Dick Van Dyke, Mary Tyler Moore, Danny Thomas, Andy Griffith, Don Knotts, were among the hit shows taped there. The commissary walls were adorned with photographs of all the stars, and a different sandwich was named for each of them. Instead of a pastrami on rye, you would order by name. You could order a Danny Thomas. You could also order a Marty Ingels or a John Astin. I think mine was a chicken-salad sandwich, and I took a genuine pride in it.

If I had an appointment at the studio, I enjoyed saying, "Why don't we meet at the commissary?" When we sat down, I'd point to the menu on the wall and say, "Hey, check today's menu. There's a Marty Ingels up there."

The week before our last taping, I walked into the commissary, and a line had been drawn through my sandwich. I walked up to the register and said to the proprietor, "What's going on here?"

He avoided my eyes. "Well, your sandwich has been canceled," he said.

"What does that mean, my sandwich has been canceled?"

"I don't know why," he said. "You'll have to ask the cook."

So he goes in the kitchen and calls out the cook with the big white hat. The cook says, "Whatsamatter?"

They exchange whispers, and the proprietor says, as if he were translating a foreign language for me, "He says your sandwich was canceled because your show was canceled."

I felt like saying, "Are you crazy? I don't mind them canceling the show, but not the sandwich." In truth, I was shocked. I walked into the offices of the production company, and sure enough, the news was true. So this was the way I had lost my job, and with it my professional life as a comic (although that would not be apparent for several years). They canceled my sandwich.

At least I could stop pushing so hard and think about why I had become so disliked. I knew one thing that hadn't helped was the fact that I didn't hang around after work at night. I didn't socialize. I couldn't. I used up so much energy trying to win whatever race I thought I was in, I had to go straight home and lie flat on my back in bed.

All of that was behind me now. It was nearing Christmastime, and I told Jean I had to win everybody back. "I'm not a bad guy," I said. "I want them to like me." What I decided to do was buy everyone in the company a special, personal gift, and we would entertain them with a Christmas party. This wasn't one of those deals where you hand your list to a secretary and she shops for you. I got the names of everyone in the company, and I researched them to find out their favorite things. Jean went with me to stores all over Los Angeles. If someone was into trout fishing, I found a one-of-a-kind fly rod. You needed a fancy blender, I found a blender that squeezed fresh orange juice while playing the "Ave Maria Mambo."

We must have spent eight, nine thousand dollars. I kept saying, "I'm going to win 'em all back." I had all the presents gift-wrapped, and there were so many they wouldn't fit in our car, so I had to rent a trailer. I had the trailer decorated in red, white, and blue ribbons, and a big sign lettered across the side: I'M SANTA, HE'S CLAUS. The plan was that on the Friday when they said, "That's a wrap," after the final show, I was going to signal one of the grips to open the garage door at the studio and Jean would drive our car inside, with the trailer behind it. This was going to be the day I retrieved myself, the day I absolved myself of having offended anyone, of any ill feelings I had created.

We finished the show, the director said, "Okay, cut, that's a wrap, thanks everybody. Stay in touch and good luck."

I cried out, "No, wait a minute, I'm having a little party here, guys." I jumped up myself, ran to the back of the studio, and pulled open the garage door. I ran out to the back of the trailer, yanked off the cover, climbed into the presents, and put on my Santa Claus hat, as Jean drove onto the studio floor. I had a waiter ready to set up a table with champagne and little cakes and cookies. And I had the gifts with everybody's name on them, not just the cast but the script girls and the cameramen and the electrician. I started calling out their names: "Okay, here's one for Steve . . . Janice . . . Jack . . ."

Now, John Astin bought twenty-five identical Zippo lighters, engraved their names on them, and everyone thought it was terrific. That was what he did for Christmas. Unlike me, during the year he had been a human being. He played cards with two or three guys during idle time. He became friendly with this one and that one. I couldn't get friendly with anyone.

I am standing there, and when I call out some of the names, they don't even bother to come up and get their gift. They walk past the champagne and the little cakes, and they leave. The whole scene is in front of me, and I gradually begin to figure it out. I have spent eight thousand dollars or more, and what I am doing isn't working. Some of the people who take their gifts don't open them, or leave them behind on a chair.

This has gone on for only ten or fifteen minutes, but in twos and threes they are going home. Understand, they didn't hate me. They didn't do this on purpose or because I was such a terrible person. They just didn't feel enough of anything toward me to let me make it up to them; to let me endear myself to them. My guts were in every one of those packages, but as far as they were concerned, it was just Marty Ingels doing another of his shticks. An hour later, everyone was gone. There was Jean and me and the custodians waiting to sweep the floor and lock up. There were bottles of champagne unopened and cakes and cookies that had gone uneaten and a third of the presents were still there. Some of the boxes had been unwrapped, and the gift was still inside.

I sat on the edge of the trailer in this big empty studio, like a warehouse, and for one of the few times in my life I just bawled my brains out. I turned to Jean and said, "What happened. What did I do?"

She said, "I don't know." And we drove home.

At that point, society simply stumped me. I knew how to tell a joke, but I knew nothing about earning anyone's confidence or friendship. That touch, making that connection, was a killer. Both John and I came out of the show as reasonably hot properties. Of course, he would go on to a lot more work than I would, including an unexpectedly successful long-running comedy series called *The Addams Family*. My career was in trouble because of the kind of person I was. I do not remember doing a truly wicked thing in my life. It was purely the fact that I kept pushing, I gave off this strong scent of desperation, of needing so badly to succeed, to have everybody love me.

Jean and I moved back to New York in 1964, there to continue the struggle with my career. I changed agents. I kept busy for a while appearing as a guest on different sitcoms. I had offers for bigger things, and auditioned for better parts, and did a pilot for a series or two, and nothing came of them.

The marriage, the career, everything was sinking, but in one respect nothing changed. I was still drawn into personal situations that were sometimes bizarre, in an innocent and even funny way.

I never liked my smile, and it wasn't that my teeth were small or uneven, I just had more lip than most people, and this was years before I grew a mustache. I related this in some way to my self-esteem, because the most attractive people always seemed to give you a flash of pearly whites, and I didn't show any teeth. Since my uncle Irving was a dentist, I asked him if he had any suggestions.

He said he could make me what was called a "Hollywood bridge," a small bridge designed to slip over your own front teeth. So after weeks of work, I had this bridge, which fitted over the four in front, and I could slip it on and off. Suddenly, I thought my smile was a thing of beauty. I actually felt and behaved better because I thought I looked better.

Of course, there were slight disadvantages. I couldn't eat with them. In a restaurant, I would duck down and slip them off when the food came, then pop them back in after the meal. Without the bridge, I felt like Gabby Hayes, but the minor inconvenience was worth it.

If I had to be somewhere and I wanted to be at my best, I always wore the bridge. One day in a restaurant I fumbled it, and the bridge broke in half. Still, I could slip on one side and then the other, and with a little denture glue keep them in place. However, I found that if I talked too fast, the right side would fall out. So I had to be very careful. I couldn't open my mouth too wide, and I had to avoid saying words that started with an *F*.

Not long after I returned to New York, a friend came into town who knew Barbra Streisand, who was then starring on Broadway in *Funny Girl*. He invited me to see the show with him. I had once dated a roommate of Barbra's, but didn't really cross paths with her on a professional level. Now she was climbing into the superstar ranks. I put on my best suit, pasted the teeth on, and went to the show.

Afterward, he said, "Let's go backstage and see her." I said, "Really? Great."

She was combing her hair, facing the mirror, when we walked into the dressing room. She was really unattractive, by the way. Not even unattractive in an interesting way. But this was superstardom, and I got carried away. I totally forgot about my teeth and my sensitivity to certain words. And, of course, I had to tell her how funny she was, and when she sang "People," how fantastic it was. . . .

And when I said the second *F*-word, my right bicuspid came loose and flew out of my mouth at about forty-eight miles an hour, just missed her eye, and lodged right in her hair. Now she saw something leave my mouth, and she knew it landed in her hair, but she was not about to say, "What was it that left your mouth and is now buried somewhere in my hair?"

Suddenly, I have a hole in my mouth where the other

half of the bridge is missing, and I'm talking out of one side like Buddy Hackett. I can't leave because I don't want to shell out another $188 for a replacement. So I continue to talk to her, waiting for her to say something that causes her to shake her head up and down so it will fall out.

She wasn't quite sure where it was, and soon she forgot about it. But I could see my teeth resting just on the back of her hair. So I kept asking her things where she might nod or shake her head. What do you think of Vietnam. Yes? No? Are you going to go to Hollywood to make movies? No? Yes? Maybe? How do you feel about the Holocaust? Are you going to stay with the show? Anything that would make her move her head.

My friend and I were there forever, or so it seemed, and finally she stood up and said politely, "Well, I have to get dressed now, so nice to have seen you." And, boom, the teeth fell out of her hair. I dived forward to scoop them off the carpet, turned around, and with my hand as a shield kind of stuck the caps back into my face. She had no idea what was going on, what it was that fell off her head, or why I had put it in my mouth. She had forgotten the first part. Now the second part was even stranger.

It was total craziness. I was thrilled and relieved to get it back and a little hyper. How else can I explain why I did what I did next. As I stood with my hand on the door, ready to leave, I turned and said, with feeling, "F-f-farewell, Barbra . . . no, omigod, no."

~~~~

Marty was aware that he made people nervous. They were starting to walk around him as if he were a swamp. In New York, Roy Silver, that bright and perceptive fellow, would not give up on him. Silver had found and managed Bill Cosby, Joan Rivers, and Richard Pryor, had worked with Woody Allen. Right away, he sensed that Marty Ingels would be a major reclamation project. As Roy said:

"He was perceived as being kind of kooky, but the perception wasn't his problem. In fact, he was a major wacko. This is basically a small industry, and sooner or later people will know. I mean, we all had problems when we were kids.
~~~~

You're supposed to grow up and recognize them and overcome them and go on. Marty just dragged his with him. I went through five different phases in my life. Once, I was hostile, then I became warm. I was fat, then I became thin. Marty is a constant.

"There are people who work for me, actors and actresses, who are obnoxious or whatever, and when you go into another project, you wouldn't hire them again. And there are people who might not be as talented but who make life easier, and you do.

"With Marty, I had to cover every base. If we had an appointment, I gave him a time two hours early and then had people knocking on his door every ten minutes. At one point, I tried to convert him into a stand-up comic because he was brilliant, a comedic genius. I worked with him and rehearsed him and got a booking at a place far enough away so that if he bombed, no one would read about it. It was out in Huntington Beach. On the way there, I literally had to lock the car doors and hold him with my right arm to keep him from throwing himself out of the car. He was convinced that he couldn't do it. The audience wouldn't like him. He had nine million reasons. I had long ago passed dealing with him on any kind of rational, logical basis.

"In our relationship, I became totally dictatorial. This is what you will do. This is what you will say. This is where you will go. This is what you wear. I knew that if left to his own, he would find a way to screw it up.

"I was way past indulging him. And that night he was brilliant. The club was called the Golden Bear, and by the time we got out there, he was in a state of panic. The headline act at that time was the Association, a folk-rock group. I had to lock him in the car until it was time to go on. And he was terrific. He was everything I could have wanted from him. He was nice. The audience liked him. The stuff flowed. It was funny, and it worked. It was the first and last time I ever got him on a stage to do that. That was January of 1966, and I could never again get him to do a stand-up routine. I could have run with it, and he would have been big, because he had a different perspective, an attitude, a unique talent for comedy.

"He was different, period, the only entertainer I ever knew

who could look through the lights and see people's faces. He has almost no pupils. His eyes are almost luminescent.

"I think Marty actually heard voices. I don't mean the way people roll ideas around in their own mind. One voice told him he was garbage, and the other voice told him he could be Superman . . . if he could just get over his fear of heights.

"He had all that energy and all that aggressiveness, and it was never tampered with in any way. I mean, Marty couldn't or wouldn't get high. Or relax. Or go for a weekend and not continue his onslaught to be a star. He was always on, always pushing, a word I hate. He was the kind of guy who would meet someone, and an hour later a handwritten note would be delivered to the guy's home with a photograph of himself and a friend he didn't remember from forty years ago.

"Marty could always find these things. He kept lists. Had one of the great filing systems of all time. Followed up on everything. His Christmas mailings would run to thousands of names. One year he had five thousand dollars in postage due.

"But he was brilliant. God, he was brilliant. He could do it all. He could do stand-up, which meant that he could have worked concerts and clubs and college campuses. He certainly could do films. He could do a series or be on the stage. I didn't see any area where he would not have been successful as a performer. None. I loved him as a stand-up, which he had not touched at all. That was a form I knew well, having developed Cosby and Joan Rivers and Pryor. Marty could have been a headliner in Las Vegas.

"He was bright enough and well-read enough to reach all levels, a terrific asset. All he had to do was *ein schtill*, an old Yiddish expression. All he had to do was be quiet and listen, which he was incapable of doing."

Stars are not born overnight—you knew that—nor are careers unmade in a day. Marty Ingels returned briefly to California in July of 1966, to appear in *The Pajama Game* at the Carousel Theater. The patient Roy Silver was still trying to guide him through the shoals, as both a friend and comic, and every day was a challenge.

"I used to do a Sunday-by-the-pool kind of thing," recalls Silver, "and invite people over for fun and business. I always wanted Marty to come, but he would get so frenetic with it. If he saw someone he had *heard* might have a TV show in six years, he had to know the history of his life. The guy would be locked forever in a corner, with Marty bending his ear. 'Gee, I was having a good time,' he would say to me when he left, 'but Ingels got ahold of me and it was one of those numbers.'

"At the same time, he was trying to keep one eye on Jean, who no question was faithful, but gorgeous and fun and a voluptuous woman. I guess people sensed she wasn't in a happy marital situation, and this is Hollywood, so everyone hits on everyone else.

"Jean was a nice lady who tried hard and at times could stabilize him. Marty could not accept what he had already done. My God, Dickens and Fenster. It was a popular show. There are four million actors out there who would have sold their soul to be in a series. Then you go on to the next thing. Marty evaluates. He takes every piece, why he didn't make it, and beats it to death. He looked at people and decided if they can or cannot do anything for him. I don't mean that as a put-down. In Hollywood, I consider everyone as a star-fucker, basically. Marty didn't know he was a star."

Roy tried to convince him.

~~~~

God knows, he tried. Roy redid me. He told me to stop wearing red jumpsuits and sandals, shave every day, go for walks. He sent me back to Hollywood for my first job since the series ended. I was to star in *The Pajama Game*, which was to be held in one of those elaborate tent theaters, and so I didn't feel any particular anxiety. Rehearsals were fine, I was feeling great. Of course, it hadn't opened yet.

Steve McQueen's wife, Neile, was starring opposite me. I had the Eddie Foy role, which was absolutely a showstopper. One scene in particular, the humor was very physical. The character is in the background, trying on a pair of pajamas. He doesn't know he has it turned around, and can't find the fly.
~~~~

Opening night I was ready to go. The new me. Roy stopped by to say he had chartered a bus and brought all his friends, all the guys from the William Morris Agency, and Danny Thomas and Sheldon Leonard. He saw Dean Martin and Frank Sinatra out front, too. Wonderful, swell, I hear myself saying. He slapped me on the back and gave me a poke on the arm. "Good luck."

Neile McQueen ducked her head in the door to say Steve was here with Paul Newman. Great, great. I'm higher than a giraffe's rectum. The show opens with a kind of *Our Town* setting, and Eddie Foy himself walks out and actually says to the audience: "Well, this is it. This is the factory over here. . . ." And he sings 'The Pajama Game Is the Game that Is."

Which is the cue for my entrance. I walk down the aisle, the overture is playing, and I have the opening prologue. This moment is going to be so sensational, I am having kittens.

I stood at the top of the aisle in the dark, in my costume, watching Eddie Foy do his bit. I looked out over the audience and saw the people still squeezing into their seats, men in tuxedos, heads of studios, women with hairdos like sculptures.

I stood there with the entire show in my head, every word of every part, and I began to think, Careers are going to be made and broken here tonight. Impressions formed for a lifetime. And the thought took root in my mind: *Death is here.*

Death? What was I thinking? How could anyone lay that trip on himself? All these people . . . they had made plans to be here. Had driven miles. Some had taken out good-luck ads in the trade papers. The critics were here. Their reviews would set the pace for this show. Thumbs up, down, our fates would be decided.

My mind was doing gymnastics. And the play didn't start until I spoke, until words emerged from that three-inch opening under my nose. Does the center on the football team ever think about the power he has? The game can't go on unless he snaps the ball.

And all of this led up to the unspeakable, terminal thought:

What would happen if nothing came out of my mouth? All those people, their money, their ads, their time, poof. Out. Look at the responsibility I had. That was all I needed. I quickly got rid of the thought and shook my head to clear my mind, but it was too bloody late.

The overture filled the tent, everyone applauded, and I walked to the front of the stage, turned, and faced the audience. The applause grew louder. I looked at all the important faces in the front rows, the tuxedos and the gowns and I said, "Well . . ."

That was the last word I could remember. My mind was a cavern. I no more knew my name, what theater I was in, what city, than I could recite the *Iliad* in the original Latin. I had done it. I had planted a destructive thought in my mind, and I was finished. I walked around. I paced. I talked to myself: Think how important this is. If you fail, they all fail. I stood there, and in the wings people are freaking out. The orchestra leader doesn't know whether to start the first song or not. If he does, we lose the first eight pages of the script. I'm the whole prologue.

And that was what they did. They played the first song, and the next actor made his or her entrance, and I had blown the prologue, which was a significant portion of the play. I made my way backstage in a daze, waiting for someone to run a javelin through my chest.

Instead, they patted me on the back, said, "Don't worry, it happens," and assured me the play would be okay. All of which made me feel like a sewer rat, but at the same time gave me a spark of hope. In the third act, I had a chance to recover; that was the scene where I can't find the fly on the pajamas. Of course, I immediately thought of eighty ways to embellish the gag. There were no lines to remember, just pantomime, which was perfect for me.

As luck would have it, I not only improvised for eight or ten minutes, spinning around, looking for my fly, I threw in some moves that were funnier than words. It was a freedom I never before had felt on any stage . . . nothing had to be memorized. The audience gave me a standing ovation.

In the reviews the next day, one critic said it takes a certain kind of comic genius to be able to do a joke like that, which is basically a crotch joke, and get what Marty Ingels got out of it without being down and dirty. They totally ignored the opening, and the review was just exquisite.

Jean and I were separated then, in the early stages of our on again, off again divorce. She called to tell me she read the review and cried because she was happy for me.

Even Roy said it: I was on my way. Now here's the pathetic part. I knew that it was the beginning of the end for me. For the first time, I knew I could destroy myself with a single thought.

After *Pajama Game*, I was warm again, if not hot, and went back to New York to read for a new television series. It was for big money, too. A strange time.

The state of New York had just legalized off-track betting on horse racing, and I was to be the comedy host of *The OTB Show*, which came on at eleven o'clock in New York to compete with Johnny Carson. Let's just say this was a very New York idea. The host would clown around, maybe interview a guest, and give the day's racing results. In theory, this must have sounded like an unbeatable concept.

On the air, it was a fiasco—and not my fault, not one hair of it. What the producers discovered was that among gamblers, people who bet on horse races and baseball and football, there is not a consuming interest in hearing someone tell jokes. They have tuned in for the score. They want to know the win, place, and show, what the payoff is. They didn't want Buddy Hackett. They didn't want topless dancers. They only wanted the results.

I received hate mail. The nice letters said something like, "Get that unfunny fuck off the screen." I tried not to take it personally, but it all boiled down to another defeat. No matter what they teach you at sportsmanshp school, losing does not bring out the best in people. I had an offer in California, and the producers of *The OTB Show*, who owed me a plane ticket, refused to pay it.

I did a couple of guest spots on *The Addams Family*, and that says something about John Astin, who knew I had been sick and was quietly rooting for me. At the same time John tested for *The Addams Family*, I was up for the lead in a new series about a funny forest ranger. The pilot was big and expensive, and the script was by the two fellows who wrote *The Red Skelton Show*.

Nobody I talked to at the time thought John's show could work. There was no money behind it, and instead of a pilot they did a fifteen-minute presentation with slides.

Mine couldn't miss. The forest ranger was a sensitive guy who caught poachers and freed the bears from those awful traps with the iron teeth, and to make a living he showed tours, and we could do nutty things with that. The ranger was a perfect part for me.

Now, whenever a lot of people are involved in a project in Hollywood, there is a certain point when they all believe it is wonderful. In the technical idiom of the film industry, this is called "jerking yourself off."

It is part hype, part reality, part wishful thinking. Then there is that inevitable time when it behooves us to put aside our egos and say, Whoa, we have spent two years on this project, and no one wants it. I watched the ritual unfold with the pilot about the funny forest ranger. I had mortgaged my house to keep going, and now the money was spent and they were running it into the ground.

Of course, I thought the pilot was going to be the pinnacle of my life. They had an office at Desilu, where the pilot was filmed, and the times were as good for me as they could get. I still hyperventilated, still passed out, but I had gotten to know the nurse there when we were shooting Dickens and Fenster.

I was always running to her to have my blood pressure taken, and she believed in me, knew it was not an act. She offered me medication and I refused, out of another kind of fear. (Shirley often says, "If I felt for one minute, for sixty seconds, like you did every day of your life, I would have been on intravenous morphine. There would be nothing I would not have taken to relieve that kind of pain.")

We all believed the pilot was wonderful. There was a love interest, a girl a head taller than my character, and at last I was going to be Red Skelton. Then we all assembled one day in the screening room to see the product. Nothing worked. Not the jokes, the story, the scenes. It wasn't funny.

My stomach sank all the way to Tijuana. We had worked on it for three or four months, and the script had pathos, moments that made you cry. How could it not be wonderful?

The lights came on, and I shrank in my seat, waiting for all the accusations to start. I couldn't believe my ears. "Well," said a smiling Leonard Stern, "it looks like we have a winner."

They were all congratulating each other, the writers, the film editors, the cutters, the cast. Sweetheart, baby. It was a victory party.

Stern would go on to produce *MacMillan and Wife*, with Rock Hudson and Susan Saint James. He looked at a lot of film, and I didn't think of him as a fellow given to self-deception. I looked at Jean, who was with me. "We got a winner? Is he kidding?" She said, "Well, who knows? Go along with it." People walk up to shake my hand. I am waiting for someone to say, "Holy shit, nothing worked. Why are we still sitting here?" But it went on and on. They were reaching, stretching, to find things to praise: "That was a nice hat you wore. . . . I liked your earrings."

Every few days I would hear that Lenny had a meeting with the network people. I kept saying to Jean, "When does a person, no matter how much is invested, finally say, 'It stinks. Put it in yesterday's file and we'll start over tomorrow'?"

Jean is trying to be optimistic. "Maybe you're being too hard on it. There were some cute scenes. You showed yourself to be a good actor . . . you have such simpatico."

"Oh, please, Jean, stop. What are you talking about? Forget it."

So what about me? Why couldn't I speak up and say, Hey, I'm disappointed, but let's be honest, nothing works. I just can't. I'm a hot person again. Then Lenny calls one night and says, "The network is setting up a public screening tonight, where they hook up the wires and measure the audience reactions. I'd like you to be there."

Who knows, maybe the fans will enjoy it on some kind of subliminal level. It is clear that Lenny hasn't had much luck selling the show, but in his mind, Who knows, if the audience sees something, maybe a spot will open in the network schedule and we'll be ready.

So I arrive at eight o'clock and—how is this for Hollywood agony?—what Lenny wants me to do is stand at the door and greet the viewers as they file in, heading for the room where they punch the cards with the questions. They watch the show, and there are no laughs. Not even polite applause.

They walked past me. "Hi, I'm Marty Ingels." Our eyes met. They knew I was the face on the screen. They moved on quickly, because they had nothing to say. What was I supposed to say? "I got a family. I'm a veteran, I have shrapnel wounds. I'm a recovering alcoholic. We plan to reshoot a lot of the scenes."

I hated standing there, trying to suck the blood of nice people who had just wasted two hours of their time. And these were the moments that finally hardened me some, made me a little jaded. The show was dead. Then came the call I thought was months overdue. Lenny said, They didn't have the room, there were some logistical problems, our timing was unlucky. Blah, blah, blah. Everything except the truth: There was no show. To this day, no one has said that.

The spot we had hoped to land on the network was filled by a show called *The Beverly Hillbillies*. John Astin had a fabulous run in *The Addams Family*. And from that moment on, there wasn't a chance that Marty Ingels would ever be up for a starring role on network television. The heat was gone.

Not far behind were my wife and house. Jean soon went back to New York, complaining she could no longer face the creditors who kept coming to the door.

On the strength of the series, we had built a beautiful home, for more than we could afford, on a hillside in an area called Sierra Bonita. We ran out of money before we could finish the swimming pool.

Don Adams had just moved to the Coast to do a pilot for a series called *Get Smart,* and I offered to rent him the house for the cost of the monthly note—$670. That was less than half what the rental would have been on the open market.

I had moved into a small apartment not long after Jean

left, and the day we closed the deal was one of the saddest of my life. Don wanted to have a big party for his friends, and he asked if I would build a deck around the pool. I told him I couldn't afford it.

"What if I build it," he said, "and you pay me back half?" At the time, that sounded like a good deal for both of us. *Get Smart* was a runaway hit. Adams would build a more elaborate house, and I still didn't have my share of the cost of the deck.

I returned to New York, hoping to take another bite out of the Big Apple. A few months later, word came down that Filmways was preparing another bumbling detective series called *The Double Life of Henry Fyffe*, and they were reading star candidates in New York. It seemed perfect for me, and Roy got me an interview.

I will never forget that day, mainly because the actor reading right before me was a tall, dark, curly headed fellow who showed up in a silver Rolls-Royce.

"Who the hell is that?" I asked the receptionist.

"Barbara Streisand's husband," she said.

It was Elliott Gould. (He hadn't yet done the film that was to make him, *Bob and Carol and Ted and Alice*.)

What makes that day even more memorable for me is that *I got the part.*

It was celebration time. And back to Hollywood in triumph. *The Double Life of Henry Fyffe*. It was better than *Dickens and Fenster*. It was better than *anything* before. It was the comeback *after* the pitstop I thought was gone forever. And I was delirious.

The calling and moving and changing and planning that followed, I did in a haze while three feet off the ground and clicking my heels. I hadn't been back in Hollywood long when I phoned an old Hollywood columnist I knew, Army Archerd. (I'd been keeping Army apprised of all my bicoastal doings and misdoings, and I was anxious to give him the good news.)

"Guess what," I said to him. "Filmways is doing a new detective series called *The Double Life of Henry Fyffe* and guess who's gonna be Henry Fyffe?"

"Red Buttons," he said.

"Funny, funny," I said. "But you're a little out of touch. It's Marty Ingels."

"Ingels," he said, "I'm afraid you're the one who is out of touch. Red Buttons was officially signed this morning for that role. And, if you read my column tomorrow, you'll see it in print."

Boom. Crash. Bang.

He was right. Somehow, some way, Buttons's agent, a hotshot shaker by the name of Marty Baum, had maneuvered Buttons into my spot as a trade-off for some big-name client Filmways wanted from Baum for another project.

I was all moved back to Hollywood. And I was out again, broke, and beaten to a pulp, not knowing, now, what to do or where to go or what to think or who to hate or when to cry. I was beyond all that. I was numb.

Don Adams was still on top of the TV ratings, and still on top of my mountain for less than seven hundred dollars a month. His payments were just enough to keep me solvent at the mortgage company.

One day I received a phone call from a neighbor telling me that a moving truck was parked in front of my house, and she had seen the movers taking out my living-room sofa.

I drove to the top of the hill in what I was then driving, a used car, a compact with a faded paint job, and parked across the street and in front of my neighbor's house. By then I was a little paranoid. I wasn't working. Every day I read in the papers about someone else's success. So now Don Adams is moving, and I see my white couch in the back of the truck. Don wasn't there. His wife was in the yard, directing the movers.

I jumped out of my car and said, "What are you doing? Why is my couch in there?"

She was clearly made uncomfortable by my sudden appearance. "Well, Don said you owe him some money, so he's taking the couch until you pay."

I could feel myself losing it. I said, "Wait a minute, you can't take my—no, that's part of my house—no, I only have a few pieces left." Rage. Rage. Rage. Rage. I ran down the hill to my car, jumped behind the wheel, and swung in between the truck and the easement so the movers couldn't leave. I yanked the keys out of the ignition, slid out the door, and shouted to the driver, "Fuck you! You're not going anywhere with my couch. Take it out of there! I'm not moving until you do."

Mrs. Adams, frightened, tearful, ran into the house, and I knew she would call her husband, tell him Ingels was crazy, on a rampage. A few minutes later, a late-model car pulled up, and out of it stepped Don Adams, Don Knotts, Louie Nye, Bill Dana, and Larry Stern, who was the producer of *Get Smart*. I looked at them, and what I saw were five people who represented the Wide World of Success.

I no longer recall who spoke first. I only know that someone said, "What the hell do you think you're doing, Ingels? What are you, some kind of nut?"

I stood there, and to that point it was probably my closest moment to really tipping over the line of being deranged. I saw red. I saw all the power of achievement, and the puzzlement of why it had to come to this. Why was I standing on a hill begging for my couch back, from five guys who could afford their own factory and who couldn't light a candle to me in terms of talent? Sour grapes, of course. Don Knotts was wonderful, and Bill Dana was a genius. But I considered Don Adams a fluke, a likable, hardworking fluke. I never understood what he was doing in his scenes.

I heard myself screaming, "It's not right! You can't take my couch away from me." The tears started to flow, and their heads were swiveling, first at me, then each other. They were thinking, Oh, God, how important can a couch be?

All I could see was the symbolism, Hollywood taking what little I had left and hurting me. The five of them just quietly climbed up in the truck, carried out the couch, left it on the lawn, and drove away.

I had never seen Don Adams before that day, but for years afterward, whenever he met Shirley or one of the boys, he would ask, in a whisper, "How's Marty?" He said it the way you would ask about someone who was in Synanon, because he still pictured me standing on the top of a hill, crying for my couch back.

~~~~
~~~~

The last word belonged to Roy Silver:

"It was such a waste of talent. After that, Marty was always getting sick or coming down with something. He and Jean finally split, the career stopped. That was when I would go over to his apartment and he would be lying in the middle of the floor. He would stay on the floor weeks at a time.

"I used to walk in and completely ignore him. 'Oh, hi, Marty.' And I'd step over him and say, 'Listen, I'm going to get something out of the refrigerator. I have an appointment for you tomorrow at ten if you want it.' I mean, I would go on like it was nothing to talk to a man curled up on a rug staring at the ceiling.

"But he didn't keep the appointments. And things got a bit testy between us, because I always considered that another role. Once he was into a role, he could play it to the hilt. So if Marty was going to be catatonic and curl up on the floor, he was going to be the best curled-up-on-the-floor person in the history of show business."

10

A Fear of Flying

THEY WERE THE COUPLE Who Had Everything. She, Shirley Jones, had glamour, charm, an educated mind, hair like sunlight, a sweet temper, and a voice made to sing love songs. He, Marty Ingels, had paranoia, manic depression, hyperactivity, phobias not even his doctors could pronounce, and a disorder known as compulsive-obsessive.

Most of his life, Marty would be baffled by the source of his problems. If only it had been as simple as knowing that they were rooted in the conflicts of boyhood, in the complicated memories of his mother and his father. Doesn't it start there for each of us, the seeds of whatever we are going to be? The answers would elude him for thirty years or more, depending on when you decide the meter started running. He did not really overcome these conditions. Rather, with Shirley's help, he outlasted them. He adapted in such a way that he could function around them—a different kind of victory, but a victory still.

The wonder is that anyone could go through what Marty Ingels did, endure, survive, and actually become a nice if ruthlessly self-analytical person. He cannot really remember a time when he did not have these weaknesses. He routinely accepted the notion that he was crazy, but if you think you are crazy, can you really be crazy?

It was his catch-22.

~~~~

A phobia is nothing more than a fear. Unfortunately, I didn't realize in my early years how phobic a person I was. I only knew that I was hyper, hyper, hyper. With my first taste of success, the anxieties began to build, became more pronounced and unbearable, until my public crash on the Johnny Carson Show.

They take all forms, defy logic, and grip you without any apparent warning. I was afraid of height, of looking up or looking down. Afraid of crowds. Afraid of open spaces, any direction where I could not see a place or structure. I was afraid of being away from my home, my "central place."

And I am still afraid of flying. I have not flown since 1960. This is a constant phobia, but not nearly as painful as others, because I don't have to deal with it day by day. I have alternatives. This is, I might add, the last one I still needed to kick as the 1980s ended.

Quite simply, I would like to get on an airplane and go somewhere, anywhere, with Shirley. I haven't been able to do so. We meet on the road, and depending on what the destination is, she flies, and I go by boat. She flies, and I go by RV. She flies, and I go by burro.

I don't blame them if people are skeptical when I describe how helpless I was after my breakdown: crawling around on the floor for all those months, unable or unwilling to stand up. What you have to understand is that I was in a total state of anxiety. Little by little, I had to learn how to find the courage to start over again. Even if I succeeded, I was aware that my recovery would not be a sympathetic one. There seemed to be nothing wrong with me medically. Yet my health, my career, my wife, and most of my money were gone.

~~~~

It had happened too fast, nor was Ingels at the top long enough to be rated as a has-been. Yet he could recognize the truth in the words of Willie Pep, the longtime boxing champion, explaining how he knew when he was washed up: "First your legs go. Then your reflexes go. Then your friends go." Marty never deceived himself, at least not for long.

~~~~

My performing career was finished by 1976 or 1977, and I had to confront the fact that the business, show business, had sort of decided to let me lie there and die. I mean, the minute my TV series was canceled, my mail dried up. You immediately fall off a lot of computerized lists for premieres and openings and benefits. A cold, cold town, Hollywood is. One month I was tooling around town in a limousine and had all these friends. When I couldn't go to the discos and boogie all night, it was over. No one wants to be around you when you are weird and sick and it is not part of your act.

That cynicism taught me a lot about business and made me a success the second time around. That I was able to pick up the pieces of my life at thirty-eight and start over I still find unbelievable. I tell the story, to groups and in interviews, to let people know they can begin again.

My immediate needs were obvious. I still had to earn a living, and I had to work at eliminating these phobias. You feel so pitiful. You want to be loved, and no one loves you. You want to be successful, and you're not. You can't move. You try to catch your breath. Your chest hurts. Your neck hurts. Everything hurts.

I was not on drugs, and I resisted taking medication. My brain was telling my body, "It's terrible out there, and nothing is working for you. On the floor, you'll be safe."

Can a healthy, well-adjusted person imagine any of this? I didn't turn off my television set for nine months. I don't mean I watched it; I seldom did. The set was just there, always on, like a night-light in the room.

Once I confronted my problems, there seemed to be no end to them. I had a phobia about looking up, and because of it, I couldn't walk around New York. As silly as that sounds, if I looked up, I would be scared witless. The jokes came. People who knew me said, "Ingels, you're afraid of height. You're afraid of depth. There is only one dimension left that you're not afraid of—and that's width."
~~~~

You remember the scene in almost every World War II movie where the captain asks for volunteers to storm a machine-gun nest and face certain death? That's how I felt just going out the door. While I was still living in New York, I was invited one night to a party too prestigious to miss. I dressed, quivering and shaking and terrified, but I went with two friends. When we reached the apartment building, the doorman said the party was on the forty-third floor.

I not only didn't want to visit the forty-third floor, I refused to get in the elevator. That was another phobia—elevators. The quieter the night, the fewer the people around, the slightest jerk of the car or the grinding of the cables, and this scenario popped into my head:

EX-COMIC FOUND DEAD IN BROKEN ELEVATOR; STARVED TO DEATH.

This is how a phobia works: We all have little fears that are natural, even fairly common. Most of us are a tiny bit afraid of heights. Of speed. The more fears you have, the less your psyche can resist, and the more neurotic you become.

My ambitions won out that night. The party was important to my career. So I stepped into the elevator, and when I opened my eyes, we were getting off at the forty-third floor.

I walked into my host's apartment, and naturally, the walls were all glass, floor to ceiling. No matter where you walked, you could look down and see the pavement, the street, forty-three floors beneath you. The food was arranged on long buffet tables in such a way that you had to walk nearly around the room, directly in front of the windows.

I did not eat that night, partly because I thought I was going to die and saw no point in it. If you know nothing about people who have fears of height, the devilish part is this: If you stand near a cliff, you are drawn irresistibly to the edge. It draws you.

So it was with me. I began to perceive that the room was tipping downward, and I was being drawn to the glass walls. While the other guests grazed on the buffet table or mingled, I found a seat at one end of a couch and literally hung on to its arm. People were sitting around me trying to make polite conversation, trying to be cute, and I'm clinging to the arm of the couch as though it were the side of a boat.

Finally, someone said, his voice revealing only a touch of puzzlement, "Marty, what are you doing?"

"Oh, it's okay," I assured him. "I'm just holding on."

Everyone laughed. I laugh when I think about it. But imagine yourself in a room that seems slanted, and you feel yourself sliding to an open door and beyond it is darkness. Now that is terror.

All of which led me to conclude that fear is the meanest disease of all. Think about it. If you had cancer and your doctor gave you three months to live, you could make your peace and accept your fate and use the time you had. It's not so terrible. Now imagine yourself sitting down with your wife in a movie theater, and you're so terrified of crowds that suddenly you start to sweat and pant and you can't catch your breath. You think you're going to pass out, or, worse, your heart will stop and you will die.

Not only does this happen every time you walk into a theater, you *know* it will happen when you buy your ticket. Still, you have to try. You have to believe that one day these attacks will stop. Maybe this time.

As I developed these problems, I began to build my defenses in my own way. I became the president of all kinds of agoraphobia clubs, of all kinds of fear.

Fear of Everything, Inc., Marty Ingels, president. "Is he in?" "Yes." "Will he speak to me?" "No, he's too frightened to take the call."

There is a bitter, bitter truth in that little dialogue. Every time I would appear on television in the 1970s, on a talk show or an awards show or a quiz show, I would receive calls from other agoraphobics all over the country, calling from their living rooms. Understand, agoraphobia is a fear of the marketplace, and there would be an accusing tone to the calls . . . distrust, disappointment.

"We saw you on television. We thought you were agoraphobic."

"It's okay," I would reassure them. "I had a car waiting right outside with the motor running and two guys ready to cart me out."

In many ways, the automobile became the symbol of my dependency, and yet it was my best means of escape. No matter how sick one is, there must be a link, an umbilical cord, to one's home base. When I would on rare occasions go to my psychiatrist's office, my big question of the day was, would I be able to get a parking space in front of his building? I never trusted it to a garage attendant, because I was certain that when I was ready to leave, I would have to stand there with eighteen other people and wait an eternal eight minutes until my car came. And to a phobic, waiting, in a crowd, is a kind of death. Which is why so many agoraphobics pass out in the lines at a supermarket because they know they can't move, they're stuck, trapped.

When I parked my car at the doctor's office, I climbed the stairs and I dreaded each step, knowing that each one was taking me farther away from my car. One day, weary of my fidgeting, he said, "What exactly are you afraid of?"

I said, "I don't know. I just want to get downstairs. I'm afraid I won't find my car."

The doctor, of course, knew me to be a reasonably intelligent person, and there I was, sounding like a nitwit. "You know what I'm going to do?" he said. "I'm going to hold your arm, and we're going to walk around the block, even to the point where you won't see your car."

I recoiled. "Oh, no. I can't just go for a walk. I've got to be where I know I'm mobile, so I can get back to my house."

Whether or not that answer made any sense, he said firmly, "No," took my arm as if I were his grandmother, and led me out of his office and down to the street.

Here we were, two grown-ups, holding on to each other like two tall winos. I had co-starred in my own television series, had been around the world three times—and I couldn't walk around the block alone. We started walking down Rodeo Drive, the ritziest street in Beverly Hills, the two of us, and I kept twisting my head so I could see my car at the curb. Then we turned the corner, and it was out of my line of vision. I started to hyperventilate. I started to panic. He tightened his grip on my arm. "It'll be okay," he said. "We're just going to make one full swing around the block."

We had not gone far when we ran into a couple I knew, an ex-comic and his wife. The husband had read in the paper that I was now involved in some other kind of business. "Marty, how are you?" he said. "How are you doing?"

"Oh, fine," I said. "As a matter of fact, this is my doctor, my psychiatrist. We're going around the block."

The ex-comic turned to his wife and howled, "Is that terrific or what? Boy, the life of the rich. They go out walking with their doctor. Only in Beverly Hills!" They waved and moved on, thinking how great Ingels must be doing, having fun, hanging out with his doctor.

As I thought about that scene later, I realized what a microcosm of society it was. Everybody thinks the other guy has it made, even when the other guy needs a keeper. I drove home in tears that day. To be so in the clutch of some invisible force that will not let you enjoy the sun and the air, that keeps you in terror, is no life at all.

I do not mean to offend those who have been maimed, born with or stricken by crippling diseases. I had to find a twist of humor in my circumstances to overcome them. Physically or mentally, to be disabled is to fight an unending war against feeling helpless.

Phobias are intensely real to me, even when I turn them into a resource, into humor, and your stories—you end up with great stories—make you more interesting at parties. They are a curse because they keep you from your full potential—and in the end because they are painful.

~~~~

When he isn't being the comic, when he is telling the story straight, you cannot escape the pain, the desperation, the scream in Marty's voice. The Gestapo could not have devised the kind of torture Marty Ingels inflicted on himself.

What is remarkable is not what it cost him, what he lost or gave away. You marvel at how long he was able to cling to the edge of the cliff. That he was able to function at all through those years is a tribute to his own will, his inner self. That he eventually overcame his ordeal is largely to the credit of two people.

The doctor's name is Leonard Schwartzman, and he practiced general medicine. Nothing against psychiatrists, but Marty tried them once. One wanted to keep him sedated.
~~~~

All Marty could think about was not passing out, or how fast he could get to his car. The shrink wanted to know how he felt about his mother when he was two years old.

Dr. Schwartzman waited for him. He pointed Marty toward recovery by not always following medical orthodoxy. He did not invent a cure for the chronically phobic person, but he proved that a treatment based in part on common sense was compatible with science. A lesson in anatomy helped—knowing where to find the funny bone.

What medicine could not supply, Shirley Jones did, just by being herself. As Marty tells it:

~~~~

I was with Shirley once in Chicago, following her around as she did her shows, and petrified of nearly everything. I started to dress to go out for the evening, and I started to sweat. That was one of the physical symptoms when I was very nervous. I mean, before I even got out of our room, I had to change my shirt. The sweat was pouring off me, and there was nothing I could do except to keep going from the theater to this famous supper club, the Pump Room, where we were among a party of fourteen.

I'm just dripping on everything, I am mopping my face with my napkin, it is unbelievable. I am unable to focus my mind on whatever I am supposed to be doing or saying. Then a waiter put a telephone down in the center of our table, one of their VIP courtesies, and I thought, Hey, I can call Dr. Schwartzman in California.

He was used to my calling at all hours of the night, so I reached for the phone and I dialed his number, and I reach his answering service. I told them it was an emergency, left my number, and waited. I am sitting at this table in Chicago, and the phone rings, the doctor returning my call: "Marty, is everything okay?"

I said, "Well, I'm in Chicago and I'm at a table, and we're having dinner and I'm sweating."

Long pause. "That's all?"

"Yeah, but Lenny, I'm not just sweating . . . I'm pouring. I look like I didn't towel off after a shower."
~~~~

He said, "I'll tell you what. Don't drink any milk."

"Milk? What do you mean, milk?"

"Just trust me when I tell you—don't order milk, and everything will be fine."

I put down the phone and looked around the table. It was noisy in the room, no one paid any attention, and when the waiter came around, I didn't order milk. And the sweating stopped. He simply had given me a placebo by long-distance, the first thing that popped into his head. He could have told me not to eat the bread sticks. The main thing was, he gave me an instruction and said the problem would go away, and it did.

Of course, the tricks, the psychology, can take you only so far. There came a point when he said, "Listen, you have got to let me prescribe something that will at least help balance your body chemicals."

I knew nothing then about the theory that anxiety attacks, even manic depression, may be caused by a serious chemical imbalance. But I am convinced today that in the not-very-distant future this will be the accepted diagnosis for most mental illnesses. After a time, you can have so many anxiety attacks that certain chemical levels are just off the meter. When you are frightened, it sets off a chain reaction in your body. Suddenly, you can't breathe, the room is spinning, you're seeing double, and you're dripping so much sweat your coat turns a shade darker.

That was me. I believe now that I was not a mental case, that what I needed was a medication that would regulate the flow of adrenaline in my system. I disliked the idea of relying on pills. I needed the illusion of being in control. Now I had to swallow my pride, along with a pill called Imipramine, well known and accepted today as a mood-elevator. Having come to believe that it was acceptable for a comedian to be crazy, I fenced with Dr. Schwartzman long after I should have been ready to try anything.

"I don't want any sedatives," I said.

"It has nothing to do with sedatives. It is for people who get depressed."

"I'm not depressed," I argued. "I'm shivering and quaking."

"No," he said, "you're having anxiety attacks, and those are a form of depression."

I took the pills, still fearful, but the physical symptoms stopped. I have been taking Imipramine for the past ten years, and I am able to cope with things that used to stop me in my tracks.

I want to be careful not to suggest that this pill, any medication, is a miracle drug. But the medical record seems clear in my case: I was extremely susceptible to any imbalance of the body chemicals that influence our behavior. Once we were able to restore and control that balance, I was able to rely on logic and reason. And human nature.

If anyone asks me how I am today, I am tempted to reply that my life is sensational . . . and why not? I married Shirley and acquired a family and was able to succeed in a new and innovative business. But that isn't my usual answer.

I tell them I feel wonderful, and if they ask why, I say, "I can go into a restaurant and sit and talk to you. I can take a ride somewhere, I can go for a walk by myself, travel out of town with Shirley, and not faint or hyperventilate or extinguish candles with the sweat running down my chin. I don't have double vision, and I don't feel the room sliding out from under me." This is my definition of happiness: a nice house you're not afraid to leave, a little action, and an understanding wife.

When I first met Shirley, she had never heard of an anxiety attack. In those days, I would pray for her to have a mild one, maybe hyperventilate for a minute, so she would know how it felt. She just doesn't experience such things. At one point, early in our marriage, she had to make a trip, and I went upstairs and stayed there for three months. Shirley didn't understand. She didn't see a splint. She didn't see anything cut open. She didn't see a graph with a bad heartbeat. All she saw was a big strapping guy who was just lying there saying how scared he was. She stuck it out.

Of all the misconceptions about Shirley, the one I enjoy most is the picture of her as America's Goody Two-shoes. Not so. Shirley is the wild one, and I'm the conservative. If I said, "I want you to slip into a black negligee and meet me on Wilshire Boulevard at two o'clock in the morning next to a picket fence," she'd be waiting for me by the time I got there. She is just open and wonderful about love and people and risk-taking. I'm the one who always says, "Wait a minute. Maybe we shouldn't. Should we?" And Shirley is the one who says, "Why not?"

I was asked once in one of those celebrity roundups, who would you most want to be with if you could have your fantasy fulfilled on Valentine's Day? I said, "Well, I would get Linda Evans, and Daryl Hannah and Joan Collins, put them all in one room, lock the door, and go have dinner with Shirley." Which is true. Shirley is the end of the world for me.

We try to do something interesting every Christmas, whatever the cost. We have reached that time in our lives when money is something to spend and enjoy and get a little goofy with if you want. I decided one year that it would be great if Shirley and I stood on the roof of our house all dressed in red, with a big, twenty-foot canvas sign that said, JOY. I had the sign made, and I talked Shirley into crawling out onto the roof—that was the hard part—while a helicopter pilot hovered above the house and a lady photographer leaned out and took three hundred pictures of us holding up the sign. We finally got the one I liked, and reproduced it as a Christmas card showing a picture of the entire neighborhood, with swimming pools and manicured lawns and fancy cars, and if you looked real close, you saw these two little maniacs in red holding a big sign that said, JOY.

~~~~

Shirley was clearly a part of the solution. Why she went through it is the question. She had understood the alcohol-induced madness of Jack Cassidy, but the quirky behavior of Marty Ingels, the apparent foolishness of so much of it, had to exhaust the most tolerant of attitudes. At times, Shirley's frustration had to exceed Marty's own.

^^^^

It was dreadful in the beginning, of course, because I basically didn't know what a phobia was. I mean, I had never experienced anything of that sort myself, and there is no other
~~~~

way to appreciate the way they take you over. Here I had married a man who really had just about all of them.

At first, I thought it was a joke. He was a comic, and he was just putting himself through this to gain my attention—or anyone else's. I went through periods of real anger, thinking along those lines. I went through all of the mood changes from anger to resignation, just putting up with it, and finally to realizing that it was all true to him, these fears, and I needed to be able to understand them.

I found that the more I tried, the more sympathetic I was, the less severe his episodes became. The very fact that I was able to sit down and talk to him about it, to find out exactly what he was feeling and going through, had a calming effect. I learned to say to him, "I understand, tell me what I can do to help you."

Marty may or may not agree, but I think a lot of phobias come from a fear that is either bred in a child or acquired through a particular experience. The more secure he became, and the more secure our marriage became, the less phobic he was.

In the early years, when we were courting, when all of this was alien to me, I constantly lost my patience. There were times when we would be at a social function, a charity benefit, or having dinner with friends at a lovely restaurant, and he would get up and abruptly walk out. You could be in the middle of a sentence, and he was gone. I never knew why, or what went wrong. I thought everything from, He's having a heart attack, to someone said something that hurt him.

A few times my reaction was blind anger. In the car or at home, I would lash out: "Why did you do this to me? I felt so humiliated." I went through the entire range of feelings until I began to understand that he could not control what happened. As absurd as much of it appeared, it was uncontrollable.

Again and again our relationship almost cratered because of these attacks, these episodes, and the emotion they triggered in me. The turning points were gradual, slight, vague. There was a particular time when we were in the car, driving on the freeway, and he literally took his hands off the steering wheel. He said, "I can't feel my hands. There is no sensation in my hands."

It is a bizarre feeling to be the other person at such a time. There is this most basic emotion in any of us: We don't want someone we care about to die . . . and we feel even more strongly that we don't want them to take us with them.

I didn't know if he had just gone berserk or was having a stroke. I screamed, "What is it? What's the matter? Marty, please, pull the car over." He pulled over and started to sweat. Within ten minutes, he was all right. But it was mostly that kind of situation in the beginning, and they raised doubts in my mind about the kind of man with whom I was getting involved.

VVVV

~~~~

(Marty: That was the first time Shirley had seen the extent of my anxieties. It was also the first time I had undergone this kind of experience. I couldn't feel my appendages, my hands or the bottom of my feet. One moment I was driving down the freeway and Shirley is talking about something, and then I was swerving across the lanes. I started to slap myself in the face, trying to snap out of it. I pulled off the freeway and finally calmed down. Then I stopped at a roadside emergency phone and called my doctor.

I said, "I can't feel my hands. Am I going to die? Is this a stroke?"

He said, "This is a classic, textbook anxiety phobia. You lost the sensation in your hands and feet. This is actually a feeling of wanting to make yourself disappear. You have a subconscious desire to drop out, that inner voice saying you don't deserve to succeed, you don't deserve Shirley." It is almost that poetic.)

~~~~

Such moments did not exactly elevate Shirley's confidence:

^^^^

Many times there was a sense of danger, at least, to me. He reacted very much as you expect someone would who was having a heart attack or some other life-threatening condition. Sometimes he would swing the car around, head right to the nearest hospital and pull into the emergency drive, without any explanation. I would have no idea what was happening. As soon as he could get a medical opinion he felt secure with, he would be fine.

I can't honestly say what turned him around. I don't think Marty knows with certainty, either. I am not sure which came first, the chemical imbalance or his insecurity. His problems subsided with the return of his self-worth, and a maturity that took place within himself. We celebrated our twelfth wedding anniversary in 1989, and I cannot remember the last time he left a restaurant or a party in a panic.

The fact that I didn't give up on Marty had little to do with any strength of mine. It had everything to do with my weakness for his way of sharing love. He isn't good at talking about love, saying the words out loud, but he has a boundless capacity for demonstrating it.

For my birthday one year, he decided to give me a party. Not just your ordinary, traditional birthday party, with the birthday girl pulling another nightgown out of a box and everyone going "ooh" and "aah." Marty arranged a large party at a restaurant, with a red phone next to my place setting. He had researched my past, and for weeks had called all the people who had been close to me through the years: my first voice teacher, my ex-boyfriend from high school, the two aunts who helped raise me, a cousin in Canada, people I had not seen or heard from in twenty years or more.

He put them all on a schedule. And every fifteen minutes, for most of the night, the phone at the table would ring, and someone from my past would say, "Happy birthday, Shirley, we love you."

It was the most beautiful birthday anyone ever had. I didn't even want to guess what the phone bill was. Marty loves that kind of gesture. No one does it better.

vvvv

In his own find-the-laugh-in-an-open-grave kind of way, Marty Ingels would be proud to serve as the poster boy for all those who have been afflicted by fear and apprehensions they cannot define or disarm. And he is as certain that the sun and the midday news will rise on schedule, that he can offer them hope.

~~~~

I needed so much to succeed. I needed so badly to be loved. Which is a risky place to be in your life, because the very desperation of wanting these things can cause you to lose them. I used to go to parties with lists of jokes and try to make everyone laugh. I gave everybody gifts. And it all backfired, because nothing I did worked.

You feel beaten by the cycle. Not only is your rent dependent on success and money, but your feeling of survival. Then, when I least expected, I fell into incredible luck. Why fortune favored me the second time around, I don't know. It was almost as if something divine was thrown my way to see how confused I could get. I stumbled into a business—as a matchmaker for companies that needed celebrities, and vice versa—that just took off. Meanwhile, I wound up with an adopted family of four Irish-Catholic rock stars who looked for ways to agitate me, and vice versa. I lived upstairs in what I called the Anne Frank room, and claimed that they fed me through a small hole in the door. And suddenly, my life was wonderful.

My business runs itself, which means I can go where I want, when I want. Once in a while, I will be driving to a studio to do a commercial or appear on a television show, and I will start to have a small uneasiness, just a hint of a relapse. That inner voice will say faintly, "You can't drive . . . your arm is falling asleep." Only now, when the voice comes, I pull over and stop the car and say to myself, sometimes out loud: "Hey, do you *have* to go where you're going? Do you *really* need this? If you turn around and go home, will anything change? Would you have any less wealth, any less love? Any less acceptance? Would anybody really care if you went home?" The answer is always the same: It's not
~~~~

that important. At which point the feeling leaves, and I start the car and I keep the appointment. It gets done, and I feel good. I feel satisfied.

This is the message I offer to people who suffer with the same phobias. First, you are not dying. Whatever your disability, you start over every day. Tomorrow is another opportunity to get out of bed and pick yourself up. It isn't do-or-die, it is just do-or-don't.

There is no cure for agoraphobia, and no way to comfort yourself except to seek the company of other agoraphobics. There are, for that reason, many such clubs around. There is something reassuring about knowing that someone else has your problem. It's the same principle as being the last person in a checkout line, and you always feel better when another shopper falls in behind you.

I know, I have seen the look on their faces, that people feel better when they hear me tell my story. There are thousands of them out there going through the same things. And they think, My God, this guy was in really bad shape, and look at him now. He feels fine. He is cracking jokes, making fun of himself. He could pass for a normal person.

So that is the message: Make a little start. Shave. Comb your hair. Cross the street. Begin. Life is okay. A Russian poet said we are all captains in a calm sea. Let the storm come. You can ride it out. You can make it work.

~~~~
~~~~

11

Sons and Brothers

WITH THE EXCEPTION OF getting out of bed on a cold morning, nothing is harder to do than growing up—no matter how much you practice.

Of the Cassidy boys, this can be said: Whatever the ups and downs of their public selves, they turned out to be nice people. Each dealt in his own way with fame. David made it as a rock singer and television star *(The Partridge Family)*. Shaun starred in *The Hardy Boys Mysteries*. Patrick toured on the stage and landed his own TV series, a spinoff of *Dirty Dancing*. Only Ryan was not immediately drawn to the family business. He pursued an early interest in law enforcement and trained as a sheriff's deputy; he sold cars and worked in a bank.

Of them all, Ryan knew his father, Jack Cassidy, the least and the best. He was nine when Jack died in the fire. He was the last to leave home, the one who lived it day by day: the breakup of his parents' marriage, his father's death, and the arrival of Marty Ingels, an alien presence who would become his stepfather.

Others would describe Ryan as the quietest of the brothers. He wanted to stay a kid, he said, but even in the saying, he revealed a maturity tinged with sadness. As when he talked about his father:

"Just as Marty did with his mother, my father had problems with his. He and my grandmother clashed a lot. They were very much alike, just as David and my father were so similar. When you act the same, do the same things, the same ways, the same ideas, you see the friction. I look at David and I see so much of my father.

"I don't know if the public realizes how respected my father was in this business. I was talking to my brother Patrick about it when I was with him in New York. Every day, somebody would come up and say, Your father was the neatest man I ever met, such a talented actor, had so much class, so much charm. No question, my dad was a charmer, and he was very sincere, most of the time.

"I don't think Marty ever really believed in his talent. His successes never really sank in. My father had a natural confidence in his abilities. It's wrong to judge him just on his work in Hollywood. His base was New York. My mother made hers in California. As far as the industry goes, Jack Cassidy was better known on the East Coast; he was the man there. He came here as a stage actor. My mother was a movie lady. It wasn't like he didn't fit in; it was like he had a different route going.

"Toward the end of his life, his career was just picking up, and that's why it was especially sad that he died at such a time. He was becoming the traditional 'old-time' actor. He was looking good.

"He was extremely hard to live with. Of course, so is Marty, but in completely different ways. My dad didn't really know how to deal with small children. He would probably have an excellent relationship with us as grown-ups, I think. Little kids he couldn't handle, and that created bad situations. He wanted things to go his way. You couldn't talk back to him. The big problems my brothers have faced had a lot to do with our dad. I will tell you right off, if he were living now, at some point Shaun would let him have it right between the eyes. I mean, he would let him know how he feels. A lot of anger built up over the years. My father would come home and see toys lying around, he would fly into an absolute rage. I saw my brothers standing there, shaking, over toys on the floor, and that is something you don't forget as a small child. It stays in you, and when you have your own kids, you remember those times, and the anger comes back.

"He did a lot of positive things, too. He took us fishing, but basically he involved us in things he wanted to do. We had no choice. We had to abide by his rules, and we never felt free around him. For the most part, my mother had the same deal. He would scare the hell out of you with his voice. He'd yell at you, and his way of yelling used to be frightening to a little kid. I mean, at six or seven, I would wonder, Why is he doing this? He put fear in us, and then as he got older, he started to mellow out.

"My father would have money one week, and it would be gone the next. It meant nothing to him. He used to tell me it was only green paper, and maybe I took that message too seriously, because money doesn't mean a whole lot to me, either. I have had a tough time dealing with money, knowing how to spend and when to conserve.

"When my dad died, we went into the storage and found things I couldn't imagine anyone owning. He had a full keg of beer, no telling how old. He had a saddle worth probably four thousand dollars. He went on binges. He was probably going horseback riding. He went out and bought a four-thousand-dollar saddle and never used it again. He had no-telling-how-many train sets.

"He built his own sets, to scale, and he showed them at exhibits. He had a whole complicated railroad built one Christmas, put it away, and never got it out again. Sometimes he said it was for us, but he played with them himself, and we never got our turn.

"I was an antique-car buff, and he loved to buy me miniature cars, surprise me with something. He came home one day and said he had a gift for me. It was a book on the history of transportation. I'm talking about a heavy, glossy, sixty-to-seventy-five-dollar book, with color illustrations, that he bought in a store in Beverly Hills.

"He thought it over and decided, 'I'll give it to you when you turn twelve.' I never saw the book again. He was the kid in his own way, and I get that from him.

"Marty buys things he doesn't need, too, but in a different way. I don't think Marty would ever spend a thousand dollars on a suit. He knows the value of money. My dad really had no sense of that, and when he had some, he bought the best.

"Marty and Jack were almost opposites as people. If they had anything in common, the obvious one was the fact that they were attracted to the same type of lady. I do know of an incident where Marty and my father met at a party one night, and they both tried to hit on the same girl. They both liked to make people laugh, but my dad had that Irish kind of humor.

"He was a charmer, a really sweet guy, but there was a side to him that was ugly, too. As he got older, there was a period when I felt really close to him. I felt as a kid that my dad needed me, needed that love. That is what makes me sad now, because he lost it at such a young age.

"I was closer to him than my brothers at the end, because I was the youngest, the available one. Pat and Shaun were in and about, dating, spending time with friends, thinking about what they wanted to do. I was home all the time, and I was there when he called. He'd call and ask me to have dinner with him. It's almost eerie, but two of the last weeks of his life I was in New York with him. He wanted to see his family, his hometown, the house where he grew up. It was a very sad experience.

"He was depressed, which was not unusual. A year, or a year and a half, before he passed away, after the divorce, my father was always unhappy—because my mother was the one thing he really needed. He basically went through a nervous breakdown, and then he got himself together, up to a point. His business, his acting, was picking up. But just below the surface, he was an unhappy man who believed he had torn apart his family.

"A memory that haunts me still is of a night he asked me to see a movie. I hadn't been feeling well for a couple of days. I had a touch of flu and was running a temperature, but I didn't want to say no to him. The theater was warm, and I began to feel worse, but I was afraid to say, 'Dad, I really feel sick, can we go home?' I was afraid to ask because I didn't want to hurt him.

"In the car, as he was driving me home, tears started rolling down my face, just from the effort of holding back the fact that I was sick. He turned around and looked at me, and he started to cry with me. He didn't even know why I was crying; he just cried right along with me. After a minute, he said, 'What's wrong, Charlie?' That was his nickname for me. He seldom called me Ryan. I said, 'I'm not feeling well, Dad. It's the flu or something.' But in a way, we were both crying because our lives were never going to be the same again, and we didn't know what to say.

"He was unhappy when he went to New York, and he wanted to show that he loved me, and he wanted to give me something of himself. I felt sorry for him because he didn't know how to do it, and I was young and I wanted to help him because he was my dad.

"I wonder what he would be like if he had lived. My mother might have married Marty anyway, so things would be different. So you can't say they would be better or worse. He was drinking more and he was taking diet pills to keep his weight down, which isn't good. He was on that combination, you know, that night of the accident.

"I walked through the apartment with Marty in the morning. I saw everything I could see. They had taken out the body. Later, I learned a lot from working for the West Hollywood sheriff; it was their department that went to the scene. I read the reports. I even decided to check into it more, because I wanted to find out what really occurred. I satisfied myself that there were no signs of foul play."

Any writer ought to be wary of practicing pop psychology, but it is hard not to conclude that there were one or two transforming events in Ryan's childhood. They were funny, and they were touching, and if they did not affect Ryan, they did affect his mother. As Shirley remembers:

^^^^

Ryan was a wonderful baby, who rarely cried and was easy to care for, even though he was sickly. He had a respiratory problem, and would start to turn blue and wheeze. We had to bundle him off to a hospital and inside an oxygen tent. This might happen every month or two and was a major worry. To complicate matters, I traveled so much of the time, and kept him with me. I would wind up being forced to leave him in a hospital in Kansas or somewhere, and go back for him a day or two later.

He seemed to have no temper, but I came to know that he held a great deal inside. If you crossed him, he would have a tantrum, to the point that he locked himself in his room and you had to just listen to him scream. None of the other boys were into that, but Ryan was so placid and blew up so rarely that when he did, it was like a volcano erupting.

He was two, just talking, when Jack wanted to do *Wait Until Dark* on the stage in New York. We did a full dress rehearsal for some friends and family, and Ryan was sitting with the boys and the lights were down.

Jack played an archvillain, and I the part of a blind girl. In one scene, he had to strike me, really smack me. This was a tense moment, of course, and suddenly you heard a scream out of this little tyke: "Look, Daddy's hitting Mommy, Daddy's hitting Mommy." The fear and pleading in his voice was the only sound in the theater. Jack and I fled from the stage and ran up the aisle to where he was sitting. I held him and said, "It's okay, baby, it's just a play." He was bewildered. He thought what he was seeing was real, and how do you explain playacting to a two-year-old? It doesn't dawn on parents, when they take a small child to the theater, that the child doesn't know what is invention and what is real. How much worse when the parents are also the actors.

Ryan saw the two of us on stage, saw Jack as the villain he was playing. It dawned on me that we had exposed him to a dreadful ordeal, and that incident gave me second thoughts about what kind of programming children should see even at home on television. None of the boys saw *Elmer Gantry* until they were out of their teens.

I can't say what effect such scenes have on a small boy's spirit, but as far as one could tell, Ryan was undaunted. Jack and I were lolling out by the pool on a Sunday afternoon when he was six, while Ryan was out riding his bicycle. We were startled by the doorbell, and the sound of a commotion at the front of the house.

Jack went to the door, and there appeared to be one or more families of Mexican tourists standing there, holding Ryan's hand. They had apparently poured out of a car parked in our drive.

Jack signed autographs and managed finally to send them away. Then he brought Ryan out to the pool and asked him why he would lead strangers to our door on a Sunday afternoon. Ryan, who was five or six, smiled proudly and said, "They passed me on my bike, and asked if I knew if any movie stars lived around here. I said, Yeah, I have two of them right in my house."

You try to look at your children objectively, and you can't. Ryan has been at times the hardest to read. Marty talks about having felt pressured by his brother, Perfect Arthur, who grew up to be a dentist. Look at Ryan, who followed David, Shaun and Patrick Cassidy.

Ryan was not competitive at all. If anyone wants to consider that a fault, or a weakness, that would be his. I have seen him grow more secure, more conscious of his feelings. He had seen all the rejection in show business, so many creative people who didn't get a break, or whose timing was wrong. He sort of ran from it, but in high school he auditioned for *Fiddler on the Roof;* I think David encouraged him. He had a bigger voice than the other boys had at that age.

He was the one most capable of surprising us. When Ryan was sixteen, Marty and I were having a giant disagreement, a few nights after Christmas. It had been going on for days, and I was furious. I was taking down the tree, and Marty was yelling so loud the walls were vibrating, and I have no idea why we were arguing. Then Marty pulled Ryan into it, wanting him to take sides, which always sent me into orbit. He was saying, "This is what she did . . . and now she doesn't want to talk about it . . . blah, blah, blah."

I did not want my children to be put in the middle of that kind of situation, or to be hurt, and he insisted on doing it. But Ryan, to my surprise and delight, handled it with aplomb. I mean, he took on the role of psychotherapist, and he said, "Okay, Marty, why don't the three of us sit down and talk about this."

I literally spun around and stared at him. He said, "C'mon, Mom," and he positioned us on the sofa, and immediately Marty quieted down. Ryan jumped up on a barstool, truly playing the therapist. "Okay," he said, "let's really open up. Marty, you're always so eager to have everybody talk about their lives and air out their anger and orchestrate these family conclaves. I want to tell you about me. I know about you, and you want my opinion about how you treat my mother."

Then Marty broke in with a complaint, and Ryan said, "Yes, you're right, she does do that. You know, she's no angel."

Well, this went on for an hour and a half, and it was the quietest I had ever seen Marty Ingels in my whole life. Ryan never stopped talking. He told his feelings about Marty, his feelings about his father. He offered an opinion about how Marty could improve. He volunteered an opinion on how I might improve on my understanding of Marty.

He was totally objective. If life wasn't right for both of us, he said, we really had to sit down and start talking about things and work on what was at the center of the problem, or the marriage was going to fall apart. Now this is a sixteen-year-old sitting there, and he was just wonderful. Finally, I said, I have got to go to bed, and I said good night and went up the stairs.

Marty was still sitting there three hours later. The next day, I told Ryan how proud I was of him. He had a sense of humor about it, but I asked him where those insights came from. He had analyzed things I had no idea he was even aware of, much less that he could articulate them as well as he did. He used words I had never heard him use.

When I finished bragging on him, he said, "That'll be fifty dollars, Mom, for the therapy."

vvvv

All along, Ryan had a curious ability to view the world around him, the people closest to him, with detachment. He was the least disturbed of the brothers when Marty Ingels winnowed his way into their lives:

"At first, Marty tried to turn the three of us into his allies. Then, at some point, he had to shift the relationship from a friend, more or less, to an authority figure, which is very hard to do.

"It wasn't as if he decided, Well, I've moved in, so now I have to act like a father. He wanted to prove to us that he was good for our mother, and part of that involved dealing out some discipline. Each of us rebelled in his own way. Pat was like, why is another man moving into this house? Why is my father not here? Why is this other man going out with my mother?

"As young as I was, their relationship, what they were to each other, was not one of my concerns. Marty took me out and bought me things, and I saw him as a neat guy. Shaun had at least one big blowout with him, but Shaun was moving out of the house anyway, getting into show business. So we had basically three different attitudes. I could accept whatever was going on. Patrick flatly could not accept it. And Shaun didn't have to accept it, he was getting out.

"There were fights, things that got solved and some that didn't. But as time passed, we started to see what kind of person Marty was, a really good person, and things got better. And I think Pat decided, 'She's my mother and I want her to be happy. If he makes her happy, then that is what counts.'

"Our scraps were minor. I learned to talk to him, to level with him and not to back off. If I was pissed at him, I would say so, and if he blew up, that was okay. I think he really cares about me and Pat and Shaun.

"For someone who is so verbal, who loves to talk, Marty has a hard time reaching out, expressing to someone how he feels about them. There was a lot of baggage between Marty and his mother, Minnie. He didn't treat her very well, for the most part. He was cordial to her, but it was like he can't show her that he cares. There is something in his mind about his mother he can't get rid of, that she did or didn't do when he was a child. It's a shame because she impressed everyone in our family as a neat lady, and it bothered me to see how coldly he treated her. He gave her things, supported her to a certain extent, and he was there for her, I guess. That was it. He was just there.

"Minnie herself didn't seem to know why Marty felt as he did. I talked to her about it, and she thinks that maybe he can't forgive her for being so slow to see that he had problems. One or two of his early teachers tried to tell her. Maybe she just wasn't perceptive, but Marty definitely grew up feeling that he was a second-class citizen. Some of that is in his mind, and some of it is valid, especially in the Jewish culture, which places such a high value on education. Here was Arthur coming home with top grades, winning scholarships, being accepted at a fine college. And Marty was pretty much a pain in the ass.

"Right or wrong, he didn't get all the love he thought he needed, he didn't have a sense of security, while my mother was born with confidence. I understand some of what Marty went through. For a time, I felt envious of Pat; he was always in and out the door, going out with all these beautiful women, going to parties, going to Hugh Hefner's mansion. Pat is a great-looking guy. He ran, he played racquetball, he stayed in shape.

"At least I was honest with myself, I was aware that I felt some envy, and I had to ask myself why. For as long as I remember, people would say to me, 'I guess you'll follow in everybody's footsteps.' I used to say yes, to get off the subject. I was embarrassed to say I wanted to be a cop. If I did, they would say, 'Wow, that's kind of interesting.' And I know they're thinking, How much money can a cop make?

"I may wind up being serious about a career singing and acting. There is a voice there. My problem would be working at it. You really do have to want it, the success, the fame, the smell of the greasepaint, whatever you want to call it. I have seen what others have gone through, and I don't know if I want it that badly."

One of the lasting clichés of show business is the actor whose career started so early, he or she "was born in a trunk." Patrick, the next-to-youngest of the Cassidys, may have broken the record. He played his first scene in a major motion picture two months before he was born. Shirley was there. . . .

^^^^

I had signed to play Marion in *The Music Man* opposite Robert Preston, who had starred in the show on Broadway. And as so often happens in the casting of a picture, there was a disagreement. Bob Preston was absolutely right as Professor Harold Hill, but the producers wanted Frank Sinatra in the part. Meredith Willson, who created the story and composed the score, refused to give in to the money men. They argued that Preston was not a bankable name, which meant they wanted Sinatra to firm up the financing. Willson said if they insisted on Sinatra, he would cancel the film. "Nobody," he said, "is going to do that role except Robert Preston."

A brilliant cast included Hermione Gingold as the wife of the mayor, played by Paul Ford, Ron Howard as my little brother, and Jean Stapleton. I remember almost nothing of the picture or the remarkable people who made it a lovely experience. This was due not to inattention on my part, but to one overriding fact:

I was pregnant with Patrick, and scared to death to tell anyone. The producers could easily have canceled my contract, and the truth was, we needed the income. This was when jobs were scarce for Jack, and a difficult time for the two of us. I felt so guilty that I was working and he was not. He was so much more talented than I was, and he wanted to succeed so desperately. It meant less to me, but one of us had to work.

By the time the filming began, I was four months pregnant, and we were on a three-month schedule. I thought, Oh, my God, I'm going to be seven months along by the time this picture ends. What can we do?

I asked the director to have lunch with me, and of course he assumed I was unhappy with the scene we shot that morning or had a personality clash with someone in the cast.

He looked relieved when I said, "Deke, I'm pregnant."

"Is that all that's bothering you?" he asked, smiling.

"Yes, but I'm in my fourth month."

The smile disappeared. "Good grief. You know we have three months of shooting ahead of us."

I said, "I know, that's why I'm telling you now."

He chewed on a knuckle for a moment, then said brightly, "Don't worry about it. If we have to, we'll shoot you from the waist up, or we'll add a lot of panels to the dresses."

Thank goodness it was a period picture, and I had costumes with petticoats that would help hide my condition. And so it went. The wardrobe ladies kept tightening the straps, and adding a panel here and a panel there. Sure enough, I was in my seventh month when we shot the film's big love scene on a footbridge. This was my duet with Professor Hill, "Till There Was You," with the lyrics: "There were bells on the hill, but I never heard them ringing; No, I never heard them at all, till there was you; there were birds in the sky, but I never saw them winging . . ."

Then came the embrace and the kiss, which is the only really passionate moment in the film. Bob was holding me close, and it was at this particular instant that Patrick decided to kick. And Bob felt it! I mean, literally, Patrick kicked him. The look on Robert Preston's face was priceless. When we finished the scene and the director said, "Cut," Bob said to me, "What the hell was that?"

I said, "You're not going to believe this, but that was whoever is inside there."

Bob had no children of his own, and he really didn't believe me at first. He was constantly amazed as my pregnancy went along, and he could not get over the fact that my unborn child had kicked his way into our scene. When he finally met Patrick Cassidy, years later, Bob said, "Listen, I've known you longer than anybody. You gave me one swift kick—even before you were born."

Minutes after I finished the picture, I went to my dressing room and made myself comfortable, changing into a bathrobe. I walked around the set, saying good-bye, and I was huge, I mean, out to here. The director took one look and said, "My God, Shirley, where have you been hiding that?"

I laughed, and said, "Didn't I warn you? You were the one who said we could do it, and we did."

I should probably point out that I squeezed into my costumes only for the few hours I was in front of the cameras, and no apparent physical harm came to Patrick, who played football and basketball in high school.

The critical time for Patrick was after his father and I had separated, soon to be divorced, and Marty had become an almost-daily caller. Pat was twelve, turning thirteen, four years older than Ryan.

More than once, Patrick said to me, "I want to go live with my father. I don't want to live in this house with you if Marty is going to be around." It was his pain and confusion I heard, not a threat.

I said, "Do you know if your father wants you to live with him?"

He said, "Yes, we talked about it."

"Then, Patrick, it's your decision. You're old enough now to make that decision. I'd be very unhappy without you here. I love you and want you with me, but if you're not happy in this house and you feel that you would be happier with your father, that is a decision only you have the right to make."

And every time he made his announcement and we had that conversation, he would start to cry and say, "No, I want to stay here." We would hug and cry and wait until the next time.

Of course, he was rude to Marty, who never knew from one day to the next what his response should be. He wanted to be the daddy, really thought he should try to fill that position. Mixed up in all this was at least a bit of jealousy. He knew that if I had to choose, he would always lose to my kids. No woman wants to make that choice, but he was at least a little competitive with them. So his need to control them to any degree had to do with that sense of wanting to be number one.

Patrick worried me the most. He couldn't understand why I was getting a divorce. I refused to defend myself to my sons by putting down their father. I never told them that Jack was the one who left, and when he changed his mind, it was too late for us. Patrick suffered the most, and he blamed me for what had happened. "It's all your fault," he said, "you didn't love Daddy enough."

We went through some rough times, after Jack moved out. *The Partridge Family* it definitely was not. Shaun had picked on Patrick until Pat got too big—he was a six-footer at fourteen—to pick on. It started with pillow fights and graduated to fists, with one or the other winding up with a broken finger.

They were sweet boys who grew into good men, and if this sounds contradictory, so be it. They were just being brothers. As time passed, it became harder for me to referee their bouts. Here was this little mother stamping her feet and looking up at these two healthy lads, each a head taller. But when I had to, I let them have it. There was no man around to do it for me. Fortunately, long hair was in style, and if the rough stuff went too far, I just grabbed a handful of hair and yanked.

Once, Patrick pulled his fist back, and I went up like a flare. I said, "Don't you dare! Don't you dare even *think* about striking me. You'll find out what a fight is." I don't believe I frightened him, but I made him think, and he dropped his fist.

Patrick had not witnessed his father's breakdown. Shaun had. Shaun was old beyond his years, ready to make his own decisions at eighteen. He knew what he wanted to do in terms of what he wanted to do with his life, who his friends were, when to gamble on a career move. We didn't always agree, and I tried to guide him in matters that were potentially self-destructive. But right or wrong, he was willing to accept the consequences. Shaun never felt threatened by Marty. He did not take him seriously, certainly not as his mother's next husband.

To Patrick, however, Marty was a threat. And that was where we were, emotionally, when I received a devastating call one Monday afternoon from Jack. Patrick had spent the weekend with his father, and I was working on the picture *Winner Take All*, filming in Gardena. Jack did not try to cushion the blow: He had taken Patrick to a doctor after Patrick complained again of chronic back pain. X rays had revealed a tumor close to his spine, and he had been admitted to Cedars-Sinai Hospital. The doctors were to operate in the morning.

From the time he was a child, there had been this curious tenderness in the center of his back. It would come and go, but he winced when other kids gave him a friendly slap on the back. I took him to a series of pediatricians and doctors, but no one ever found anything. The pain was attributed to his activity in sports; he had probably strained a muscle, they said.

Jack's words on the phone were ominous. He did not have to dramatize them. "It could be malignant," he said. "They won't know until they operate. If the growth is not, but it touches the spine, well, we don't know how he might be affected."

It gnawed at me to know my son had been plopped into a hospital bed and I still had a full day's work to do. They were going to operate the next morning, and I wasn't sure I could stop my tears. I managed to get through the scenes because of a poetically simple reason: The movie was about a woman who becomes addicted to gambling, and if I looked and felt a wreck, just miserable, it went with the part.

The next morning, I went to the hospital early, and waited while Patrick underwent his surgery. Jack arrived. Marty wanted to come, but Jack made his disapproval clear, and I said I would call when Patrick was out of the operating room.

They removed a tumor the size of an orange, but it was benign, the doctors said, and not attached to the spine. There would be no paralysis.

Patrick was in agony. Even before the surgery, he had undergone a battery of excruciating tests, including a spinal tap and dye injections. He does not take anesthesia well, and required more than normal dosages. He is in that medical risk group of people sensitive to drugs or alcohol, even beer, and is subject to a severe reaction.

Once he was wheeled into intensive care, Jack and I could visit him only a few minutes at a time. Later in the day, he was moved into a private room, and that night Marty stopped by to visit. Dear, well-intended Marty brought him a sculpture of a basketball player, and when he walked into the room, Patrick turned his back on him. At that moment, groggy and in pain, what he didn't want was a kind gesture from the new man in his mother's life.

Once he was back home, Patrick's recovery went smoothly, when not everything else did. My divorce from Jack was final, I was in the last season of *The Partridge Family* and had narrowed my social life pretty much to Marty. I had for a time dated another, older man, an actor I had not seen in close to ten years. I think he had been in love with me once, briefly, but we were both married at the time, and nothing came of the attraction.

This was the man whose X rays Marty somehow obtained, and sent them to me mounted on art paper, with arrows pointing to all the potential disabilities of age. Nothing Marty did surprised me. He found out my favorite color was green, and sent over a dozen green carnations with a photograph of himself retouched in green. He knew the name of every person I dated, and he didn't find out from me.

We had not yet moved into the house, although he was quietly smuggling his clothes in a shirt at a time, and his toiletries. For someone who wanted me, cared about me, and obviously was in love with me, he was still fearful of that step. I was fighting it, too, struggling with the idea of living with a man and having three sons at home. I wanted to do the right thing, whatever that was, but I had also concluded that I could not go on living the way we were, with him sneaking out of the house at four in the morning and the boys not knowing what he meant to me. I thought I was too honest a person to continue with that kind of deception.

What really settled the issue was the unexpected advice I received from the boys. I came home late one night after a date with Marty, and Shaun and Patrick and a couple of friends were playing pool.

Shaun took me aside and said, "Mom, what is this charade you're putting on here?"

I was not sure I liked the direction of that question. "What are you talking about?"

"I mean you and Marty." He went on to say that he was worried I might remarry on the rebound, that I was accustomed to having a man around and would be unable to handle being alone. This is my seventeen-year-old son talking. He was keenly aware that I was now seeing no one but Marty, and he knew, or thought he knew, what was going on (whatever ground that covered).

And at that point, he floored me. "Mom," he said, "why don't you just live with the fellow?"

When I could get my mouth to work, I said, "What do you mean?"

"First of all," said Shaun, "I don't want you to get married, so please don't run off and jump into something you'll regret. If you're even thinking about it, live with him first. It's okay. This is 1975, not the forties. I'd rather see you live with him and really get to know him."

I said, "How can I do that with your two younger brothers in this house?"

He said, "Mom, Patrick and Ryan agree with me. They would rather have you live with the guy before you make some big mistake. I've discussed it with them."

I said, "You have?"

"Yeah. They're not blind. They know the score."

"And it wouldn't be a problem with you and your brothers?"

"No. We want you to be happy."

That was when I broke down and cried, happy tears.

vvvv

Now Marty was in the act, with results that were sometimes poignant. In his approach to the Cassidy family, Marty imagined himself each day crossing an alligator pond on a high wire.

"The idea of being able to have a fight with someone," he said, "or maintain authority, after you have said 'koochi koochi koo,' is just untenable to me. I watch people hugging in the park—I mean friends, fathers and sons—and this is absolutely another language to me. I would love to be able to tap into some of that."

Marty tried. The summer of Patrick's senior year in high school, Ingels swung a deal—"one of my cute little arrangements"—for a cruise to London on the *QE2*, two first-class suites each way and two weeks to bounce around Europe, France, Germany, Italy, Belgium, the works.

He threw himself into the project. This was going to be a *family* event, and Marty was going to restore the family. There was only one possible glitch. As a junior, Patrick had been the first-string quarterback for Beverly Hills High School. He didn't want to risk his starting role as a senior, and teams did begin conditioning drills in the summer.

"Aw, don't give me that bullshit," said Marty. "It's the summer. You don't have any games. In no way is there a conflict with this trip. It's a family trip. You have to go. Don't screw it up for us."

Predictably, Marty called Patrick's coach to ask if the trip would jeopardize his status on the team. The coach said, "To be very honest with you, he could go, but our scrimmages start a week or so after he gets back. If he doesn't measure up, as far as his timing and his passing, yes, I could go with somebody else. It's up to him. If he stays in shape, it ought to be okay. I don't want to blow the trip for him."

With that, Marty went back to Patrick and said he had cleared the trip with his coach, so now there was no reason for him to say no. Patrick still wasn't sure.

Marty was getting annoyed, not with Patrick but with himself. "Why should I have to beg him? Here I am, making calls, checking out his story with the coach. Let him stay home. What's the difference? While we're gone, he can have orgies in his room. Then it struck me. I wanted Patrick to go with us because I knew his being along would mean I'd have a better time. I could fool around with him, talk man-talk."

This he could not do with Ryan, still a bit young, or Shirley, the wrong gender. (Man-talk, in the traditional sense, of course, includes unnatural sexual practices and locker-room philosophy.)

So Marty made up his mind to confront Patrick. What am I going to tell him? he thought. That I like him? Well, maybe that's a step forward. He called a family meeting, and then he wasn't sure he could say the right words, and he tried to back out. "We can do this another time if you're busy," he hedged.

"No, no, let's do it now," they all insisted. "What did you want to tell us?"

Marty had never imagined it could be so hard to say anything so simple. He turned to Patrick and said, "Look, we've been having this fight, with me trying to pin you down and you making excuses why you can't go to Europe. And there is one big reason why you ought to go." He looked at their faces, and everyone was grinning, waiting. Finally, Marty said, "I want you to go. I want you to be with us."

Patrick was still grinning. A canary feather all but fluttered from his lips. He cocked his head as if to say the previous declaration wasn't quite good enough. "Come on, Ingels, admit it. Say it. You love us, right?"

Marty said, mumble, mumble, mumble. It sounded very much like, "I love you," and these handsome Irish-Catholic Cassidys, Patrick, Ryan, and Shaun, and their beautiful blond shiksa mother, laughed and gave him a spontaneous cheer.

The story had a sequel: Marty suffered a toxic reaction to a medication, fell ill for weeks, and had to cancel the trip.

Every artist or entertainer must wonder on occasion, could they avoid the sometimes bizarre things that happen if they led ordinary lives? Shirley's concern was usually related to her sons:

^^^^

Shaun was a late baby, my God, overdue nearly a month. Jack and I had a date set for a nightclub act, and six weeks after I gave birth, I was stomping on a stage in Dallas. We had to leave Shaun with a nurse who had been highly recommended to us. Mrs. Webber was German, very strict, and worked by a definite set of rules. We also had a housekeeper, Maria, a friendly little Mexican woman who spoke very good English.

We were to play four cities and then open in Pittsburgh, which was home to me, and I planned to have the nurse fly in with the baby so my parents could see him for the first time.

Wherever Jack and I were on the road, we called to see how the baby was, and from the first night the nurse and the housekeeper clashed. I would get one on the phone, and the other would pick up the extension, and I could not carry on a conversation. They would both try to tell their side at once, and then they would address each other while I waited on the line. "You keep the baby locked up all day," Maria accused her. "The child is in my charge," said Mrs. Webber, "and none of your business. You take care of the kitchen and stop telling lies." Maria: "It is not a lie, you German pig."

I was frantic, thousands of miles away, and out of my mind thinking about this infant, six weeks old. I decided to bring in an intermediary, and I called my friend Sari, who was newly married and living in a tiny apartment. I called and said, "I don't like having my baby in the middle of a fight between these two women. Would you mind doing me a huge favor and move into the house until I can bring the baby to Pittsburgh? Maybe you can calm things down."

As I knew she would, Sari dropped everything and moved in, bag, baggage, and bridegroom. That night, when I phoned, I was relieved by her report: "I have to tell you, Shirley, I haven't heard that baby cry once. The nurse brings him out, and we play with him. He must be the sweetest baby in the world. You don't hear a peep out of him."

"Thank goodness," I told Jack, "everything is fine."

A few nights later, Sari sounded uneasy. "I have to tell you, Mrs. Webber is a rather odd lady. I am inclined to believe that Maria is right in her suspicions. She goes and closes the door, and I don't see her all day. She keeps the baby hidden in the room, and whenever I want to go in and hold him, she says it's not the right time. She'll let me know when I can hold him."

Oh, God. The woman is a nurse, I reminded myself. She knows about these things. I told Sari to keep an eye out and let me know if she drew any conclusions.

Sari didn't wait for my next call. She phoned me and put my pediatrician, Alfred Lang Stanley, on the line. Dr. Stanley said, "Shirley, I have taken it upon myself to fire your nurse."

I said, "*What?!!*"

He said, "Let me explain what has been taking place here." Sari was on the extension, and she broke in. "Shirley, I walked into Mrs. Webber's room, and she had a spoon in the baby's mouth. I demanded to know what she was doing, and she tried to hide the spoon. She said, 'Oh, I was just seeing if his teeth were coming in.' I said, 'Don't hand me that. This is a six-week-old baby. They don't begin to get their teeth until they're three or four months old.'

"And she said, 'Oh, he's so bright and advanced for his age, I thought he might be getting a small tooth.' Shirley, this was such utter nonsense it scared me. I noticed traces of what appeared to be a brown syrup on the sides of his mouth. That's when I decided to take him to the doctor."

Dr. Stanley spoke up: "Shirley, I tested his reflexes, and

had some concern. We did a blood test, and I must tell you she was giving the baby small doses of phenobarbital, not enough to really hurt him, but certainly enough to keep him happy and keep him from crying. To the people who gave her those good references, she must have seemed the best nurse alive."

The doctor saw to it that her license was suspended. Sari stayed on to help care for Shaun until Maria flew with him to Pittsburgh.

To this day, I shudder at that recollection, of a nurse who was doping my baby to keep him quiet.

That was an isolated incident, I hope, the actions of an incompetent woman, not a dangerous one. Protecting a child is a scary business. Nor is it any easier, I suppose, to accept that point at which the child no longer wishes to be protected.

Shaun began his rebellion at thirteen. He was not as intimidated by Jack as David was before him. He stood up to his father, who reacted by finding constant fault with him. He was in his freshman year of high school, at Beverly Hills, and Jack disapproved of the entire environment, the hard-rock music, the long hair, the tacky clothes, the scuzzy-looking friends, the drug talk, and the possibility that it was more than talk.

I didn't like it, either. This was the early 1970s, a time when many teenagers found it unnecessary to please their parents. Shaun was absorbed with getting his rock-and-roll band going, and they were playing all the school gigs. Marijuana was all over the place. Jack didn't try to understand why a kid would rebel, smoke grass, adopt this other lifestyle. He just wanted to stick him someplace where he thought those things would be out of reach.

He decided to send Shaun to boarding school. "I've found a wonderful place," he said, "it's in Bucks County, Pennsylvania. It's beautiful there."

I said, "You know, Jack, that may not be the answer."

He ignored any reservations I had. He loved Bucks County, loved the idea of a private school in a country setting, an all-male school. "It's not military," he said, "nothing like that. It's rather progressive. They can wear blue jeans to classes, but they have to keep their grades up. It'll be better for him. If nothing else, it will get him away from the Beverly Hills syndrome. I want him out of here."

Whatever Jack wanted, I could never dissuade him. Of course, there was a certain logic to it. There always was. He sometimes did the right things for the wrong reasons, but he always believed he was doing whatever he did for the boys' own good.

Jack had been the youngest of five children, including a brother who died early. His mother was a tyrant with all of them, especially Jack, her favorite. She beat him constantly. He grew up with that and the nuns in the Catholic schools who were always rapping his knuckles. His father was an amiable Irishman who loved to drink, and who always brought bottles home. He was an expert at ringing doorbells with his elbows.

He inherited his mother's aversion to a house that had any appearance of being lived in. Clean, neat, everything in its place, Lottie Cassidy would have it no other way.

Jack became a man of impeccable grooming and living habits, but his mother beat his religious faith right out of him. On her deathbed, she begged him to come back to the church. He denied her, and stayed away from the funeral. In his later years, and I predicted it then, he carried with him an awful lot of guilt and inner conflict. He too often took these out on his sons, and expected them to be not boys but little adults.

When Jack made up his mind to send Shaun to boarding school, the decision was not open to discussion. I drove him alone to the airport, and he wept the entire time. I couldn't hold back, either, riddled with mixed feelings. I was weak in my role as a wife because I couldn't say to Shaun that sending him away was the right thing. But I felt a failure as a mother because I had done nothing to defend him. I could only say, and I kept repeating it, "Honey, Daddy is really doing this for your own good. He wants it to be a good experience for you. He thinks you will come home a stronger person."

He looked right at me and said, "I hate him! I just hate him!"

If I ever needed to know how it felt to have my heart ripped right out of my chest, that was the moment.

Shaun stayed only one semester. We learned later that he was in more trouble there than he ever could have concocted had he been in the Beverly Hills school system. Drugs were rampant. He and a friend or two would sneak onto a train, hide in the rest rooms, and spend their weekends in New York, roaming the streets and panhandling for money.

He was fifteen years old. He took a fierce delight in the irony of it, in exposing the folly of his father's decision.

After Jack and I separated, his father tried to regain Shaun's affection, and to an extent he succeeded. He never did make his peace with David, which was so unfortunate for the two of them.

Shaun's feelings about his father improved, but he disliked the weekend visits. Jack could not resist being critical of him, as he had been too long with David. The sloppy look was in; boys spurned suits and ties and crew cuts. If Shaun didn't make A's in school, if he cut classes, he knew he would feel his father's wrath. When he co-starred on the Hardy Boys and had his taste of real success, Jack told Shaun he was proud of him. I don't know if he had ever said so before, nor would he again. He died not many weeks later.

But they talked, and the relationship was better at the end than in the middle. Shaun had no misgivings or guilt about his father, the way David would.

∨∨∨∨

He was a bigger star in his time than his father, a man of stunning talent, was in his. He earned more money in a year or two than his famous stepmother had in her career. David Cassidy became a teeny-bopper idol around the globe, riding the success of *The Partridge Family* on television. While David inched closer to discovering who he really was, the show created a certain confusion among his fans.

"The irony for me," David reflects, "is the fact that during *The Partridge Family* years Shirley really became my 'mom.' To the people who watched us on TV, I became Keith Partridge, and David Cassidy became the son of Shirley Jones.

"And this is really important to me—that Shirley understood how frustrating that had to be for my mother, and she respected her feelings. I was an only child. My mother gave up her own career when she remarried, and she gave it up to raise her son, and I can never thank her enough for that.

"Shirley and Marty had us over for Christmas, so it's a good situation. Having kids of her own, she knows what it means to Evelyn Ward to be recognized as my mother. Shirley didn't try to play that role. She was my father's wife.

"The first time I met her, I was six or seven, and not impressed with whether she was famous. She had been performing in *Carousel.* Now Mickey Mantle would have impressed me. I lived in a small town, and my parents had split up, and I was kind of oblivious to the rest of it. You have a basic resentment because you want your mommy and daddy to be together. I wanted to dislike her, as I guess any child would.

"We met in their apartment in New York. She walked into the room with this beaming smile, bright-eyed, just so warm and real and loving. There was no way you could ever hate this person. The resentment lasted, like, six seconds. I saw who she was.

"Later, coming from my environment, I didn't know if I would like my brothers. I was a product of West Orange, New Jersey, raised by my mother and my grandfather until I was eleven. I was the soloist in the choir, very WASPy, but solid in terms of the values in my life. I grew up very much as Shirley did.

"And my brothers were Beverly Hills High, Brentwood, and movie-star heaven. They came from such a different place and consciousness. I'm nearly nine years older than Shaun, eleven years older than Patrick, and fifteen years older than Ryan, so there was a serious age gap. There had been another life they knew nothing about, when Jack Cassidy was married to Evelyn Ward.

"For a long time, I felt as though they were the family, Shirley and the boys, and I was the guy they let in the door now and then. Probably the way Marty felt, but that was just my insecurity.

"*The Partridge Family* had a lot to do with changing how I felt. I drew closer to Shirley than to my father, because he was having a hard time. He was a brilliant man but frustrated, and his frustration was compounded by the fact that his wife sort of had "it" happen to her, and he was fighting and struggling and could never get over the hump. Then I go into the business at eighteen, and in two years I'm on the cover of *Life* magazine and I've sold twenty million records.

"Where was the justice? After his death, people who knew him would stop me on the street and tell me how great he was. I had people tell me he was a great stage actor, a genius. I would look at them and think, Where were you when he was alive? Why didn't you give him a job?

"It was only in the last few years that he received any real recognition as an actor and a singer. A lot of people never knew what a magnificent voice he had. It took him so long to come up through the ranks . . . he did so many shows and so many musicals. He must have felt humiliated to be 'Mr. Shirley Jones,' but he gave her a lot. I saw it when they worked together. She would always ask, 'What do you think, Jack?' She was the star, but he was the maestro.

"When I became successful, it was tough on him, and Shirley helped me to deal with what he was going through. He was an ultrasensitive, temperamental child in a lot of respects. But I thank him for the gifts that I got from him; that I will always hold on to and embrace. I am indeed very much like him, but I think without the neurosis and the Catholic guilt he had laid on him.

"Shirley and I worked together every day, up to twelve hours a day, for four-and-a-half years. You get to know each other pretty well. That whole experience was remarkable because neither of us knew the other was doing it. There was no fix, no nepotism. I showed up with another guy to test for my part, as you do in television all the time, and I didn't know they had signed her a few nights before. It just happened."

^^^^

Shirley confirms David's version of the event: "My agent then was Ruth Aarons, and she liked the script, as I did. The fact that it was a musical family I felt might work. When

David auditioned, the producer, Bob Claybürg, liked him very much, but he had a reservation. He called me and said, 'Shirley, do you know that David is testing for the role of Keith?' I told him, truthfully, that I did not. He said, 'I don't really like the idea of a mother and son working together, because that could cause problems. How would you feel about it?' I said, 'You needn't worry. He's my stepson. I didn't raise him, and I'm not going to have to baby him. He's an actor, and he's talented, and we have a very good relationship.' So it was almost the other way around. Instead of my helping him get the job, they nearly turned him down because of me."

vvvv

Careers would be made on the show. A pretty young girl who played Shirley's daughter, Susan Dey, would be popular in motion pictures a decade later. But the undisputed winner was David Cassidy, who was all but adopted by *Tiger Beat* and the other teeny-bopper magazines. He was in his early twenties, looked seventeen, and was less than thrilled by the fact.

But there were a number of compensations, including the relationship he formed with his stepmother:

"I was fortunate because there are things you can't share with your mother that I could share with Shirley. And I think we could confide in ways that she couldn't with Shaun and Patrick and Ryan. She is really my friend and I love her, and whether we talk every day, or once a week, or once a year, I always get to the same place with her. I don't ever feel that I have to start over with her.

"I learned a lot just watching her work. I admired her professionalism. She is always so level. I'm more like my old man, volatile. She helped me to deal with the pressure of being successful. She is so very gracious in relating to the public, as my father was. There was a period in my life when I was so hot I couldn't go out, it was just mania. It was in some ways a horror to go through, and I could talk to her about my confusion and paranoia. She was protective of me, and she didn't resent the attention I was getting.

"Tastes in music had changed. It's a cycle. In the seventies, her kind of music was out, then it came back. I love to watch her perform. I love her music, Gershwin, Rodgers and Hammerstein, the themes. To watch her as an artist is a thrill for me. And there was never a time when she couldn't let go of it. She lived for Jack Cassidy. Imagine, she had to be what he wanted her to be, what she was at nineteen. She had to stay the person he fell in love with, and I can only guess at how frustrating that might be.

"And the reason my brothers are as good and as real and as together as they are is because they had a real mother, not a movie star. They had a mother who wanted to drive the car pool and go to the PTA meetings. She never in her life thought of herself as a movie star.

"I feel very close to my brothers. The day our father died, I remember feeling for the first time that we were all one. I walked into the house and I held them in my arms, the three of them, we all had our arms around each other and we were all sobbing. And I felt my father go through me, and it brought us a lot closer together.

"My brothers are great guys, and my father instilled certain things in them. He grew up on Long Island in that Irish-Catholic environment, and for all his style and charm and being a bon vivant sort of guy, he believed there were things more valuable than money, such as family and caring and affection.

"One day I had all of my brothers over to my house. We were sitting around the piano, and I was watching Shaun and Patrick agitate each other. They have this competitiveness between them, which is great. They were pushing each other off the piano bench.

"I was giving them parts to sing, teaching them harmonies. I sing every day of my life. I just do it because I love doing it. I had never heard Ryan sing, and we were having a great time, feeling very close, and I looked over and said, 'Ryan, sing this part.' He started out real soft, and as he got more confident, as he saw that he was fitting in, his singing got stronger, and you could tell he has a good voice.

"And it was interesting to me that he had resisted this gift, and I understood why. You come out of the family of Jack Cassidy and Shirley Jones and then three brothers, it's a little intimidating. There are expectations and your own doubts: Maybe I'm not as good. Not as handsome. Not this or that.

"There is some of my father in each of us. And there is Shirley in all three of them. Patrick reminds me the most of my dad, he even looks like him. Shaun and Ryan I felt had more of Shirley's temperament. Ryan is unusual, extremely sensitive, a really sweet guy. He hears a different drummer. He's turned more inward than the rest of us, more inside himself, in his own world. Shirley says when I was younger, I was much like Ryan.

"I feel close to them. To my stepmother and my brothers. I feel a part of that family, and I include Marty, and I have to tell you, that is a long way for me to come. To call Marty family. But I feel that way about him. I care about him. I admire his moxie, his guts. He can be overbearing, for lack of a better word, but his intentions are good.

"I had a real problem with Marty Ingels because I had a problem about my dad when he died. I never wanted to think about Shirley being with another person. In time, it came down to this: No one has the right to dictate how or with whom we share our lives. When it sank in that my stepmother was happy with the way this man loved her, the friction with Marty began to fade away."

In the telling of these relationships, the story Shirley wrestled with the most involved her youngest son and his trial with drugs. In the end she talked with Ryan and, together, they agreed to include it in the book because, in a sense, this could be any family's story.

Writing or talking about this plague is, of course, a part of the recommended therapy. If what follows helps anyone else to understand how to deal with it, all the better.

Ryan was sent away to a drug rehabilitation clinic. Once there, he very nearly didn't come back. This is a story with no joy in it, no anger, but long months filled with a feeling close to panic. Shirley recalls it reluctantly:

^^^^

If I could say there was any period in my life that I tried to block out, and wanted to erase from my mind, this would be it.

I am not trying to rationalize what happened. But in several ways Ryan had a rough road: an asthmatic child, in and out of hospitals, under oxygen tents; then a learning disability and the pressure of being the last down the line. He grew into a sensitive teen, never feeling that he could be as important as his brothers, or even his mother, his father, or his stepfather.

Unsettling signs kept appearing. I thought he was sleeping more than he should, staying out too late, not doing well in school. Then money was missing, including nearly two thousand dollars from Marty's cash box. Marty decided he must have misplaced it, after blaming everyone but Ryan.

In today's nervous social climate, with any suspicious behavior, one thinks about drugs. Questions were asked and denied. Our eyes contradicted what our hearts wanted to believe. One morning I looked in my purse and, instead of the two fifty-dollar bills that should have been there, I found only one. Ryan had been out with a couple of his friends the night before, and I asked if he had taken the money from my purse. He said no.

Marty looked at me and said, "I think I had better have a talk with Ryan." At that point he had put things together. I left the two of them alone. Marty didn't even have to threaten him. Ryan admitted everything, cried, and said he was sorry he had lied. Finally, Patrick came by one night, went up and ransacked Ryan's room, and found traces of cocaine.

Now, in early November of 1985, the pattern could not be ignored. We wanted to see Ryan as a casual user, but doing so only begged the issue. Small habits unchecked escalate into big ones. Stories and evasions turned into theft. Sweet, innocent Ryan had taken the money, meaning that he was in deep enough to frighten us. I realized then that I had to do something, exactly what I wasn't sure, but it had to be done without delay.

I said, "Ryan, this is very serious, and I think you're going to have to go away for a while. I don't know where, but we need to get you some help."

He said, "Please, Mom, let me stay until Thanksgiving."

I said, "No, you need to go now." I can't explain the urgency I felt. Over the next twenty-four hours, I called doctors, social workers, close friends whose sons or daughters had faced a similar shock. I considered several drug rehab centers and settled on one, called Habilatat, in Hawaii. I told Ryan we were going to leave the next day. Without a word he climbed the stairs to his room. Moments later, Marty knocked on his door and talked to him. I still don't know what they said, but it was one of the few times I ever saw Marty kind of back down.

Gently, he said to me, "Let him leave right after Thanksgiving. He'll miss the Christmas holidays, but let him stay for that." I was secretly relieved to give in.

What drives you is the fear that if you don't do something *now*, what options will you have later, and how much worse will his condition be? I took what I thought was the absolutely toughest route, the hardest choice.

I picked a clinic far from home, with a reputation for an almost Prussian kind of discipline. I needed all of my strength, and most of Marty's, to go through with it. He kept reminding me, "*You gotta do it.*" This wasn't a decision I could put to a vote. The other boys weren't living at home, so they didn't know the extent of Ryan's problem. And, truthfully, I had my own doubts and mixed feelings. There is that long period of time when you are simply not sure.

Four days after Thanksgiving I boarded a plane with my son for the long flight to Hawaii. I had decided on Habilatat for two reasons: I realized Ryan needed to be far enough away that he couldn't walk out and come home, and I wouldn't be running after him. The other reason was they had courses he could take, including vocational training. He could continue his schooling.

No sooner had I checked him in than I almost lost my nerve. I met the director, whose attitude was like a foreign language to me. He was a man who had been a street person, a heroin addict for twenty years. Here I was entrusting him with my beautiful son, still a boy to me, at nineteen.

I was not prepared for how quickly they began to indoctrinate him. The language was direct and raw. They shaved his head. He slept on the floor. He was not allowed to keep anything of his own; no clothing, not even a toothbrush. They sent everything home in a suitcase. In my moist, motherly eyes, the process went beyond culture shock: This was a boy raised in Beverly Hills.

The psychology is that of the military—tear them down and build them back up. As parents, we feel for them, hurt for them, feel tremendous guilt.

What made the experience even harder was the fact that Ryan didn't fight it. He was so passive and yet so scared. When I left, the tears were just streaming down his face. I cried most of the flight home. When I stepped off the plane, I was a basket case, far from sure that I was doing the right thing.

After that, it didn't take much for me to dissolve. Ryan's suitcase was delivered to our door, with all his belongings inside, as if he were dead. We were not allowed to contact him for the first four months, not by phone or mail. It was just as if he no longer existed. I had no sense of his treatment, whether he was being brainwashed or drugged or even where he was kept.

These measures struck me as a program for the hard-core, last-ditch, last-resort, last-chance offenders. This impression, I belatedly learned, was not far off. Ryan had been thrown in with wards of the court, the hard cases.

I didn't have that information at the time, and confused what I knew with an extreme version of the TOUGHLOVE theory. Had I been more deliberate in my research, I might have looked for something a little less Spartan. I did not get to see Ryan until he had been there five or six months. We had talked once on the phone and he had sent me one letter. He said, "It isn't anything I can describe or anything I can even talk to you about. It's rough, Mom, but I'm okay."

I was on a cruise that stopped for a day at Hawaii, and I called the director to tell him I would be there and wanted to see my son. He said they usually didn't let the parents visit their children until they had been there at least a year.

That news floored me. I said, "I'm going to be in Honolulu. I have to see him, if only for a couple of hours." He said they would make an exception for me.

I asked if I could take Ryan off the grounds. He said only if I took two other patients with him. They do that to keep each other straight. They chaperone him, go to the bathroom with him, never let him out of their sight.

When I saw Ryan I was stunned. He was thin as a stick and smoking heavily. He, and his companions, looked as if they had been in prison, or were inmates of some kind of asylum. They were all walking around with shaved heads. He seemed alert, and he tried to explain the methods to me. But his physical condition, and his edginess, alarmed me. I had never seen him so high-strung. He never stopped talking.

They had group therapy every day and fundamentally the staff tried to tear them down to a common denominator. This they accomplished. I was disturbed enough to ask Ryan if he wanted to come home, if he thought he was ready. To my surprise, he said no.

By then I knew the clinic expected to keep him there for two years. When I returned home, I made plans for another trip in December, at Christmas, a reminder that a year had already passed. In the meantime, a couple of kids had been released from the program and stopped by to urge me to get him out of there. They were afraid that if he stayed much longer he would wind up with no will of his own.

I had talked to a few parents who had heard troubling reports of their own. I felt so torn, wondering if Ryan had been beating himself with shame, and worrying that the cure was doing damage of another kind. I called around, trying to find a support group to get me through the coming weeks. I was leaving for Hawaii on the twenty-third. The center called on December 22 and told me not to come.

I asked why, and they said Ryan had disobeyed a rule, had taken a pair of pants that didn't belong to him. He didn't deny the charge. The boys would toss their laundry into a barrel and didn't always get the same laundry back. He said he grabbed a pair of work pants and then realized they weren't his. The staff wouldn't believe him when he said it was unintentional.

He was being punished, and they canceled my trip. I was beside myself. We had the rest of the family over to the house, but Christmas was ruined for me. On Christmas day I told Marty I wanted to talk to Ryan. He said sure, we'd get him on the phone. When Marty called, the person on duty refused to put him through. He was told Ryan was on detention.

As confident as he had been when we acted, Marty at this point was beginning to feel frightened. He insisted on speaking to the director, who said he could not permit Ryan to take the call. Fear turned to outrage. Marty warned him, "I'm going to talk to Ryan if I have to get the police to beat down your doors."

Marty did call the police department, and it sent an officer to the clinic. He called from there and said Ryan seemed well. Marty said he wanted to speak to him. Soon Ryan was on the line, baffled by whatever was going on.

I took the phone and said, "They wouldn't let us talk to you. I wanted to be sure you were okay and we wanted to say Merry Christmas." He said he was fine, not to worry about him, he was only sorry that I couldn't come. Then he added, with a giggle, "When the cop came, he really put a scare into the staff." I said that had been our intention.

We still felt too much in the dark. Every two months, the clinic sent a report, but it was never very detailed. Shaun had gone over once since I had been there and spent a day with Ryan. He concluded that there were some good things about the program, and some bad, but Ryan was healthy and handling it.

After the Christmas day episode, Patrick said, "Mom, I think it's time to get him out of there." I said, "So do I."

He said, "I'm going over. I'll pay my own way, and I'm going to call the director and tell him I'm bringing Ryan home."

I said, "Pat, there's nothing I'd like better. But don't go in like Rambo. You mustn't force him. For his sake, he has to know that he's ready to come home."

He had been there nearly thirteen months when Pat showed up. To his big brother's dismay, Ryan said no, he didn't feel ready. The more Pat saw, however, the more convinced he was that he had to get Ryan out of there. He told Ryan, "Listen, my plane leaves tomorrow. I've got a ticket for you, and I think it's time for you to go. Mom feels the same way and so does Marty."

Ryan kept hesitating. It was as if he thought he'd be copping out, and his friends there would turn on him if he left. At the last minute, as they ate dinner in the cafeteria, Pat tried one last time. He said, "My car is outside, and I'd still like you to come."

Ryan stood up and said to whatever staffer was in charge, "I'm leaving, sir. I'm going home." Everyone in the room turned their backs on him. They form close relationships, they help each other, and a strong bonding process takes place. The administration counts on it.

I was waiting by the phone. Pat told me, later, how Ryan walked up the stairs to get the few belongings he had. He took his shoes off and crawled on his hands and knees into the room. They aren't allowed to walk where the bunks are. He put his belongings in a trash bag and, when he came out, Pat, my big football-player son, said he couldn't hold back. He cried like a baby, watching Ryan do this.

We gathered up the whole family and drove out to the airport in Marty's van to meet them. While we waited, my mind flip-flopped between thinking "Thank God" and fearing that we would be responsible if Ryan had a setback. When he got off the plane with Pat, I could see that his hair had grown back an inch or so. He looked like he had been in boot camp, with a plastic trash bag over his shoulder, wearing torn jeans and a torn T-shirt. It was an unbelievable moment. I didn't know whether to laugh or cry. He looked a mess, but a wonderful mess.

When we reached the house, Ryan went into every single room, touched everything, and cried. It was a scene. I choke up today when I think about it.

For several months after that he had a need to talk about it. There is no doubt in my mind that he was somewhat brainwashed for quite a while. Today he's fine.

Marty and I had to reconcile our own feelings about people who are given a chance to play God. Power takes over, and I have never trusted that. I understand that tenderness will not undo a lifelong drug addiction, and for some the cure really must be as rough as the disease.

I accepted what Pat had said: If they couldn't solve Ryan's problem in a year, they were not going to solve it. I am grateful that he came back to us clean and healthy, but I don't regret bringing him home when we did. Getting a child off drugs, without killing his spirit, should not be mutually exclusive.

I knew Ryan was well when he said, "Mom, I took my family for granted until I was around people who had nobody. For the first time in my life, I realized what a loving family I have . . . a mother who adores me, brothers who love me, a stepfather who loves me. That was what kept me going."

vvvv

12

The Plumber Played Cupid

WHEN THEIR PATHS CROSSED, that day on Michael Landon's lawn, neither Shirley nor Marty was exactly down-and-out in Beverly Hills. The mortgage on her house was paid, and the house was furnished with antiques. Her savings had been depleted, for one reason or another, but she still commanded nice fees when she worked.

With no visible income, Marty lived frugally on his residuals, while in New York his uncle Irving quietly ran up the value of his investments. Money was never a factor in their relationship, neither the lure nor the lack of it. Once Marty moved into the house, they were more likely to differ on matters of convenience, and even propriety.

Marty had put away his shaving and grooming articles and adopted Jack's bath, opposite the master bedroom, as his own. Certain fixtures in the room, unoccupied for two years or more, had fallen into disrepair. And Ingels was meticulous about lists:

~~~~

Each time I found something wrong—a leaky faucet, a broken toilet handle, a drip in the shower—I showed the list to Shirley. I offered to call the plumber myself. She would insist on taking care of it.

One day, Shirley said, "I called the plumber. He's coming tomorrow." Great.
~~~~

The next morning, I heard the van pull into the driveway, and I looked out and saw the sign on the side. I was in my bathroom, shaving, and I immediately unfolded my list and smoothed it out.

I heard Shirley talking to him in the hall, so I waited for him to come in, checking to make sure I had not overlooked any of the leaks or broken parts. I splashed on a little cologne, finished cleaning up, tied the belt of my robe, and admired my reflection in the mirror. And then I heard the sound of a van driving off.

I looked out the window, and he had already swung into the street, heading north to his next clogged drain.

I threw open my door and said, "Shirley, he's gone. What happened? Didn't you tell him about my list?"

She had this funny, sheepish look on her face, almost a blush. She said, "Marty, I've known this plumber for twelve years, and the truth is, I didn't know what to call you, how to introduce you. And . . . and . . . then he left." She raised her hands, palms up, and half-smiled, as if she had no other choice.

I said, "You mean, I'm gonna have to live with a leaky toilet because *I don't have an official name*? Okay. That does it. We have to get married."

And that, more or less, is what happened. There was romance, and a little night music, along the way. In 1977, three years after we had met, Shirley Jones and I were married. A few days later, the plumber came out. I said, "Hi, I'm Marty Ingels, her husband. My toilet leaks."

~~~~

"And they lived happily ever after" is the line that leaps to mind after such an uplifting tale. The truth is, they lived together for a rocky, bumper-car kind of year, with no idea what the outcome would be.

To begin with, Marty made two ghastly blunders in his campaign to win the hearts and minds of her sons. After he settled in, Marty was able to maintain his apartment as an office. It was more than adequate for the purpose: two bedrooms and two baths, renting for a reasonable $590 a
~~~~

month. He kept a desk there, but in the main the apartment served as a backup, a retreat in case he and Shirley fought.

Of course, boys being boys, and Marty being Marty, he soon was slipping the key to Shaun when the young man had a date and needed privacy.

How Shirley found out about this arrangement isn't clear to this day, but the best guess is that something Marty said gave it away. She was furious, which surprised him, which made her even more furious, which led to a long and heated philosophical discussion.

Marty: "He's a young, vigorous boy, and he's got a girlfriend. He's certainly old enough. . . ."

Shirley: "It is wrong for you to be encouraging him."

Marty: "What? Don't blame me. That's nature. Do we fight that every step of the way?"

Shirley: "No, you don't forbid it, but you're not a hotel, and you don't provide him with a room. They have to find their own."

Marty: "That sounds like we're sending him into the streets, telling him to use the back of a car, do it on the beach or in the garage."

Shirley: "Fine, let him. That's the way of nature. Let 'em find their own places. But they are still kids, and you don't make responsible adults out of them by setting up a love nest."

Marty went away puzzled, aware that society had not yet resolved a timeless dilemma. "We are in the middle of a huge shift in what constitutes acceptable behavior. There is the generation that grew up being told you don't do it at all until you marry, and the current one, which says you can have all the sex you want as long as you find a place to do it."

And on he plunged. . . .

~~~~

I was going nuts, wooing the kids to get closer to Shirley and at the same time running the risk of losing her. I did things for them that I had to keep from their mother. Stuck
~~~~

in the middle of that funny maze was my morality and my ethics. So you readily see why I didn't tell her I had also given the key to Patrick.

One day Patrick was with me, I had forgotten my key, and the manager was out. I really needed to get into my desk and Patrick offered to climb up the outside wall. My apartment was on the fifth floor, and there were balconies outside each unit.

Of course, I said no way, out of the question. But Patrick said, "No, I can do it. It'll be great." Before I could stop him, he was edging his way up the side of the building like a monkey. I couldn't believe it. I was shouting, "Be careful, don't slip." It had occurred to me, and I had this brutal vision in my head, what to expect if he fell. I could see myself driving back to the house, and carrying his broken body up to Shirley, and saying, "It's Patrick. He broke his neck. Are you mad at me?"

I stood there, rethinking my approach to life. If anything happened to that kid, I was going to blow a year and a half of intensive courtship. Okay. He made it without a hitch, raised the window, and let me into the apartment. The fact remained, for most people every adjustment, every moment of growth, is maybe two and a half inches high. For me, it was two and a half feet, because I magnified everything I did, everything I saw. That was how I pursued Shirley—and lesser things in my life.

~~~~

In his next misjudgment, Marty was a victim of the times, the times having been turbulent and unclear, as times usually are.

~~~~

A competitor of mine flew in from the East to meet with me in the hope of borrowing money—he must have believed the publicity about the success of my new company (much of which I had generated).

We had talked on the phone, but had never met. He was

tall, very nice looking, tanned, black hair, gold chains, no sense of humor. He had come out of friendship, he said, which lasted right up to the moment I indicated I wouldn't float the loan. "Oh, by the way," he said, "I brought you a present. I don't know what your or Shirley's habits are, but I think you'll like this."

He took out a letter-sized envelope and turned it over, and a small pouch spilled out. Inside was a vial containing a white powder. "This is the best," he said, "A-one gold, terrific stuff." It looks like sugar—so help me—and tucked inside the envelope is a poem on friendship. I had no earthly idea what to say, how to respond, what sense to make of this gesture, whatever it was. He's rattling on about friendship and what prime stuff this is, A-1 gold.

And I don't know if that is a product name or what, and I said, in what he clearly took to be a joke, "Well, great, when I have my coffee, I'll remember that," and is there a B-one quality, too? Then, suddenly, as if I had just witnessed the dawning of the twentieth century, it occurred to me that cocaine is white—like sugar. And I said, out loud, "Holy shit."

I believe he accepted that reaction as a compliment, but I was thinking; I don't do drugs. I don't even drink. What would Miss Manners say? Is it an insult to give back a gift? In certain Hollywood circles, and I suppose even in cities and towns and villages not so sophisticated, it is the ultimate compliment to have a guest bring you a premium grade of dope. And I could guess that it was expensive.

Meanwhile, I still didn't know what to say. In my head, I'm doing comic things: "Great, I'll shove it up my nose, but I won't inhale, so Shirley and I can have it for tomorrow." Instead, I keep raving about the poem, how nice it was, how touching, all about friendship, and he wants to tell me how tough it was finding cocaine of this quality on the street. They have to practically fax it from Colombia.

When my visitor left, I was still unsettled about the encounter and unsure what to do. I only knew that I couldn't keep the details to myself. So I told Patrick, who was then a senior in high school. And his eyes got big as manhole covers. He said, "Marty, can I borrow it? Not to use. But this is prom night."

"What do you mean," I asked, "borrow?"

"To impress people," he said. "It's kind of a status symbol."

As if I were bucking for the Fool of the Year Award, I said, "Listen, I'll give it to you, but bring it back. If your mother finds out, she's going to cut off my balls."

That night, the rest of the boys, David, Shaun, and Ryan, met us for dinner, and I had to open my mouth and tell the story. I get to the part about thinking it was sugar, and everyone was laughing, and suddenly, David and Shaun, being of this generation, looked at each other. "Uh, Marty, you still got any on you?"

"Oh, no, no, no, of course not."

"What did you do with it?"

I feel every eye at the table drilling me, and I said, halfheartedly, "Well, I just, you know, threw it out."

Her voice very cold and steely, Shirley said, "Where—is—it?"

I swallowed and said, "I gave it to Patrick."

"You did what?!!"

"Don't be upset. I gave it to Patrick, but he promised not to use it. It was just a kind of joke."

What a miserable rest of the night that was. All I could think about was what I had done to poor Patrick on his prom night. We get home, and of course no one wants to leave, everyone is waiting for Patrick to come through the door. And if he doesn't have the stuff with him, the feeling in that room was, Shirley is going to bust him for a year. We had agreed to be super-cool when he walked in, talking and joking, but looking for little signs of drug behavior.

But when he walked through the door, the whole family rose en masse and said, "Okay, *where is it?*"

To my relief, he reached into his pocket and whipped out the vial, handing it to his mother with a composure that, under the circumstances, I had to admire.

Only Patrick and I knew that the vial he handed her was not the one I had given him. This one was considerably smaller. That remained our secret for some time to come (or until Shirley reads my half of the manuscript. Of course, I intend to tear this page out of her copy).

~~~~

The courtship of Shirley and Marty zigged and zagged and squiggled, much like an electrocardiogram. And much of the time, her sons were in the thick of the activity, challenging Marty, fencing with him, giving and taking with sometimes hilarious results. Marty makes it sound like a Tom and Jerry cartoon, one side constantly trying to outwit the other:

~~~~

They used to laugh at me because I would make myself sound like Abe Lincoln, talking about how I rode on the back of a shovel through ten miles of snow to get to school. Of course, I lived in the inner city, and walking to school was the least of my worries.

But each of them had chores to do, and I was unyielding in that respect. I believed in giving them a work ethic, and a sense of responsibility. Patrick's job was to take out the garbage. Ryan fed the dogs. Shaun brought in the firewood in the winter. And nothing was ever done when I told them to do it. At least not without an argument.

Patrick was the philosophical one. "Why me, why is it my job to take out the garbage?"

I said, "Look, don't give me that business of why. Why is there air? Just do it, that's all."

"But what if I don't want to do it? What if I really believe I have better uses for my time?"

I said, "Don't challenge me, because there is one thing I am that you are not, and that's crazy, which means you can never win. So when I tell you to do something, do it."

That worked for a certain length of time, and then, one day, Shirley and I had dinner with friends. I mentioned my contests with Patrick, and one of the ladies, a family counselor, chided me. "Oh, you mustn't," she said. "That is a terrible thing to say, it sends absolutely the wrong message. You should take a page out of Moss Hart's book *Act One*.

"Whenever a youngster asked, 'Why should I?'—this was Hart's answer: He looked him right in the eye and replied, 'Because I am taller than you, I am richer than you, and this is my house.' "

"Hey, that's terrific," I said. "I'll remember that." I couldn't wait for the next time one of the boys balked. They foiled me by being on their best behavior the next several days. Finally, my opportunity came when I asked Patrick to put liners in the trash cans. He said, "Why do I have to do this now? I have somewhere to go."

I puffed myself up to quote Moss Hart, and then, just before the words came out, I realized that none of those things applied to me. I was no longer taller than Patrick. He had more money in the bank than I did. And the house belonged to his mother.

So I said, "Because I'm crazy, that's why."

~~~~

The wonder of a good marriage is not that the right people actually find each other, but that they somehow learn of their rightness, in the face of all the evidence to the contrary.

There are, of course, the obvious, minor differences. For one, the room is too warm, for the other too cold. One wants it dark, the other light. One prefers the silence, the other needs the noise.

Says Marty, "I like activity. I sleep with two television sets going and sometimes the radio, and I leave all the lights on. Ideally, Shirley likes a room to be pitch-black, with no sound.

"(She actually hates music when she sleeps, even soft music, because . . . and this is true . . . she keeps thinking of the lyrics, and feels the need to sing them, which evokes the irresistible picture of her leaping up on the bed in the middle of the night and singing 'Climb Every Mountain.')

"Little by little, this is how it starts: 'Honey,' she says, 'if you would turn off one of those lamps it would be nice.'
~~~~

"Then: 'Sweetheart, the ceiling light is in my eyes.' And: 'I can still see the crack of light from under the bathroom door.' Even the light from the now-silent TV screen has to go.

Now, one of my lifelong habits is working at night, in bed. I have a work tray and files, and by this time I was down to a special little sensor light that clipped on the top of a book.

"Still, she twisted and turned and made those whiny little sleep noises. I knew I was in trouble. I needed the newest technology. My secretary found it in the Hammacher-Schlemmer catalog: a fountain pen with a tip that lit up when you pressed down to write. It ran on one triple-A battery. My marriage had been saved. I couldn't wait to try it out.

"That night I turned off everything: ceiling, lamps, bathroom, sensors, all of it. Smiling in the dark, I reached for my clipboard and turned on the pen light. The tiny, two-inch beam was all I needed. I was in heaven until Shirley rolled over, fluffed her pillow, and yawned: 'Please, honey, turn out the pen.'

"Turn out the pen. Now that was unbelievable. I had to give up trying to work in bed."

Then there are the differences not so obvious, or minor.

Shirley has an honest tolerance for unhappy people, for the complaints and petty regrets of others. But everyone has a choke point, and she has hers. She reached it the week that Marty, in his understated way, considered the most critical of their lives—if they were to have one together.

It was the week his patron and surrogate father, his uncle Irving Crown, and his aunt Toby flew to California to meet Shirley and give (or withhold) their approval. "We had been together a year and a half," explained Marty, setting the scene. "We were not married yet, and it was an important time for me. I still can't figure out that side of her, that she would pick that time to make a scene, when I was trying to show her off to my family."

(Editor's note: You know this to be true, and somehow you know Marty will never understand it.)

The night, which was planned around a large family dinner, began with Marty presenting Shirley with roses and reading his card out loud to the guests. Then he led everyone outside, where, at the curb, waited another surprise for his lady, a four-wheel-drive truck. "Now I still had my apartment," said Marty, "and I came from there, and I was late to my own party. My aunt and uncle arrived ahead of me. I burst in and right away started with the gifts, and there was this yellow truck with a ribbon around it. She had wanted one for her cabin in the mountains at Big Bear. I thought she would be thrilled. Instead, I made her feel it was not a gift, just part of a show. I looked in her eyes, and I knew that this was not going to be a good night."

Shirley concurred. "First of all, I came home after filming a scene in a made-for-TV movie called *Yesterday's Child,* in which my character murders her own child. Marty ordered the roses, and he read the card out loud. It was a poem called 'Tuesday's Child.' So I was playing a murderess, not in a good frame of mind, very tense, in no mood for a party, and certainly not in a mood for the kind of display he made of the truck. I hated that. I felt he was doing it to impress his uncle.

"It was the issue we used to fight about the most, his need to make things a production, to do them in public, to ignore someone else's privacy. He would read my mail. I couldn't stand that, and I would really tear into him. Not that I hid anything from him; I shared everything. It was a question of ownership. I do not want anyone to give me that feeling, that they own me. So he couldn't quietly drive the truck around, take me aside, give me the keys. He wanted to make a show of it. He wanted to be thanked for this big present that everyone could see. I mean, how dare he even buy that truck for me, that expensive a gift. I didn't want that kind of commitment yet. Boy, I was ready to give up on him completely that night."

At one point, a subdued Marty Ingels took Shirley by the arm and led her into the backyard. She had gone out of her way, he felt, to ignore him and his uncle. She had planted herself among her friends and made snide remarks about the truck.

Marty: "She wasn't being her, she wasn't being gracious. I said in a whisper, 'I don't understand what's upsetting you.

Please, hit me now. Get it out of your system. This is an important night for me. This man is like my father. This is my family. Hit me, but goddammit, don't make a scene in there.' "

Shirley: "I pulled away from him and said, 'You don't tell me what to do.' I came running inside, and he grabbed me again in the dining room. I went over to his uncle and I said, in a little-girl voice, 'Would you tell your nephew to leave me alone? I can't stand him. I don't like him. And I just want him to leave me alone.' Poor Irving. Oh, God. He took Marty into the dining room for a private talk. His wife, Toby, sat there with her mouth open. They were flying back to New York in the morning, and finally she said, 'Irving, I think we better leave.' And Marty, he was just—"

"Like a bomb had been dropped on me," he said, completing the sentence. "There was this total silence. Nobody said a word. You know, old Jewish people, you have to sweep things under the carpet. No one knew what was wrong. I stood there like a terrible person, and my uncle went into another room and put a pill under his tongue for his heart condition. People just began to disappear. The night was a disaster. I drove my aunt and uncle back to the hotel, and believe it or not, the next morning Shirley got up and we met them for breakfast.

"She said to them, like a dutiful, wonderful lady, 'I want to apologize to both of you for last night.' And they said, 'Last night? What was last night? Something happened? What do you mean, apologize? It was fine, last night, we didn't see nothing.'

"Shirley and I laugh about it now. This was the other side of the coin for her, the independent side, the woman who won't be pushed. We drove them to the airport in her new truck."

"Actually, I was crazy about the truck," she said. "It became my favorite thing."

Of course, she felt the fights were never fair. "He could do something so sweet," she said, "and be so obnoxious about it. But when we fought, it always ended with me either laughing or feeling sorry for him. I would be mad at myself for putting him through it."

Marty was shrewd enough to know that the courtship would never be a safe one; and the blessing of sons and uncles would go only so far. Something else would be needed for him to succeed with Shirley Mae Jones: a sense of his own worth. In short, he needed a job.

Ever since the night of the party for the ski instructor, Marty had been angling for a new career. As an actor and comic, he had burned the bridges and blown up the fuel depot. What now?

The idea for Ingels, Incorporated, celebrity brokers, the first company of its kind, was born the way really good ideas often are—it floated into his lap from out of nowhere. The roots of the business actually dated back to 1972, when an old army buddy named Larry Crane called Marty from New York. He describes Crane as the sort of guy "who could create a need across the country for old shoes."

That night, Larry was somewhat beside himself, calling from a restaurant in New York, where sitting at the next table was the Italian actor and baritone Rossano Brazzi. It had occurred to Crane that Brazzi would be a terrific spokesman for a record package one of his companies was about to produce.

The call puzzled Ingels. "Look Larry," he said, "your net worth is around sixteen million dollars. You have a little white card with your name on it. Go over to the table and introduce yourself."

His friend insisted, "No, that's your thing." He gave him the number of the restaurant and hung up. A few minutes later, Marty placed a person-to-person call to a startled Rossano Brazzi. "Before I tell you who I am, Mr. Brazzi," he said, "you should certainly give me the Nobel Prize for tracking you down."

"*Fantastico! Fantastico!*" agreed the man with the classical looks and voice. "We laughed," recalls Ingels, "which is a great ice-breaker. In less than five minutes, I had made the deal. Now came the punch line. He asked me how we would be contacting him. I said, 'Listen, you're not going to believe this, but after you hang up the phone, my man will tap you on the shoulder and hand you his business card.' "

"*Fantastico,*" Brazzi repeated. He never did figure out

how the arrangements were made, but Ingels had found a celebrity for a friend. In his own mind, an idea was taking shape.

Crane kept calling, asking Ingels to recruit other artists to sell his wares on TV. And so he did, not far removed from the phone on the floor, making deals and delivering stars to Larry in New York. Rudy Vallee, Fats Domino, Buddy Greco, Trini Lopez, Jerry Lee Lewis, Louie Prima, Don Ho, Arthur Fiedler—there was even a Bing Crosby package.

Marty was getting good at it, and Larry was getting richer.

He had quietly noted over the years that companies seeking the services of a celebrity often ran into roadblocks thrown up by agents. Jaded and indifferent, most agents were helpful only in terms of their own client list.

Nowhere was there anything resembling a central, one-step, celebrity service that would have, at its fingertips, every well-known name on the scene. The seeds of such an idea had been in Ingels's mind for some time. His emotional crash had convinced Marty that he was no longer equipped for the performing part of show business. What else could he do? He was always a good talker; putting a phone in Marty's hand was like putting a microphone in Sinatra's—the instrument of choice.

Ingels emptied one of his bedrooms and put in two desks and two phone lines. He was in business. A friend's four-word retort—"No, that's *your* thing"—had redirected him, had given him another incentive, after Shirley Jones, to inch his way up from the floor.

Step-by-step he began what was to be the world's first celebrity brokerage, a service dedicated to cutting through the tangled lines that separated celebrities from celebrity shoppers.

Besides Larry's projects, Marty needed some of his own. A friend at *Advertising Age* (the Madison Avenue bible) did a brief story on the new celebrity tracker, and the two phones started ringing off the wall. At first, they were mostly public service requests from nonprofit causes that wanted famous pitch-people for their TV spots. Ingels knew it was a starting point from which a reputation could bloom, and he went right to the top:

He lined up Robert Mitchum for the Job Corps, Burt

Lancaster for UNESCO, and John Wayne, for the American Cancer Society. He was on his way.

The next call was to be his most ambitious test yet (and nobody called Ingels now, unless he had tried it first and struck out). Lincoln Continental wanted Orson Welles for a series of magazine print ads. One day's shoot. Good money. Quality exposure. Why not?

The problem was finding Welles, a legend ever since he wrote and directed *Citizen Kane*, but by now a virtual recluse, always in some remote or far-off place.

For openers, Ingels made the usual calls and got nowhere. Then his stage two list. No luck there either. He kept calling until he reached an old grouch in New York who handled certain business affairs for Welles. Ingels laid out the proposal. The old man cleared his throat and harumphed a few times, said he would run it by Welles and get back to him.

For Ingels, that answer wasn't nearly good enough. He knew that wherever this mountain of a genius was hiding, there had to be a phone nearby. Indirection was never Marty's style. He remembered that Welles had recently hosted a Dean Martin "roast" that had been taped and edited for television. He rang up the Martin office, and explained his problem to a sweet old dear who liked Marty's raspy voice.

"Well," came the reply, "we can't give out Orson's private number. But if you tell me where you are, and if you can stay there for twenty minutes, I think you'll be in luck." Nineteen minutes later, the phone rang. It was Orson Welles.

Marty made his pitch. When he hung up the phone, he had closed his deal.

It was so sweet, so easy, Marty began to believe that there was room, perhaps even a need, for an aggressive, bare-bones, get-it-done celebrity headhunter. At the moment, Ingels, Inc., was one guy with a phone line, but the future was beckoning.

He had all but forgotten the old prune in New York, when he heard from him nearly three weeks later. His message was brief. "Regarding that print ad for Orson Welles," he said. "I had met with him, and there is no way he would be available for that kind of campaign."

Normally, such news would have left Marty a hollow shell, but he knew something the caller did not: Orson Welles had completed the photo shoot eight days earlier.

There were other, more basic obstacles. Hollywood's agents, big and small, were instantly suspicious, and opposed him on general principles. No one knew whether to classify Ingels, Inc., as a talent agency or an employment agency. He called himself a talent broker, and he differed in this crucial way from the standard agencies: He charged only the people who bought the talent.

The first few years just about covered the bills. By the time Marty and Shirley were married in 1977, the business was turning the corner. Halfway through the eighties, he was operating one of the most successful endorsement-promotion companies in the world. (The list of stars Ingels, Inc. has connected to advertising campaigns runs into the thousands, from Jimmy Stewart and Joan Collins and Arnold Schwarzenegger to Muhammad Ali and Scott Carpenter and Joe Montana.)

Marty Ingels was a long way from the floor.

Marty even stumbled into a second career in 1980. He came back to the public ear, if not the public eye, as the voice of Pac-Man, a cartoon favorite of millions of American grade-schoolers.

Of course, he thought he was through with that end of show business. His return was the kind of fateful accident that seemed to characterize so much of his world. He was sitting at his desk one morning, hustling one of his clients, Robert Culp, who had starred with Bill Cosby in the *I Spy* series. He heard Universal was casting a film, and he dialed what he thought was the studio's number. He was a digit or two off, and instead he reached Hanna-Barbera, the producers of animated cartoons and other Disneylike features.

Instead of hanging up, Marty figured why waste a phone call? He asked who their casting director was, and the operator put him through to a man named Gordon Hunt. No sooner had he introduced himself than a baffled Ingels heard Hunt tell him, excitedly: "You know, after two years of trying, we finally landed the rights to Pac-Man."

Here's Marty with the rest of the story:

~~~~

And I said, "Wow!" I had not the foggiest idea what Pac-Man was. For all I knew, it was a luggage company. So I said, "Well, that's wonderful," and he goes on: "We have all the other characters, Pac-Baby and Mrs. Pac-Man and the ghost monsters, and the only person we don't have is Pac-Man himself. It's very difficult. We've listened to a hundred and seventy-three voices, and it has to run through all these approvals."

He mentioned this whole bureaucratic system: ABC, and the top brass at Hanna-Barbera, and Bally-Midway, the company that owned the patent, and a little Oriental man in Hong Kong who invented the machine.

So I said to him, "Robert Culp would be sensational for you." And Hunt said to me, "Would you say that again?"

I said, "Say what again?"

"What you just said, the thing about Culp."

I repeated myself: "Robert Culp would be perfect for the part." I felt as confident as one can feel, without knowing anything at all about the part itself.

Hunt asked me what I was doing at that moment. I told him I was sitting in my office. He got as far as "Could you come down to—" and I cut him short. I said "I don't come anywhere. I don't go anywhere."

He said, "Well, I would like to put your voice down on tape, because I think you have a great voice."

I said, "You don't understand. I don't compete anymore. I don't get disappointed anymore. I don't get hurt anymore. I don't have to shave anymore. I hang around in my pajamas all day. I don't have to be Tom Selleck or Robin Williams or anybody."

It turned out he was taping my voice while we were talking. Two days later, my secretary said, "A Mr. Gordon Hunt, with Hanna-Barbera, is on the phone." I said, "Yeah, that's the guy who may have a job for Robert Culp."

I picked up the phone and said, "You find anything for Culp?" He said, "No, but I have a job for you, starting tomorrow at ten o'clock in the morning."

During the nearly two years it lasted, Pac-Man turned
~~~~

out to be a dream job. I could drive to the studio in my pajamas and do three weeks' worth of voice-overs in one afternoon. I made more money as a cartoon than I did in my entire career as a comedian.

~~~~

It seems only fitting that the symbol of Marty's business success, his most remembered personal triumph, would be one of his few product failures. He received an otherwise routine call one day from a company that wanted to hire Cary Grant to narrate a documentary on the American presidency. Marty swung into action.

~~~~

I told my office people to get in touch with Grant any way they could. He always kept a low profile, so we knew we would probably run into a layer or two of the talent reps who shielded him. I said, Just tell them you think it is a good, patriotic assignment and would be done with taste.

The next day, we had been in touch with Cary Grant's right-hand man. I assured him, "It will probably be all narration, just voice-over, with a shot or two on camera to establish him. Of course, they'll shoot it any way he wants."

One day later, my secretary answers the phone, I see the blood drain from her face, and her voice goes up nine octaves. She said, "Uh . . . uh . . . Cary Grant, on four. He wants to talk to you."

My voice only went up seven octaves. "For me? What would he want to talk to me about? Have someone else talk to him."

This was ridiculous, of course. I'm as star-struck as my secretary, and literally tongue-tied at the idea of talking to Cary Grant. This was eight or nine years before his death. He was turning seventy-five that week, still the symbol the world over of style and elegance.

It wasn't possible to hear that distinctive accent without feeling as though you were listening to someone imitate him. "Hello, Marty? Cary here. How are you? I have been wanting to tell you, I read a story about your courtship, you and Shirley, and I cried. Yes, I truly cried. I love Shirley dearly, and the things you did, the crazy ideas, they were just wonderful."

Before I could sputter a polite response, he went on: "Now, Marty, on this other thing, I'm going to turn you down. It's a documentary about the American electoral process, as I understand it. And you know, people still think of me as a British subject. I don't think it would be right, for many reasons, for me to do it."

For reasons not entirely clear to me, I was relieved.

"But there is something I want to talk to you about," he said. He asked if he could drop by the house in the morning around eight, before he went to the racetrack. Of course, he was on the board of directors at Santa Anita.

I said we would be delighted to have him, but I was thinking, Why don't I come to his house? I'll bring in his milk. His newspaper. I'll mow his lawn.

The next morning, as I waited for him to arrive, I thought how hard it must be to convince people who you were, once you achieved a certain stature. "Hello, Domino's Pizza? This is Cary Grant. . . ."

He arrived in a silver Mercedes driven by his lawyer. Grant was wearing a cashmere sweater, and the tanned face, under the perfectly groomed white hair, looked twenty-seven. He had appeared in films with both Jack Cassidy and Shirley, and when she joined us, the conversation flowed easily.

I wasn't quite sure in my own mind how we were going to shift into the business talk. I wasn't certain what he had on his mind, although I thought I might be able to guess. Then I heard Shirley say, "So, you want to do a commercial, Cary?"

I couldn't believe it. You are supposed to bring up that subject with some delicacy, especially among stars of another era, to whom the idea still seemed offensive. He put down his coffee cup and said, "Well, to tell you the truth, I have been thinking about it. And that's what I wanted to discuss with Marty."

He said he wanted to find the right kind of commercial, something to do with progress. He brought with him an envelope stuffed with articles about General Electric—"Better Living Through Chemistry." The idea of progress excited him. He talked about plastic alloys. He picked up the gadgets on our kitchen table.

At one point, he went into one of the guest bathrooms, and when he came out, he said, "My, what a wonderful thing you have there. People don't do that anymore. The most marvelous thing." I tried to remember what was in there that could possibly have impressed Cary Grant. Well, yes, we did have a sink and a toilet in each bath. . . .

"That's such a nice touch," he said, "keeping a hanger behind the door. If you wear a jacket, there is no place to hang it. I told them at the racetrack, they ought to have hangers in the rest rooms."

I ended up going to a special place and having a gold-plated hanger made for Cary Grant to keep in his bathroom. He called to thank me, and said, "You're so resourceful, Marty. Where do you find such things? What a wonderful gift."

The kicker to this story is the fact that I could do nothing for him. I could not find a company interested in having Cary Grant as its spokesman, which tells you where we had come to as a country. People who sell products in America want them identified with the average schlepper in the street. Cary Grant was never a person you could describe as average. Most of us wouldn't feel that we belonged within the same cosmos.

Robert De Niro can speak to the guy in the street. Robert Blake. Betty White is everybody's housewife. Shirley can do it. But Cary Grant, who would identify with him except for a few members of Parliament and some multimillionaires who travel on their own corporate jets?

I tried desperately to make a connection with Hallmark Cards, thinking he would be perfect for them—"When you care enough to send the very best." Hallmark, I learned, didn't use celebrities. Nor do the products with the most prestige even advertise on television. Not Rolls-Royce. Not diamonds from Tiffany.

I couldn't listen to him or look at him without thinking of *Gunga Din*, or *North by Northwest*. And it bothers me still that in a society obsessed with celebrities, I failed to find a company that needed Cary Grant. It must not have been a very good year for a quality called class.

~~~~

As Ingels involved himself more and more in the business, into following up calls, developing leads, adding to his client list, the staff grew to eight—including, at one point, Larry Crane, the man whose call from a New York bistro started it all. The Cassidy boys, repelled at first, began to take an interest in what he was doing.

"He was on the phone all day, every day," said Patrick. "I couldn't stand it. Half the time he was shouting at someone. He sounded like a used-car salesman."

Marty had taken over a desk in a corner of the study, where the piano was. Shaun would wander in, sit at the piano, and idly peck out a few notes. Whenever a moment of silence intruded on the room, he would ask, "Can I play now?" And most of the time, Marty would growl, "No, I'm doing business."

Then an interesting turn took place. Shaun became curious, and Marty began to explain what he did, and how, and the strategy, when there was one, behind the shouted conversations and the occasional calmer ones and the flowers and gifts he often ordered by phone. And in time, Shaun, followed by the others, would go to him and ask, "Ingels, what should I do?"

And, of course, something else happened of equal or greater consequence to change the standing of this displaced person who had moved into their home. Each of the boys fell in love. "And for the first time," said Marty, "they began to look at Shirley and me through those eyes."

Her movies, his deals, their families, the wins and losses, the gift-wrapped trucks, a Cary Grant, the parade passed. After a year and a half of courting, and another year and a half of living together, Shirley Jones and Marty Ingels were married in August 1977.

In keeping with the welding and blending of their two different worlds, the wedding was half-secular and half-re-
~~~~

ligious. The ceremony was performed under a *chuppa* (a canopy) in the elegant Bel Air Hotel, with a rabbi presiding—and the men of the wedding party wearing the yarmulke, or skullcap, of Jewish tradition.

Shirley: "Marty wanted the rabbi, and I thought that was fine. I objected at first to the yarmulkes, only because the rabbi said they were not required. That was the only point we had any disagreement about, and I gave in. Obviously, Marty was not an orthodox Jew. He was not marrying a Jew, and I had a minister there, too. Still, he wanted a certain amount of tradition. This was his way of making up for the last thirty years of not going to the synagogue, and the fact that his first marriage was first performed in his living room."

Marty: "In the Jewish religion, you want to have a rabbi. That was the big thing. Her family was not going to be offended. She was a little uncomfortable about the hats. I assured her that there was nothing in yarmulkes that would seep into their brains. They would still be able to have children."

Shirley: "It was an authentic Jewish wedding, with the crushing of the wineglass at the end of the ceremony. We had fifty to sixty people, as intimate as we could keep it, and the whole thing was just lovely. Shaun gave me away, Ryan and Patrick were our attendants, and my goddaughter, Sari's daughter, Nancy, was my maid of honor. That was the key decision. I had several women friends, but only one had a daughter. Sari had been my maid of honor when I married Jack."

Marty: "My uncle Irving was my best man. My mother and brother were there. I didn't know the rabbi, so I wrote out what I wanted him to say about us, how these people had met at a time when the world said no, and they said yes. It was just beautiful. I wrote it in the second person, and I told him to read it as though he were saying these fine sentiments—but I forgot to tell the rabbi not to mention that I wrote it. So, right away, he says, 'This wonderful speech was prepared by the groom,' and I have to admit, it was hysterical. Nothing else mattered after that because, when he said, 'This remarkable person,' and 'this loving husband,' every word was an embarrassment.

"And then, as I stood in front of the rabbi, suffering for my sins, there was a blissful moment of pure elation. I happened to glance over my shoulder, and there were all these Irish Cassidy kids, David, Shaun, Patrick, and Ryan, watching so intently, faces like angels, all of them wearing a little white yarmulke.

"For me, that was happiness, fulfillment. That was acceptance."

The Pushkie

IN JEWISH LORE, the *pushka* fund was a way of tithing. Going back to the Inquisition, to the Russian czars, and the pogroms, and possibly back to Moses, Jewish families kept a can around the house into which they would drop spare change. The money would go to the poor, to those less fortunate; later to build trees in Israel, in special cases to be tapped in times of personal emergency.

Tevye in *Fiddler on the Roof* had a *pushka* fund, and the Woody Allen character in *Radio Days* was slapped around by his rabbi and his parents for blowing his on toys or candy.

This is an account of how this tradition—called a "*pushkie*" by some practitioners—helped solidify, in a roundabout way, the marriage of Shirley Jones and Marty Ingels. It is all true, sometimes funny, and to those who knew of it, the effect was an uplifting one, surprisingly so.

Not that Marty ever thought he would need a fallback position, but. . . .

~~~~

Money always had a curious place in my life. It was never "an end," as it is with so many others. And there were never any extravagances I couldn't live without. But I knew from the first, as I watched my father live and die without it, that money was a must, that it was freedom and independence
~~~~

and power. It also meant dignity and peace, and I needed that.

Watching those sad old actors hanging around Schwab's Drug Store, living in some faded past and waiting for casting calls they knew would never come, made me more sure than ever: There had to be money.

Finally, falling in love with an American princess, only to find that her first marriage had left her close to busted and ready to sell her home of eighteen years, made me crazy. I could never let that happen.

But just how was I going to prevent it? I had my comic's savings stashed in New York with my uncle. (It made me a rich kid in my singles complex in West Hollywood, but on Oakhurst Drive in Beverly Hills, I was a peanut.) On top of that I was starting out, fair or otherwise, in the public dog house. I had been tagged as the slick Jewish hustler moving in on the naïve shiksa to tap her fortune and leave it at the racetrack. They had me cast as Nicky Ornstein in *Funny Girl*. The so-called Hollywood crowd thought I had found my perfect meal ticket, when nothing was further from the truth. The little I had saved was more than Shirley had; her career had been neglected and, without a plan, we were both headed for the Actor's Home. There had to be money.

The house was all that Shirley really owned. And she was set on leaving that to her boys. So we put together a prenuptial agreement, making her house and what I had in New York separate and independent resources, exempt from all the other community assets (of which only we knew there were none).

With all the sweet daffiness of our courtship, Shirley had her private doubts about us. While her heart still ruled, it was hard not to hear the cynical, strident voices around her.

And so she tested me, maybe even without knowing it. Little fights about nothing, but clear messages that she was her own person. She doesn't throw things up to you; she is very good about that. But there were times when I had my luggage in the hall, and she said, "Please close the door on your way out." Funny. She loved me, but emotionally, deep down, she would never let herself be Jack Cassidied again.

Once during a mindless squabble we went to the usual grounds. I said, "Yeah, you don't care if I do leave." And she said, "I care, but that has to be your decision." Then, very softly, she said, "By the way, it is my house, you know."

Something automatic went off in my head. She had the house. Any trouble along the line, and I was back in my skimpy little condo. Immediately, I saw myself as Larry Flynt and a nurse is rolling me out in a wheelchair. I'm Gary Morton holding Lucille Ball's coat.

No, sir. I couldn't let that happen, either. I needed a way to protect myself. And I decided right then to start a secret *pushkie* for me, my own little Marty Ingels mad money, my Save-Me-from-the-Midnight-Mission crisis fund.

~~~~

Marty approached his *pushkie* as he did most of his projects—with energy and imagination. His plan was based on a concept alien to most people. "I have a special way of doing things," he says. "I believe in giving to yourself first, and *then* paying all the bills second. You *have* to pay your bills. Society makes sure of that. No phone payment, no phone. No car payment, no car. But nobody forces you to put money away for yourself. That is the last thing most of us do. So you end up paying all of your bills, and you are stuck with nothing.

"But try it the other way: If a check for four thousand dollars came in, and you could force yourself to put three in the bank and live on the one, even if it meant having to go out and hustle up three more to pay bills, you'd be moving toward real solvency. You do that ten or twenty times and suddenly you have money tucked away producing sweet little baby monies. Now the fun begins."

When a friend told Marty about the *pushkie* tradition, Ingels laughed: "Imagine that. I've been practicing Jewish folklore all my life and I never knew it." Marty had been hiding money all of his life. He just never knew there was a name for it:

~~~~

The *pushkie* takes a lot of forms and leaps across ethnic boundaries. Jackie Gleason used to keep twenty-dollar bills hidden in various New York subway toilets, taped under sinks. W. C. Fields's nameless and numbered accounts in Switzerland are show business legend. So people do that for security.

I needed a plan. And I gave myself some tough rules; I would take no money from any of Shirley's income. Nothing that came in officially, on the books. Any cash given to us for anything was fair game. If I had lunch with four friends and three of them paid their share in cash, I picked it up and put the bill on my credit card. If I charged Shirley's travel on my American Express card, I had the promoter reimburse me with cash. If I gave someone a loan, I wrote a check and got it back in cash.

Whenever I saw green, zap, it went into the treasury. Gifts, prizes, purchase refunds, anything we sold, zap, out of sight. And, of course, interest on anything accumulated anywhere was gold.

It was not only neat, it was safe and sound and 100 percent legal, yet totally unrecorded. And untraceable. No hotshot divorce lawyer could ever come in and point any larcenous fingers at me. There would be no Doris Day and Marty Melcher stories in this house, no widow waking up one morning to discover that her husband had left her nearly bankrupt.

I started with a little metal box I kept under my desk. Six or seven weeks later, I opened the box to find inside almost eight thousand dollars in cash. Jesus, this could turn into serious money. By the end of that month, I needed a bigger box. Soon, it got to be fifteen thousand. Too risky to keep at home, but I couldn't open any bank accounts. Even safety deposit boxes can be tracked.

Remember, this was all money that had been earned, spent, taxed. I wasn't concealing anything from the government, only from Shirley and the kids, so I thought. This was another of my comic nightmares. Her will provided that, if she died, the boys had to let me stay in the house the rest of my life. I pictured them keeping me upstairs in the Anne Frank room.

Months went by. Then a friend told me how he was preparing himself for the Big War (or the Big Quake, or any great upheaval). Banks would be out, the economy would be shaky, paper money worthless. Gold would be the only negotiable form of trade—bullion, coins, even jewelry. On top of that, it was a good investment. Gold and silver prices were rising. When the cash was about to overflow the box—fifty thousand dollars' worth—I went to one of those metal marketplaces and put all of it into gold and silver. The dealer helped me carry out sixteen bags of coins. I could hardly lift them into the trunk of my car.

They stayed there until Shirley's next trip, then I slowly and tediously dragged the bags one by one up to the attic. It took forever.

I hid them behind the luggage pieces and covered them with old tax records. The attic was not a solid floor. The ceiling was attached to beams spaced across the sheetrock, with beds of soft insulation in between. I sat the bags along the beams. One night in bed, I looked up to see a crack in the ceiling over our heads. When I climbed into the attic, I saw that three bags had toppled off a beam and dropped to the ceiling.

I thought, "Shit, I can't have a bag of silver falling on Shirley."

The attic was out now. I sold the coins for just about what I paid for them, and began to look for another location. I had been seeing newspaper ads for private security boxes. No government link, no big facade. Just a little store-type place with gates and guards and special keys and code machines that admitted you into the box area. So I rented a box and locked my money in there, and as I drove out of that shopping center in the valley I wondered: What is to keep whoever owned the place from packing it all up one night, all those people's valuables, and fading to Argentina?

One day, I drove by (I used to do that from time to time to reassure myself), and there was a pizza parlor where the safety box place had been. I had apoplexy. Worse. I didn't know who to call. A few days later I received a notice that they had moved, apologizing for the secrecy, which was necessary for security.

But that was it for me. I took everything out of there. Had to find another option.

Someone said "tax-free bonds." My loot was growing. (Out-of-town cash-per-diem monies on location shoots became another bonus.) So tax-free bonds sounded great. (You are actually loaning dollars to municipal projects all over the country, on which they pay you tax-free interest.) There are no deposits and no withdrawals. They just send you the numbered bond, which you keep wherever you want. Nobody knows you have them. And, to top it all off, it's insured by the federal government. It was perfect.

So I began buying these bearer bonds. They came in five-thousand-dollar increments. Whenever the metal box under my desk got full, I called my bond man and told him to find me something. Then he'd call me back and describe the bond. I'd approve and we were off to the race.

What amazes me even now is how good I was with my plan. I was obsessive. There were times I was sitting with up to twenty thousand dollars in my drawer, and my bookkeeper would call about being overdrawn at the bank, and I'd go through all sorts of gymnastics to find the eight or nine thousand I needed to cover. But go to that drawer? *Never.* It was like a different color money to me. The instant I put it in the box, it was gone. And it just kept growing.

Here's where the story takes a weird left turn. Without knowing it, little by little, I had become so good at my Marty Ingels Security Fund game that I lost sight of the fact that my marriage had become too sound and solid to *need one.* Shirley and I had virtually melted into one person. There was almost nothing we didn't share. And, suddenly, the thought, the possibility, of our splitting—or certainly *fighting* about who got what if we *did* split—was outrageous.

So what now? What about my beautiful *pushkie?*

Well, I didn't want to just blow it all at once. Too much time and effort had gone into making it. What I did was adjust my brain a little, still keeping this meticulous plan, now grown into impressive numbers, a secret, but now seeing it as the Marty *and Shirley* Security Fund. There was only one problem there: Shirley had gotten so used to overhearing me struggling to "pay the bills," hustling to move this amount to cover that overdraft, and this check to wait for that deposit, she was convinced we were destitute. I hated that.

But I also didn't want to tip my surprise (no, "our" surprise). It made for some absurd moments.

There was the time we were at Sloane's to buy a new couch for the den. The one she liked was "entirely too expensive," so she walked away to look at another one.

"What are you doing?" I asked.

"We'll get the beige couch," she said. "It's fine."

"Why not that nice white one?" I asked.

"It's way too expensive."

"No, it's not."

"Yes, it is."

"I'm telling you, Shirley, *it's not too expensive*!"

This went on and on, my voice getting sterner and sterner, and Shirley getting more confused. Finally, I just walked her over to the white couch, sat her down on it, and called the salesman.

"We'll take this one," I said.

There were very few times in our marriage that I made such dogmatic noises, and Shirley knew that. She had no idea what was going on—or that, in some other place across town and down the street, we were loaded.

I tried explaining it in the car, without giving it away:

"You see, Shirley," I said, "you have to trust me on some things. Money is a game."

"You don't play games with money," she said.

"Yes, you do. That's the only way you win. And when the game is over, all those bankers and tailors and milkmen you put on hold along the way will be right there at your victory party with their hands out, kissing your shoes, with absolutely no memory of those bad old times."

Shirley was quiet. Still confused, no doubt. But quiet.

And so, in the Ingels's household, it gradually became known to everybody that Marty had a secret.

A few times there, when the kids had a serious squeeze (one was for $38,000) I mysteriously appeared with the cash. And wonderful as that was, it produced another complication: If it didn't come from money Mama knew about, it had to be money Mama DIDN'T know about. And that meant Ingels was stealing from Mama.

That did it. I had to come clean. Not the *secret*. Only the *name* of the secret. (And it took me the better part of six weeks to teach all those confounded Gentiles how to just pronounce *pushkie*.)

And so, the on-going family joke, when any money came in to anybody for anything that had to be passed through me, was: "And where is *this* gonna end up, Ingels? In the *pooshky?*"

Shirley would hand over some expense money and say, arching an eyebrow, "Where is this going, Martin, into your"—pause—"*pishkie* fund?"

Of course, the ongoing, burning question was *How much?*

The truth was that I wasn't sure myself. I had instructed my bond guy never to tell me the total. And I never checked my monthly statements. I had given him some outlandish figure way back at the beginning, and said, "Just call me when we hit it."

By now I was promising everybody that we would have a grand and glorious *pushkie* party one day and reveal everything.

The next part really gets eerie—like there was some kind of *pushkie* fairy up there pressing all the buttons and making all the phones ring.

A week later mine rang. It was my bond guy calling—five years, almost exactly to the day, since my first little cash deposit. I had started on December 12, 1982.

"Guess what?" he said.

"Don't tell me," I said.

"Yep. You got it," he said.

Wow. Yippee. Hallelujah. And I'll be a son of a bitch. I had reached my goal. Keep in mind, we had done this during a period when Shirley did not have a network television show, and I wasn't Michael Jackson. Now I had to have my party.

I set to work on it, probably with the same energy and intensity I had given the *pushkie* itself. But now there was joy and excitement and surprise. Now there was victory.

I couldn't have done any of it without my "runaround" girl, Jhoni. She was in on everything from the beginning, and I put her onto the task of setting up my whole choreographed production.

First we reserved the banquet room at Yamato's, my favorite party restaurant (little private rooms with curtains, long, low Oriental tables). We arranged party-favor settings for each guest—piggy banks, little rolls of money, chocolate coins, miniature *Wall Street Journals*. There was a special pad and pencil at each place, for later. And, on the entrance arch, a giant hanging banner that said, in big green letters, MARTY'S *PUSHKIE* PARTY."

Then, the show: At one end of a long, low table was a natural raised stage. On either side of it I had placed a large black easel, covered over with green silk drop cloths. And in the center, my podium, on top of which was a big glass bow and beneath that a broad cardboard box. Behind the podium, the entire wall was cleared for the main attraction (for which the contents of the broad box waited):

Nine green eighteen-inch vinyl numbers
Two green three-inch commas
One green half-inch period.

Jhoni had spent two weeks trying to find the prerecorded sound of a great Buddy Rich drumroll, finally having to get a drummer friend to cut one live for us. Then, a tape of Sousa's "Stars and Stripes Forever." And we were ready.

When my party arrived, nineteen in all, they were ushered into the room, shoeless, of course. I got up to explain why they were there and just what a *pushkie* was. I went through the whole genesis; why I did it, how I did it, why it changed, how Shirley didn't know—and explained that it was now time to reveal how much I had been able to put away in exactly five years.

Act One: *I wanted them to guess exactly what that figure was*. (Hence the pad and pencil.) And on the second page, another guess, as close as they could come, to exactly how much the dinner tab would be.

Prize for the *pushkie* guess: $1,000
Prize for the dinner guess: $500

The guess sheets were collected and placed in the bowl on the podium, and it was cocktails and music.

Some minutes later, Jhoni, poised and ready at the tape machine, hit the button, and the first of a series of extended drumrolls, spaced at twenty-minute intervals, startled the room. I walked up to hang the first green number on the wall, way over to the right, to make room for the others upcoming. Twenty minutes later, and I was at the wall with the second number. Now we had forty-four cents on the wall.

A few more drumrolls and we had:

9,856.28

BY 10:00 P.M., the figure was $49,856.28—and the crowd was starting to wonder if that was all. We held the next roll to *thirty* minutes, just for fun, and then we hit it:

$149,856.28

—and I said that was it. That was the figure. There were hoots and howls, some cheers, a few puzzled faces.

"I really thought it would be more, Ingels," Patrick said.

"Hey," I said. "You think it's *easy* to do that from *cash?* Saving twenties and fifties and hundreds at a time? *You* try doing that. See if you could even get *near* a hundred sixty-eight thousand dollars!"

He bought it, maybe. Then we all settled down and ruffled through the guess sheets to see who won the grand. Suddenly above all the buzz and clamor, Jhoni hit the drumroll again. Everybody stopped. Wide eyes. Total silence. Could it *be?*

I shuffled to my feet and started toward the wall as Jhoni hit the switch and drowned the room in "Stars and Stripes Forever." It was some scene. I walked to the stage, and to the box for the last comma and the final unthinkable number:

$1,149,856.28

And, with that, I ripped the two easel cloths off to reveal a pair of newspaper headlines:

UNLIKELY JEW HITS BIG ONE

and

SHIRLEY JONES MAKES EARLY RETIREMENT

The place went absolutely cuckoo. One million dollars, from funny little nickels and dimes. Even the Cassidy boys, who had *seen* millions in their hot rock days, were incredulous.

"How the hell did you swing *that?*" they said. "It's unbelievable."

And soft, quiet, not very street-smart Ryan, juggling his little dollars every week to make ends meet, took me aside and whispered in my ear, "Say, Marty, would you show *me* how to do it?"

Shirley was stunned, for real. Everyone, of course, thought she knew. But she kept shaking her head and swearing, "I had no idea." (Shirley, who knows me better than anyone on earth, had guessed $450,000.)

The next explanation was to all the people who cupped their hands to their mouth and hushed out the dire warning: "Be careful of the IRS."

"You still don't get it, guys, do ya?" I said. "This is not *dirty money.* It's not washed Mafia loot, unearned dollars the IRS doesn't know about. And that's what makes the total figure even more astounding. It's all clean and has already passed whatever reporting requirements were needed. It was Shirley I was hiding it from, not the government."

And that's the way it went. We laughed and marveled and hugged and drank. Shaun's mother-in-law wept. I gave out the dinner-tab prize. And everybody made dumb jokes when I paid the bill and tried to figure the tip.

And we all went home in a kind of Disneyland tooth-fairy dazzle. Shirley, stunned, happy, and proud of her crafty husband, was still half-rattled for all those white couch times when she thought she had to squeeze her pennies.

~~~~

You might find this a curious, maybe even unseemly, way to end a book about two people, fated to pass through their storms and fall in love. And neither of whom was very good with money. But this is the point that Marty makes:

~~~~

Life is always a series of tomorrow goals: "I'll get mine, I'll put my feet up, and I will have arrived." Nobody ever says, "This is it, I'm done." Somehow, Aaron Spelling gets up in the morning and fights to put one more show on the air. Donald Trump gets up in the morning and wants to battle Merv Griffin one more time to take over a hotel or casino or office tower.

I once thought, If only I could get a million dollars, boy, then I'd be able to get up each day and enjoy how nice the house looks when you're not working in it. The pool would look clearer; in thirteen years, I had been in it twice, and once because I slipped and fell in.

And I reached the goal and, sure enough, our lives didn't change except in one major way. If Shirley wants to turn down a movie or a series she doesn't like, she can do so. And while it had nothing to do with my socking away the cash and the coins and the bonds, during the five years I chased that goal, the marriage just got better and better.

I thought I wanted the money for the dreams my father missed and the ones all the losers never reach. I wanted it for my own security and peace, neither of which I had.

Then, along the way, I learned that, sweet and grand as they were, the reasons had changed. It was no longer for my father. It was no longer for inner peace. In fact, it was no longer for me. It was now for *us*, my wife and me, the *us* I was never really sure of.

The *pushkie* story was my Christmas gift that year to Shirley. Later, the night of the party, she said, and her eyes were a little moist, "No, Marty, that's your money."

I said, "Shirley, you don't understand. We've gone way beyond that. This is *our* money."

And, of course, we can keep the white couch.

Postscript

THREE YEARS AGO, on our tenth anniversary, I made up a special greeting card for Shirley which turned out to be much more than a Hallmark wish. It has stayed with me, and with her, for all this time. It not only sits in a special place that I can call upon when I lose my way with my wife, I often share it with anyone who feels a cloud passing over their home.

It is *The Ten-Word Manual for Marriage.* We learned it one word a year. Maybe we can save you some time.

1. TRUTH The only way to go, with anything, especially love. And there is absolutely no defense against it; it is the purest communication there is. Try it, with yourself first, then with your person. Work on it. It will lift all the weight off your shoulders.

2. STRATEGIES These are the learned disasters we brought from high school; produced only by fear and insecurity. Builds only walls between you. Makes strangers of people you thought you knew. Enemy of truth and sincerity and everything permanent. Dump them.

3. HUMOR Easier said than done, but do it, find it, feel it, look for partners with it. Life's absurd as it is. Try laughing at it. Just make the *sound* first. It's contagious, and medicinal, and addictive.

4. REPRESSION The *real* cancer of our time. And an irresistible trap. "Suck it in." "Save it." "It'll go away." *No, no, no.* It never does. It just rumbles and simmers till the big quake. Repress *nothing,* neither the sweet nor the bitter. Let it out, no matter how unsettling. *Today's small eruption is better than tomorrow's doomsday!*

5. VULNERABILITY It's a *virtue.* Big one. Trust me. But it's hard. (You'll feel like you're the world's number-one target.) Not so. Start. Open up. It's lovable, it's disarming, and it's courageous.

6. SELF-ESTEEM The magic words. If you won't muster any for you, nobody else will. And it's like Western Union: If you don't have any, they all get the message. Any spare time, work on liking yourself better. It'll put a new paint job on everything.

7. CHANGE There's always someone to tell you you have to. *Wrong. Don't.* Rather, spend the time finding out who you *really are.* Work on being more of *that.* A lot better than the futile "gotta-change" treadmill, which really never ends.

8. SPACE A lover's most precious gift. Most of us don't offer it, for fear of losing control. Fight that. Find the guts to hand some out, the kind you'd like for yourself. Don't be afraid to trust it. It can only make you look better, and be loved more for it.

9. FRIENDS Terribly overlooked "balance" for a twosome. And necessary: Make sure your "mutual" ones include some from *both* sides. (One-sided friend lists, no matter how intriguing or comfortable, invariably mean trouble down the road.)

10. PRIVACY Save some for the both of you, no matter how pressing your commitments. Be alone together. Talk, touch, stare, think, read, but do it with the world on the other side of the door. It's not only healthy, it'll "test" what you've got.

—MARTY INGELS

Index